OVID'S ART *and* *the* WIFE *of* BATH

THE ETHICS *of* EROTIC VIOLENCE

MARILYNN DESMOND

CORNELL UNIVERSITY PRESS
Ithaca and London

First published 2006 by Cornell University Press
First printing, Cornell Paperbacks, 2006

Printed in the United States of America

Library of Congress Cataloging-in-Publication Data

Desmond, Marilynn, 1952–
    Ovid's art and the Wife of Bath : the ethics of erotic
violence / Marilynn Desmond.
        p. cm.
    Includes bibliographical references and index.
    ISBN-13: 978-0-8014-4379-4 (cloth : alk. paper)
    ISBN-10: 0-8014-4379-2 (cloth : alk. paper)
    ISBN-13: 978-0-8014-7317-3 (pbk. : alk. paper)
    ISBN-10: 0-8014-7317-9 (pbk. : alk. paper)
    1. Literature, Medieval—Roman influences.
    2. Literature, Medieval—History and criticism.
    3. Sadomasochism in literature.   4. Ovid, 43 B.C.–17
or 18 A.D.—Influence.   5. Ovid, 43 B.C.–17 or 18
A.D. Ars amatoria.   6. Chaucer, Geoffrey, d. 1400.
Wife of Bath's tale.   I. Title.
    PN681.5.D47 2006
    809'.933538—dc22
2005037802

Cornell University Press strives to use environmentally
responsible suppliers and materials to the fullest extent
possible in the publishing of its books. Such materials include vegetable-based, low-VOC inks and acid-free papers that are recycled, totally chlorine-free, or partly
composed of nonwood fibers. For further information,
visit our website at www.cornellpress.cornell.edu.

Cloth printing   10   9   8   7   6   5   4   3   2   1
Paperback printing 10   9   8   7   6   5   4   3   2   1

❧ OVID'S ART *and the* WIFE *of* BATH

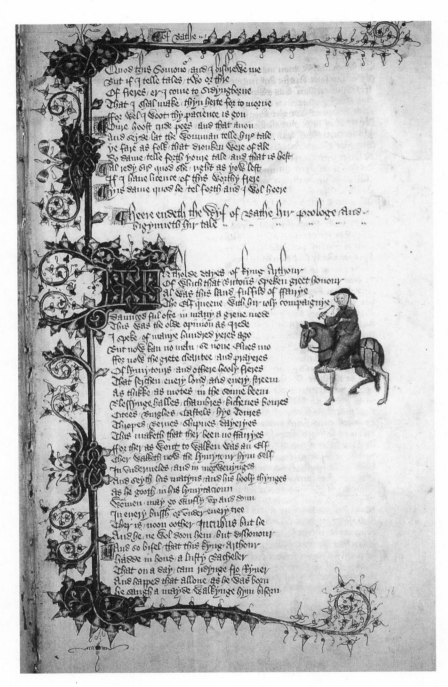

Frontispiece: *The Wife of Bath's Tale. Canterbury Tales*, Ellesmere 26C9, fol. 72r. By permission of the Huntington Library, San Marino, California.

For Sheila Desmond Schultz

✒ CONTENTS

✦ ILLUSTRATIONS

✒ ACKNOWLEDGMENTS

Ovid's Art and the Wife of Bath: The Ethics of Erotic Violence is an analysis of the reception of Ovid's *Ars Amatoria* in a specific literary trajectory that includes the letters of Abelard and Heloise, the *Roman de la Rose*, Chaucer's *Wife of Bath's Prologue*, and Christine de Pizan's contributions to the *Querelle de la Rose*. Since the *Ars amatoria* programmatically addresses the uses of violence in the erotics of sexual difference, this book is likewise a study of the representation of erotic violence in classical and medieval literary texts.

This book has taken shape over several years. I began work on this project as a Visiting Fellow at Clare Hall, Cambridge University, during 1999–2000, and I completed it during the first few months as a Marta Sutton Weeks Visiting Fellow at the Stanford Humanities Center during 2003–4. I am extremely grateful to both Clare Hall and the Stanford Humanities Center for the vibrant intellectual communities they foster and the exceptionally warm welcome both institutions extended to me. I must also acknowledge the Medieval Reading Group at Cambridge University, whose participants included William Burgwinkle, Jane Gilbert, Miranda Griffin, Cary Howie, Sarah Kay, and Nicole Zeeman, for lively discussions that helped shape the direction of this project.

I have benefited from the generosity of readers and friends who have contributed in a variety of ways to the refinement of the argument in this book. Several individuals, in particular, sustained me over the years of my work on this project. Pamela Sheingorn made early suggestions that changed the direction of this project, and she later read drafts of portions of the manuscript; Jongsook Lee offered sharp critiques of each chapter in this book; as editors, Deborah McGrady, Barbara Altmann, David Townsend, and Andrew Taylor provided critical readings of early versions of chapters that appear here in revised form. Robert Clark and Barbara Altmann kindly answered questions about Old French, and Karen Winstead, Jonathan Schofer, Elizabeth Archibald all generously shared information with me. Three anonymous readers for Cornell University Press offered critically engaged readings, and Bernard Kendler's support for this project in its early stages was crucial. John Ackerman has likewise been exceptionally supportive as this book moved through production. The editorial assistance of Gavin Lewis has been extremely valuable, and Lys Ann Weiss's work on the index is greatly appreciated.

An earlier version of chapter 3 appeared as "*Dominus/Ancilla*: Rhetorical Subjectivity and Sexual Violence in the Letters of Heloise," in *The Tongue of the Fathers: Gender and Ideology in Twelfth-Century Latin*, ed. David Townsend and Andrew Taylor, Philadelphia: University of Pennsylvania Press, 1998; and an earlier version of chapter 6 appeared as "The *Querelle de la Rose* and the Ethics of Reading," in *Christine de Pizan: A Casebook*, ed. Barbara K. Altmann and Deborah L. McGrady, New York: Routledge, 2003. Both are reprinted in revised form by permission.

Over the course of my research for this project, I have had the privilege of working with manuscripts in the Bibliothèque Royale Albert Ie, Brussels; the Bibliothèque nationale de France, Paris; the Bodleian Library in Oxford; the British Library; the Cambridge University Library; the Fitzwilliam Museum, Cambridge; the Getty Museum, Los Angeles, the Huntingdon Library, San Marino, California; the Morgan Library, New York; and the Biblioteca Històrica, Universitat de València. I am grateful to the curators and librarians at these institutions for access to manuscripts and for permission to reproduce photographs.

I have presented material from this book at Bristol University; Clare Hall, Cambridge University; Cornell University; Indiana University; the Medieval Club of New York; the University of Oklahoma; the University of Pennsylvania; Queen Mary University of London; Tulane University; Seoul National University; and the University of York. In addition to individuals already mentioned, I am grateful to Miri Rubin, Alastair Minnis, David Wallace, and Rita Copeland for invitations to speak; the resulting conversations have left traces throughout this book.

While I have been the beneficiary of the various academic communities I have just acknowledged, this project has also drawn heavily on my classroom experiences over the past decade. The responses of my undergraduates at Binghamton have been critical to my assessment of the texts under study here, particularly the *Wife of Bath's Prologue*. In addition, a remarkable group of doctoral students, especially Helene Scheck, Rhonda Knight, Adale Sholock, Mary Sokolowski, Joseph Pappa, and Robert Wasilewski have challenged me to continually rethink my theoretical approaches. Christian Beck and Rhonda Knight both assisted with research at different times in the course of my work on this project.

As colleagues and friends, Susan Pollock and Reinhart Bernbeck have been extraordinary. Peter Mileur, Dean of Harpur College, Binghamton University, provided a subvention to support publication of photographs, as well as extremely generous funds for travel and research assistance, as did the Francis X. K. Newman Fund in the Department of English at Binghamton University. As always, I am pleased to acknowledge the daily support of Gerald Kutcher, my best reader, my best friend.

This book is dedicated to my mother, Sheila Desmond Schultz.

OVID'S ART *and the* WIFE *of* BATH

Introduction
All under Correction

But nathelees, this meditacioun
I putte it ay under correccioun
Of clerkes, for I am nat textueel.

—Chaucer, *Parson's Prologue*

For myne wordes, heere and every part,
I speke hem alle under correccioun
Of yow that felyng han in loves art.

—Chaucer, *Troilus and Criseyde*

In the fall of 1997, the Women's Studies Program at the State University of New York at New Paltz sponsored a conference, playfully entitled "Revolting Behavior: The Challenges of Women's Sexual Freedom," that was designed to "examine a broad spectrum of women's sexuality in a political and cultural context." One particular panel was entitled "Safe, Sane and Consensual S/M: [Sadomasochism]: An Alternate Way of Loving." In the program available to registered conference participants, the workshop was described in more detail: "Safe, Sane, and Consensual S/M: An Alternate Way of Loving. Have you ever wondered what S/M is, but had no one to ask? Join Sonya, Carol, Helen and Lois to explore society's perceptions of S/M and find out what it means to the people within the S/M community, discuss our experience of S/M with an emphasis on safety and communication." This one informational panel on same-sex S/M generated a media firestorm throughout the United States, although most of the journalists and editors who reported or opined on this conference did not check facts or interview the conference organizers. The intensity of this reaction prompted the governor of New York State, George Pataki, to demand an investigation; simultaneously, a trustee of the university system called for the dismissal of the president of SUNY–New Paltz; and the chancellor of the SUNY system publicly denounced the conference as a whole for "promoting lesbianism and sadomasochism." The subsequent in-

1

vestigation found that no laws had been broken, and no taxpayers' money had been misused. The report of the investigating committee specifically appealed to free speech and academic freedom—two principles that have come under enormous political pressure in the few short years since September 2001. In retrospect, the reaction to the New Paltz conference now appears to mark the beginning of a new phase in challenges to academic freedom, particularly in the context of the discourses on sexualities that have emerged from feminist and queer theories in the last few decades.

The committee charged with investigating the New Paltz conference reported that the program planning committee had several long debates about the S/M panel before deciding to include it in the conference program, a discomfort that points to the contested status of discourses regarding power erotics within feminist communities even in the late nineties. In a memo sent to the university president before the conference, the program coordinators note: "Many of us were deeply disturbed by the current interest in S/M activity, since as feminists we are committed to egalitarian relationships in all aspects of life."[1] The review committee further reports: "Some members were apparently guided here by what they described to us as the 'principle of lesser harm,'—the notion that discussing how S/M was performed in ways that participants regarded as consensual and safe would reduce the likelihood that women might participate in nonconsensual, unsafe S/M activity." In representing S/M as a problem of ethical negotiation, the report highlights how general anxieties become attached to S/M—whether as a discourse or a practice.

The New Paltz conference is only one recent example of the ways in which the discourse of S/M has historically troubled the categories of feminist thought in provocative and highly productive ways. In 1982 the anxieties surrounding female sexuality were dramatically staged at an earlier conference, the ninth annual "Scholar and Feminist" conference at Barnard College entitled "Towards a Politics of Sexuality," and known in its published form as a landmark collection of essays entitled *Pleasure and Danger.*[2] That conference was planned to offer a "framework which recognized what often seemed to be contradictory impulses in feminist theory and women's lives that would alleviate the need for a forced choice between pleasure and danger." (2) The Dworkin-MacKinnon antipornography activists of the day took exception to the Barnard conference and applied enough pressure on the Barnard administration to have the program notes confiscated. Women who called themselves "antipornography feminists" picketed the conference and labeled it a conference on "sado-masochism, pornography and butch-femme roles among lesbians," even though there was no one panel at the conference that specifically addressed S/M. The conference itself generated a tremendous amount of commentary, and as Carol Vance states in the introduction to *Pleasure and Danger*: "For many feminists the Barnard Conference signaled the beginning of the 'sex wars,' the impassioned, contentious, and to many, disturbing debates, discussions, conferences and arguments about sexuality that continued unabated until at least 1986."[3] Vance characterizes the controversy surrounding the Barnard conference as a "sex-panic": "an operation in which irrational fears about sexuality are mobilized by the effective use of alarming symbols".[4] The New Paltz conference fifteen years later demonstrates that S/M remains an "alarming symbol," even when its practitioners stress its contractual and consensual nature—as they did in the conference program—and even though popular culture, especially advertising and fashion (Versace, Gaultier) is saturated with S/M imagery.[5]

Despite the difficult polarities that emerged from the "sex wars" within feminist theory and women's communities, these controversies generated some of the most exhilarating writing on sexuality, desire, and identity in the past few decades. The work of a range of cultural theorists as diverse as Kaja Silverman, Eve Kosofsky Sedgewick, Mandy Merck, Anne McClintock, Sue Golding, Lynda Hart, and writers such as Dorothy Allison and Pat Califia,[6] demonstrates not just the efficacy of a variety of discourses on masochism and S/M but the centrality of these discourses to any theoretical understanding of the performative quality of genders and sexualities. Same-sex S/M has been celebrated for its potential to challenge heteropatriarchal roles; for Parveen Adams, the lesbian sadomasochist "has separated sexuality from gender and is able to enact differences in the theater where roles freely circulate."[7] Same-sex S/M simultaneously highlights the erotic potentials of power and violence, a fact that does not always fit comfortably within the antihierarchical discourses of many feminisms. According to Lynda Hart, "It is not only . . . that S/M lesbians *play* with power and hierarchy configurations *within* their sexual practices, but they also pose a challenge to mainstream feminism's ethical ground." (47) Tania Modleski puts this challenge into words: "the defining . . . features of S/M—the infliction of pain and gestures of humiliation by one individual on another—are features requiring explanation even if they *are* desired by all parties."[8] The explanation Modleski requests would address the performativity of S/M, the means by which pleasure rather than pain is elicited through gestures that *appear* violent. Most writing on S/M emphasizes that the categories of pain and humiliation take on meaning through references to scripts or scenarios that mime rhetorical or physical violence. S/M handbooks emphasize negotiation and consent so that much writing on S/M actually reads like a rhetorical manual. Indeed, S/M is frequently discussed as a theatrical performance: "S/M is any mutually pleasurable sexual activity between consenting adults that involves dominant and submissive role playing, physical restraint or erotic (i.e. pleasurable) pain. A sexual encounter for which roles and S/M activity have been negotiated is called a 'scene.' "[9] If S/M stages the erotic possibilities of violence without actually constituting violence, it consequently points to the cultural scripts that render all forms of intimate violence legible.

The scandal generated by S/M effectively obscures the everyday violences that work to organize gender and sexuality. By contrast to the cultural anxieties generated by the theatrical evocation of violence in consensual S/M, the most pervasive form of intimate violence in contemporary Western cultures is domestic violence, otherwise known by the sociological term "violence against women."[10] The category of violence against women became culturally intelligible in the legal and medical discourses of the late twentieth century as a direct consequence of second-wave feminist activism,[11] although as such violence became more visible within the social and cultural imaginations, the assumptions about the nature and meaning of that violence have been highly contested.[12] As terms that emerge from social science, "domestic violence" and "violence against women" refer to the gendered nature of a specific form of intimate violence that performs the category maintenance work of contemporary heterosexualities by naturalizing hierarchy and power. As such, violence against women constitutes a form of "structural violence"[13] in the contemporary West. By contrast, the theatricality of S/M demonstrates that such hierarchies are inventions, and unstable inventions at that. Commercial and consensual S/M are aggressively policed in Britain and the United States while domestic violence has generally been tolerated in both countries as part of the status quo; perpetrators of domestic abuse, unlike S/M practitioners, are not classified as sexual outlaws.[14] Indeed, domestic violence is not commonly considered to be a sexual transgression, whereas S/M remains an "alarming symbol," as the New Paltz conference amply demonstrates. Perhaps S/M is so intensively policed because it exposes the status of domestic violence as nonnegotiated, nonconsensual violence and humiliation. As a category of cultural analysis, S/M creates a space in which to consider the ethical challenges posed by violence against women.

While S/M scripts parody the formations of power and fetishize the instruments of violence, such parodies and fetishistic operations frequently rely on historical configurations. Michel Foucault described S/M as a form of courtship, in which "sexual relations are elaborated and developed by and through mythical relations."[15] In his book *The Mastery of Submission*, John Noyes cites a recent socioethnographic study of the contemporary German S/M scene where "the entire spectrum of popular culture and a wide body of historical sources serve as scripts." Among them, configurations drawn from premodern cultures appear frequently: "slave auctions in the ancient world, crucifixions, the martyr scenes of the Christian saints, tortures from the Inquisition . . ."[16] Premodern history offers intense opportunities for staging power in theatrical erotics since the semiotics of power relations in premodern cultures are popularly thought to be crudely figured in terms of dominance and submission or starkly organized into social institutions such as feudalism or the Church. As one S/M practitioner longingly writes: "For years I was actually unhappy about the civilised times I lived in, full of envy for people who had lived in the Middle Ages, in the days of witch-hunts and the Inquisition."[17] Perhaps this is why Slavoj Žižek sees masochism and courtly love as direct reflections of one another: "It is only with the emergence of masochism, of the masochist couple, towards the end of the last century that we can now grasp the libidinal economy of courtly love."[18]

While masochism makes medieval erotics legible for Žižek, an essay by Anna Freud from the 1920's illustrates the role of the medieval in erotic fantasy. In this essay, entitled "Beating Fantasies and Daydreams," Anna Freud extends some of the issues posed by her father in his famous essay "A Child Is Being Beaten." Freud describes how a girl in her analysis creates a superstructure of daydreams over the beating fantasy, so that "nice" stories replace autoerotic fantasies of being beaten by substituting rituals of humiliation for the physical violence: "the girl accidentally came upon a boy's storybook; it contained among others a short story set in the Middle Ages. She read through it once or twice with lively interest; when she had finished she returned the book to its owner and did not see it again. Her imagination, however, was immediately captured by the various figures and their external circumstances which were described in the book." The girl "takes possession" of these fantasies, elaborates extensively on them, and produces a framework for all her future fantasies: "The material she used in this story was as follows: A medieval knight has been engaged in a long feud with a number of nobles who are in league against him. In the course of a battle a fifteen-year-old noble youth (i. e., the age of the daydreamer) is captured by the knight's henchmen. He is taken to the knight's castle where he is held prisoner for a long time. Finally, he is released."[19] Within this framework, the girl fantasizes about the knight of the castle, who is "sinister and violent," and the noble youth who is vulnerable and good; each fantasy revolves around threats and humiliation only to be resolved in relief and happiness when the knight releases the youth from his threats. Anna Freud's case study suggests that narratives adapted—however loosely—from an identifiable past such as the medieval West provide a superstructure of fantasy that facilitates an erotic paradigm. If medieval scripts can be read through masochism —as Žižek sees it—or if they facilitate masochistic fantasy—in Anna Freud's terms—perhaps the constructs of the medieval past might elucidate specific performances of contemporary heterosexualities, particularly in terms of erotic violence. The term "erotic violence" denotes interpersonal violence in intimate or marital contexts; as a critical category, erotic violence refers to the construction of subjectivities around gestures of dominance and submission, or the construction of desire or pleasure around violence, pain, or abuse—whether for the subject or the object.[20] Erotic violence as such is distinct from sexual violence or rape.[21]

While medieval texts frequently represent violence as erotic,[22] no literary text better exemplifies the paradoxes evident in medieval representations of erotic violence than Geoffrey Chaucer's *Wife of Bath's Prologue*. As a fictional, literary character, the Wife of Bath presents herself as a woman on top, yet she simultaneously describes herself as the object of Jankyn's violence at the end of her *Prologue*. The Wife of Bath is nonetheless frequently cited as an alarming symbol of female sexual autonomy, as though she were a historical figure who offered what the New Paltz S/M panel describes as a "different way of loving." One particular incident will illustrate the sort of sexual notoriety that attaches to Chaucer's most recognizable figure. In 1983, the city of Minneapolis held a public hearing before passing the highly contested Dworkin-MacKinnon Ordinance banning pornography. In the course of these hearings, S/M was often invoked, frequently by Andrea Dworkin herself, as though S/M somehow formed a link between pornography and violence against women. One person who testified, Mr. Osborne, offered his concern that the definition of pornography in the ordinance was so broad and could be applied so widely that even the *Wife of Bath's Tale* might be banned; after quoting the last few lines of the tale in a modern English translation, he attempted to unpack the potentially offensive aspects:

'He took his wife in his arms and kissed her, overcome with joy. Thereafter she obeyed him in everything that might add to his bliss, and thus they lived for the rest of their lives in perfect happiness' It is sexual, it refers to her as a wife, as a woman, that is explicit. . . . She is definitely subordinate. . . . By someone's definition that she is being treated as an object, a thing, or a commodity, it might mean she is being presented in a posture of sexual submission because we don't know what he meant, Geoffrey Chaucer means, when she is overcome with joy. The problem is, we don't know if that material is going to be covered by this ordinance. [23]

Mr. Osborne cited the *Wife of Bath's Tale* as an example of a canonical text that is innocuous and alarming at the same time, and he questions whether the "sexual submission" in the tale might be deemed—under the Dworkin-MacKinnon Ordinance—to facilitate violence against women. His invocation of the Wife of Bath as a cipher for questions of mastery and submission accurately poses a recurring question about the character of the Wife of Bath: is she a scandalous and/or subversive figure, or does her performance of desire ultimately reinforce the status quo?

The representation of violence as erotic in the *Wife of Bath's Prologue* marks the culmination of a textual tradition that developed specifically around the medieval reception of Ovid's *Ars amatoria*. While Ovid's *Metamorphoses* offers frequent examples of sexual violence or rape, erotic violence—as it emerges in the *Ars amatoria*—is a category of desire shaped by power erotics. Ovid's *Ars amatoria* was repeatedly translated into French in the high Middle Ages; it was cited by Heloise and adapted by Jean de Meun in his continuation of the *Roman de la Rose*. Christine de Pizan critiqued the Ovidian discourse of erotic violence in the *Rose*; Geoffrey Chaucer appropriated it for the *Wife of Bath's Prologue*. The *Ars* ironically explicates the potential of violence in the heterosexual contract as facilitated by Roman colonial power, and the medieval citation and adaptation of Ovid's *Ars* elaborate on violence as a formative component of eros. The representations of erotic violence in these texts participate in what William Burgwinkle has identified as a "cultural shift in which some of the complex of practices and desires we know today as heterosexuality . . . were codified in tandem with new models of masculinity at the dawn of vernacular writing in Europe."[24] As we shall see, the *Ars amatoria* parodically proposes that masculinity is achieved through a particular performance of heterosexual desire, and vernacular poets such as Jean de Meun or Chaucer reiterate the Ovidian precept that categories of heterosexual desire might be linked to gendered identities. The structures of medieval desires thus carry the traces of ancient Mediterranean sexual regimes: the textual trajectory of the *Ars amatoria* required that the sexual categories of Ovid's poem be adapted to medieval sexual ethics; consequently, the power erotics in the *Wife of Bath's Prologue* are haunted by the imperial structures of desire as they originate in the *Ars amatoria*. Indeed, to appreciate the texture of the *Wife of Bath's Prologue* as an

Ovidian construct is to consider how the colonial structures of the ancient Roman world shaped the erotic discourses of the medieval West.

The medieval reception of the *Ars amatoria* took place against a proliferating set of discourses on *amor* and eros in the high and late Middle Ages. In order to sketch out the contours of these erotic cultures, chapter 1 opens with a survey of the "mounted Aristotle," a textual and visual tradition of power erotics that depicts Aristotle being ridden like a horse. While the tradition of the "mounted Aristotle" informs the language of erotic horsemanship employed in Chaucer's *Wife of Bath's Prologue*, the status of the Wife of Bath as an object of violence at the end of the *Prologue* ultimately contradicts her claims of mastery. The chapter thus juxtaposes the scandal of female sexual dominance represented by the "mounted Aristotle" to historical evidence regarding marital violence against women in canon law, customary law, sermons, and conduct literature during the medieval period. Chapter 2 analyzes Ovid's *Ars amatoria* within the early years of Roman imperial rule under Augustus. As a handbook for heteroerotic performance, the *Ars* ironically instructs its readers in a masculinity that is calculated and predatory, and in a femininity grounded on submission. Medieval readers of the *Ars*, however, tended to overlook its irony and to unproblematically embrace the premise that violence is erotic. Chapter 3 considers Heloise as a reader of Ovid: the exchange of letters between her and Abelard acknowledges the erotic significance of violence in their relationship, and it likewise enacts a textual and rhetorical play of power erotics. Throughout the correspondence, Heloise performs a submissive role in an erotic dynamic scripted by Ovidian amatory poetry and structured by epistolary rhetoric. Chapter 4 examines the most supremely Ovidian poem in medieval literatures, the *Roman de la Rose*. Compared to the medieval French translations of the *Ars amatoria* that circulated in the thirteenth century, the *Rose* extends the directives of the *Ars* with a rhetorical flourish and excess that test the limits of Ovidian irony. The representation of violence as erotic animates Jean de Meun's section of the *Rose*: Ami addresses the issue of marital violence and cites the letters of Heloise in quoting the speech of the Jaloux, and the Vieille implicitly returns the reader to the violence of the Jaloux when she tutors Amant in the possibility that a successful lover might effectively deploy violence as part of eros.

Chapter 5 examines the Ovidian discourse of the *Wife of Bath's Prologue*: in following the precepts of the Vieille, the Wife of Bath ultimately celebrates a sexual relationship with her fifth husband, Jankyn, whose "book of wikked wyves" includes both the *Ars amatoria* and the letters of Heloise. Chaucer's text implicitly endorses the lessons on erotic violence that emerge from Ovid's *Ars amatoria* to become codified by the Vieille in the *Roman de la Rose*. Chaucer's contemporary, Christine de Pizan, took exception to the representation of violence and sexuality that structures desire in the *Roman de la Rose;* chapter 6 examines her critique of Ovid and the *Rose* in the exchange of letters known as the *Querelle de la Rose*. Like Heloise, Christine's rhetoric in the *Querelle* is enabled by the *ars dictaminis*, which allows her to identify marital violence as an issue in the ethics of reading. In order to construct an ethical framework, Christine draws on Nicole Oresme's translation of Aristotle's *Ethics;* she focuses specifically on the Ovidian discourse of the Jaloux and the Vieille in order to intervene in what she considers the grammar of violence in the *Rose*.

This study of the *Wife of Bath's Prologue* situates Chaucer in relation to Jean de Meun and the reception of Ovid's *Ars amatoria* in medieval French. The epistolary texts composed by Heloise and Christine offer alternative perspectives to these canonical reworkings of the *Ars amatoria*, so that these two collections of letters signed by women expose the gendered nature of the French and Ovidian textual traditions that produced the *Wife of Bath's Prologue*. Central to the textual circulation of erotic violence is the concept of correction whereby each text cites earlier texts in order to acquire authority. In the Chaucerian corpus, the narrators of *Troilus and Criseyde* and the *Parson's Tale* use the Middle English term "correccioun" to invite readers to make rhetorical adjustments to their statements. In such a context, "correccioun" suggests the ethical agency of the reader whose knowledge or obsessions—whether amatory or textual—might dominate the text. "Correccioun," like its Latin counterpart, *disciplina*, also refers to punishment, rebuke, or chastisement. Both *disciplina* and "correccioun" invite an ethical reading at the same time that they belie the presence—and power—of textual violence in the disciplinary acts of interpretation. Both terms also point to the eros of reading as well as to the allegorical potential of readerly erotics to mimic larger cultural dynamics of erotic violence. As Ivan Ilich has noted, reading texts in a manuscript culture was an intense, even erotic experience.[25] In addition, Stephanie H. Jed has suggested the connections between the discipline of philology, with its "correction" of the text, and the reader's implication in scenes of sexual violence.[26] As we shall see, Ovid's *Ars amatoria* initiates a discourse of erotic violence that is put under correction by a specific set of medieval poets and readers, and the heteroerotics that animate the *Wife of Bath's Prologue* are the consequence of that correction.

✒ CHAPTER 1

Sexual Difference and the Ethics of Erotic Violence

> The hardest lesson is the impossible intimacy of the ethical.
>
> —Gayatri Spivak
>
> Sadomasochism is precisely the technique of sexuality by which the bare life of a sexual partner is brought to light.
>
> —Giorgio Agamben

In *Totality and Infinity*, his seminal work on ethics and violence, Emmanuel Levinas employs the most traditional of heteronormative categories when he invokes the domicile or dwelling as the place of the feminine.[1] He likewise invokes the "caress" as the erotic gesture of the masculine subject addressed to the feminine other. In Levinas' terms, the caress brings the subject "face to face" with the *visage* of the other; the recognition of the other that results from this encounter activates the prohibition on violence that is the foundation of ethical behavior. Yet lurking in Levinas' language is an awareness that this caress, in the privacy of the domestic space, encodes the very possibilities of violence, since it is the violent potential of touch itself that renders physical contact potentially ethical. Levinas' paradigm implicitly suggests that ethics emerges from the potential for domestic violence inherent in the caress. In her critique of Levinas' notion of the caress, Luce Irigaray interrogates the place Levinas assigns to the feminine (the *aimée*) in relation to the "aesthetics and ethics of the amorous gesture."[2] In claiming a space for the female as subject rather than beloved or object of desire, Irigaray revises Levinas' heteronormative paradigms for erotic agency and subjectivity in the Western imaginary. Irigaray proposes that sexual difference itself opens up a space for a consideration of the "ethical."

If an ethics of sexual difference must start with the caress and the potential for erotic violence it encodes, an ethical approach to categories of erotic violence must go beyond normative values and moral systems. The notion of an ethics outside regimes of normativity is the legacy of Michel Foucault, who employed the term "ethics" to designate the concept of self-cultivation and self-mastery that he explored in his final works. Beatrice Hanssen demonstrates that he grounded that notion in an understanding of ethics as "an attitude, an ethos, a philosophical life in which the critique of what we are is at one and the same time the historical analysis of the limits imposed on us and an experiment with the possibility of going beyond them."[3] In its Foucauldian sense, "ethics" is a heuristic approach rather than a prescriptive discourse. Detached from languages of morality and prohibition, ethics becomes a critical category for examining the contingencies of eros and human conduct in a historical trajectory.

Chaucer's *Wife of Bath's Prologue* explores the ethical implications of the uses and limits of erotic violence. As narrator, the Wife of Bath does not assume that the recognition of the other in an intimate, domestic context leads to a prohibition on violence; rather, she describes erotic violence as a form of recognition of the other. In order to appreciate the interpretive implications of erotic violence in the *Prologue*, it is necessary to examine the textual traditions that animate Chaucer's text as well as the cultural contexts from which it is derived and to which it refers.

The *Wife of Bath's Prologue* develops and elaborates on the discourses of erotic violence as they emerge from Ovid's *Ars amatoria* in the course of its medieval appropriation as an ethical treatise. Since the patrimony of the medieval Christian West included pagan Latin texts, medieval reading practices relied on a notion of ethics in order to accommodate the alterity of pre-Christian Latinity; thus the study of ethics and the study of Latin literary texts were intertwined.[4] Throughout the Middle Ages, Ovid was known as *Ovidius ethicus*, ethical Ovid, and his texts were read for their potential to elucidate or explain conduct.[5] As a didactic poem, the *Ars amatoria* particularly lent itself to an ethical reading, as we shall see in chapter 2. In addition, theories of reading in medieval cultures assumed that reading itself is an ethical activity, and that the act of reading is implicated in the construction of agency and subjectivity for the reader, an assumption evident in the *ordinatio* of a medieval manuscript.[6] Mary Carruthers has argued that texts acquire their ethical urgency through their memorability, and highly memorable texts encourage readers to meditate on the actions represented therein.[7] Brian Stock has shown that medieval literary cultures emphasized the ethical value of narratives and linked narrative to categories of self-analysis.[8] Descriptions of erotic violence frequently form particularly memorable units of narrative, some of which are illustrated and thereby all the more memorable—as we shall see when we take up the case of the Jaloux in the *Roman de la Rose* in chapter 4. The "experience" of erotic violence narrated by the Vieille in the *Rose* or the Wife of Bath in the *Canterbury Tales* becomes a constitutive element of self-analysis and even gendered identity for these two vivid literary characters.

To focus on representations of erotic violence in medieval texts requires that we examine discomforting scenes that are all too quickly passed over in many readings,[9] such as the violence Abelard and Heloise describe in their retrospective account of their love affair, or the celebration of erotic violence voiced by the Vieille in the *Roman de la Rose*. In the *Wife of Bath's Prologue*, the narrator speaks of herself as a woman on top when she depicts her dominance over her husbands with the resonant phrase: "myself have been the whippe."(175) When she claims mastery over her fifth husband, she describes their negotiations in similar terms: "He yaf me al the bridel in myn hond." (813) Chaucer's choice of an equestrian metaphor for the Wife's self-presentation neatly encapsulates an iconographic convention for representing the sexually threatening female as a woman capable of riding a man like a horse. This metaphorical depiction of the Wife derives from the textual and visual tradition of the "mounted Aristotle," an exemplum that expresses the scandalous possibilities in the erotics of sexual difference. As in contemporary cultures, however, the scandal that attaches to representations of power erotics obscures everyday violences, particularly marital violence, a quotidian feature of medieval cultures. The cultural fantasy of erotic violence as imagined in the texts and images of the "mounted Aristotle" and evoked by Chaucer must be read against the more mundane realities of marital violence as encoded in legal texts and conduct literature. In order to articulate the cultural intelligibilities of erotic violence, this chapter first explores this fantasy of the woman on top as it emerges in the tradition of the "mounted Aristotle" before considering the social limits on violence against women set by prescriptive discourses.

The "Mounted Aristotle"

In *Madness and Civilization*, Foucault asserts that "sadism is not a name finally given to a practice as old as Eros; it is a massive cultural fact which appeared precisely at the end of the eighteenth century, and which constitutes one of the greatest conversions of Western imagination: unreason transformed into delirium of the heart, madness of desire."[10] While sadism may be historically specific to the eighteenth century, a cultural fantasy of power erotics as the triumph of delirium and desire emerges in the high Middle

FIGURE 1. The "mounted Aristotle." Roman missal, Seminario Arcivescovile Maggiore, MS 325, fol. 260v. By permission of the Biblioteca del Seminario Arcivescovile, Firenze.

Ages in the proliferation of texts and images of the ancient philosopher Aristotle mounted and ridden by a woman. In the course of the thirteenth century, pictorial depictions of the "mounted Aristotle" begin to appear in the margins of manuscripts, on choir stalls and capitals, on tapestries and ivory caskets. More than one hundred examples of the "mounted Aristotle" survive from the medieval period, and the image appears with similar frequency throughout the early modern era.[11] This image occurs in highly public spaces—both courtly and religious—and in the more private spaces of Latin and vernacular books. Though only a small proportion of the surviving images of the "mounted Aristotle" come from manuscript illustration, these images share both composition and iconography. An old man, usually identified as aged and learned by his hair and dress, crawls along the ground on his hands and knees. On his back sits a woman who "rides" him; these images visualize the woman's erotic agency by a whip or rod that she holds aloft in one hand. In medieval manuscripts where the "mounted Aristotle" functions as a marginal decoration, the image bears no specific relationship to the text. For example, it appears in the lower marginal decoration in a thirteenth-century missal, a fourteenth-century breviary, a late thirteenth-century or early fourteenth-century psalter, and a French prose version of the Graal legend produced in Picardy in the thirteenth century (Figs. 1–4). Marginal illustration, however, may convey a thematic relationship to the textual material it accompanies without actually being an illustration of the text.[12] The image of the "mounted Aristotle" in BnF 95, a copy of Robert de Borron's *Histoire du graal*, illustrates the interpretative possibilities offered by marginal illustration (Fig. 4). The manuscript has extensive marginal decoration, yet these images only appear on folios that also contain illustrations within the text; these illustrations occur at regular intervals that work as chapter divisions so that the illustration in the column of text signals the upcoming narrative. The image of the "mounted Aristotle" in the lower border of the folio is compositionally similar to the illustration that appears on the same page: a two-part image depicts five messengers on horseback in the upper half and three messengers in the lower half, with the messengers on horseback and the woman on Aristotle all facing in the same direction (Figs. 5 and 6). The mounted Aristotle appears to be gratuitous, but the start of the next chapter is marked by an illustration of the humiliation of Hippocrates, a wise man like Aristotle. Hippocrates' infatuation with a woman leads to his being hoisted up, nude, in a basket on the outside of a tower where he is exposed to general ridicule (Fig. 7). The marginal image of the "mounted Aristotle" points forward to the scene of Hippocrates' humiliation, an anecdote narrated in the text. Thus the figure of the "mounted Aristotle" initiates a thematics of erotic humiliation that is later picked up by the text and image of Hippocrates. In such a visual and textual matrix, the "mounted Aristotle" requires no narrative explanation to operate as an erotic image.

At the same time that the image of the "mounted Aristotle" begins to appear in Western European visual cultures, narrative texts that describe Aristotle being ridden by a woman like a horse occur in Latin sermon collec-

FIGURE 2.   The "mounted Aristotle." Breviary, Yates Thompson 8, fol. 187r. By permission of the British Library.

tions and, almost simultaneously, in French and German verse narratives. The textual tradition appears to be completely independent of the visual tradition; taken together, both traditions suggest an extremely large dissemination for the "mounted Aristotle." Like its visual counterpart, the narrative of Aristotle's humiliation has no basis in ancient history or legend but emerges as an anecdote of power and desire that becomes attached to the historical figure of Aristotle in the course of the thirteenth century. The story is set in the imperial court of Alexander in India where Aristotle presides as tutor to the youthful ruler. When Aristotle perceives that Alexander is too besotted with his wife (in some versions it is his mistress), Aristotle chides him for his excessive desire. The wife (often, though not always, named Phyllis) sets out to seduce Aristotle as vengeance. Aristotle succumbs easily to her attractions, and he agrees to let her ride him like a horse. Phyllis alerts Alexander, who watches from a window while Phyllis mounts Aristotle and rides him through the garden. While some versions of the tale of the "mounted Aristotle" emphasize the derision and humiliation of the scene, these narratives expressly acknowledge the eroticism inherent in Aristotle's performance.

The text and image appear together only once in a narrative context, in a late fourteenth-century manuscript of Rudolf von Ems' *Weltchronik*, into

FIGURE 3.   The "mounted Aristotle." Psalter, MS 47 (Musée diocésain), fol. 74v. By permission of the Bibliothèque municipale d'Arras.

which is interpolated the *Alexander* of Ulrich von Etzenbach (1280–87) (Fig. 8). Ulrich von Etzenbach's text is unique in its addition of the story of Aristotle being ridden to the tales of the wonders of the East that constitute the Alexander cycle. In Ulrich von Etzenbach's text, Alexander's exotic and imperial adventures include his witnessing Aristander's (instead of Aristotle's) humiliation, in this case by Candace. The image that illustrates the brief anecdote (lines 23401–528) includes Alexander's face in a window. In a walled garden, Candace, wearing a crown, sits demurely on the back of Aristander. In this image, she is not accessorized with a whip; rather the spectator adds the element of observation that renders this a scene of humiliation scene for Aristander. In addition, an image of the "mounted Aristotle" illustrates a German dramatic manuscript of the play *Hie hebt sich ain spil an von Mayster Aristotiles*, one of a series of carnival plays performed in Nuremberg (Fig. 9). With these two exceptions, textual versions of the "mounted Aristotle" are not illustrated, and the image is found throughout Western Europe in a variety of contexts, all entirely separate from the textual tradition. In-

FIGURE 4.   The "mounted Aristotle." *Histoire du graal,* BnF, fr. 95, fol. 61v. Detail. By permission of the Bibliothèque nationale de France.

deed, by the fifteenth century, the image functions as an iconic supplement to narratives. For instance, illustrations of Petrarch's *Trionphi* include an image of the "mounted Aristotle" in the "Triumph of Love," even though the text does not mention the story in the panoply of loves that illustrate the triumph of Love (Fig. 10).[13] The pervasive implications of the iconography of the "mounted Aristotle" are most evident in a late fifteenth-century image in a Burgundian book of hours that depicts Catherine of Alexandria seated on the back of the emperor Maxentius (Fig. 11).[14] In this hagiographic context, the erotic iconography of the "mounted Aristotle" is borrowed to suggest the intellectual mastery of Saint Catherine, and it simultaneously implies the erotic potentials of that mastery.

In the absence of specific text/image relationships between the various narrative and pictorial examples of the "mounted Aristotle," the extent of both the textual and visual traditions suggests that the "mounted Aristotle" articulates a cultural fantasy regarding the erotic potentials of sexual difference. While Natalie Zemon Davis sees the "mounted Aristotle" as an instance of the topos of the "Woman on Top," a temporary inversion of socially sanctioned hierarchies,[15] Helen Solterer finds an example of female

FIGURE 5. Messengers. *Histoire du graal*, BnF, fr. 95, fol. 61v, detail. By permission of the Bibliothèque nationale de France.

mastery in the face of clerical learning;[16] and Susan Smith reads the "mounted Aristotle" as part of the topos on the "power of women." Smith suggests that Aristotle's performance as a horse is a "metaphor" for sexual intercourse, and she reads the "mounted Aristotle" as an inversion of the ecclesiastically sanctioned positions for heterosexual intercourse.[17] But the

FIGURE 6. Messengers and the "mounted Aristotle" in the margin. *Histoire du graal*, BnF, fr. 95, fol. 61v., full folio. By permission of the Bibliothèque nationale de France.

traire entre lui et une siue cousine
a qui elle auoit ceste cose descouure
Et coment il le uoloit ypocras dece
uoir par son sens. por ce quil se faisoit
filosofes souuerains deseure tous.

Quant il fu uenus contreuolt
iusques pres des creaus
Et la dame prist la corde

FIGURE 7. Humiliation of Hippocrates. *Histoire du graal,* BnF, fr. 95, fol. 66v, full folio. By permission of the Bibliothèque nationale de France.

FIGURE 8.   Alexander observes Candace riding Aristander. *Weltchronik*, c.g.m. 7377, fol. 213v. By permission of the Bayerische Staatsbibliothek.

"mounted Aristotle"—whether text or image—goes beyond metaphor to represent the erotic possibilities of humiliation and even flagellation. In many images, the female rider brandishes a whip held aloft in midair as though she were in the act of striking Aristotle with it. The whip is usually depicted in vivid detail as a riding crop consisting of several leather thongs furnished with metal studs. As a visual detail—or an attribute—the whip directs the viewer's attention to the physical sensations Aristotle will experience as a consequence of the rider's erotic mastery. The excessively detailed riding crop acts as a visual fetish that demands that the viewer recognize the erotic possibilities of female sexual and phallic mastery. The whip and the gesture of flagellation in the images signal to the viewer that the libidinal economy encoded in the "mounted Aristotle" is not metaphorical. In addition to the visual rhetoric of the whip as an instrument of erotic violence, the sight of Aristotle crawling on his hands and knees—often with a bridle in his mouth—offers a tableau of masochistic humiliation.

Narrative versions of the story of the "mounted Aristotle" exhibit a similar interest in the power erotics of the exemplum. It appears in Jacques de Vitry's collection of sermons, the *Sermones feriales et communes* (1228–40); simultaneously it appears in the vernacular version by Henri d'Andeli, the *Lai*

FIGURE 9.   The "mounted Aristotle." 4⁰ Cod H 27, fol. 159v. By permission of the Stadtbibliothek, Augsburg.

d'Aristote (1200–1240). The Latin exemplum of Jacques de Vitry emphasizes the intensity—even violence—of Aristotle's desire for Phyllis: "Et ita in amorem et concupiscenciam suam mentem eius eneruatam adeo induxit, quod rogare cepit reginam, vt eius consentiret voluntati" ["And thus she led his unmanned mind into such love and desire for her that he chose to ask the queen to agree to his wish"].[18] The queen asks him to abject himself for

FIGURE 10. The "mounted Aristotle" and Samson and Delilah. [Detail] *Trionphi d'Amore* 315., Stroz MS 174, fol. 19r. By permission of the Biblioteca Medicea Laurenziana.

love of her: "In hoc sciam quod ex corde me diligis, si ea que tibi dixero, pro amore meo facere non recusaueris. Cras hora matutina domino meo adhuc dormiente ad me in ortum istum exibis et super pedes et manus ambulando, ut te equitare possim, incuruaberis" (16) ["From this I will know that you love me from your heart if you will not refuse to do what I will ask of you for my love. Tomorrow in the early morning, while my lord is still sleeping, you will come to me at first dawn and you will bend over, walking on your hands and feet so that I will be able to mount you"]. The erotics of power is evident in the negotiations between Aristotle and the queen: the exemplum emphasizes that Aristotle is so weakened by desire that he negotiates with the queen and then allows her to ride him. Jacques de Vitry does not specify that the ride is part of a larger exchange of sexual favors; instead the ride

FIGURE 11. Saint Catherine. *Crohin-La Fontaine Hours,* 86.ML. 606 (MS 23), fol. 205v. By permission of the J. Paul Getty Museum.

itself is an erotic performance, not just a testimony to the power of women,[19] but also a cautionary tale regarding the pleasures of humiliation; as Aristotle says, she held him captive ("captiuum duxit"). The French *Lai d'Aristote* presents a more extensive meditation on the erotics of pain and humiliation. The woman in this version explicitly fetishizes the whip as part of the performance; in planning the scenario she boasts: "Ainz de si tranchant escorgie / Ne fu feruz ne de si cointe / Com il aura demain acointe" (260–63)[20] ["never was he struck with so sharp nor so elegant a whip as he will encounter tomorrow"]. In negotiating with Aristotle over the mechanics of the ride, the lady adds a saddle to the whip to complete the paraphernalia of the scene. In this version, Aristotle allows himself to be saddled, and when Alexander laughs at him, he emphasizes that love made him do this. The *Lai d'Aristote* eroticizes power through the imperial setting and through the identifiably historical figures of Alexander and Aristotle, so that the "historical" framework facilitates the erotics of the narrative just as the instrumentality of the whip in the hand of a woman suggests the pleasurable possibilities of erotic violence. Alexander looks on at this scene from a tower and laughs derisively at the sight. The *lai* concludes with a proverbial celebration of the pains and suffering that must be endured by a loyal lover. Since the *lai* opens with a reference to the fact that Alexander—king of Greece and Egypt—had subjugated India, the conclusion explicitly celebrates an eroticism enabled by empire.

The "mounted Aristotle" is cited widely in the textual cultures of the thirteenth and fourteenth centuries. Brunetto Latini briefly alludes to the story in his *Livre dou tresor*,[21] and Matheolus includes the "mounted Aristotle" as an exemplum that illustrates the dangers of female sexuality:

> *Quid dicet philosophia,*
> *Cum sibi doctorem deceperit amphibolia?*
> *Summus Aristoteles equus est et femina miles;*
> *Quod patet ex istis: hec militat, hic equitatur,*
> *Pro quibus artistis confusio perpetuatur.*
>
> *(495–99)*[22]

[What will philosophy say when ambiguity will have beguiled its doctor? The distinguished Aristotle is a horse and the woman a soldier. What is shown from that: she serves as a soldier and he is ridden, by which artifices disorder is perpetuated.]

Guillaume de Machaut, Eustache Deschamps, and Jean Froissart are among the vernacular poets who cite Aristotle as a figure whose story exemplifies the power of eros.[23] Given its wide dissemination, "the mounted Aristotle" renders legible the erotic possibilities variously expressed in medieval narratives. Gower for instance, depicts the mounted Aristotle in the book 8 of *Confessio Amantis*, when the narrator views the parade of lovers:

> I syh there Aristotle also,
> Whom that the queene of Grece so
> Hath bridled, that in thilke time
> Sche made him such a Silogime,
> That he foryat al his logique ;
> Ther was non art of his Practique,
> Thurgh which it mihte ben excluded

That he ne was fully concluded
To love, and dede his obeissance.

(2705–13)[24]

This textual image of Aristotle bridled by the "queen of Greece" clarifies the form of erotic mastery that is alluded to more elliptically elsewhere in Gower. In book 7 of the *Confessio Amantis*, Genius takes up the substance of Aristotle's instruction of Alexander, since according to Genius, wisdom is essential for lovers. The wisdom of Aristotle includes astrology, astronomy, and philosophy, as well as the ethical issues raised by the conduct of kings.[25] In order to illustrate the notion that Truth is the king's most sovereign virtue, Genius tells the story of Darius, the sultan of Persia who sought after wisdom. Darius asks three wise men the question, "Which is the strongest—wine, women, or the king?" The third wise man answers that women are the strongest, and as illustration he offers the example of Apemen who mastered the tyrant king Cyrus:

Cirus the king tirant sche tok,
And only with hire goodly lok
Sche made him debonaire and meke,
And be the chyn and be the cheke
Sche luggeth him riht as hir liste,
That nou sche japeth, nou sche kiste,
And doth with him what evere hir liketh.

(1889–95)

The language of mastery in this passage—that Apemen leads Cyrus by chin and cheek according to her will—is haunted by the erotic imagery of the "mounted Aristotle" later described in book 8, even if it does not specifically cite or invoke it.[26] Likewise, in the *Roman de la Rose*, the Vieille—the prototype for Chaucer's Wife of Bath—refers to the one lover she cannot dominate, as the lover who has a "bouche tandre" (14499), a tender mouth, not suitable to the bridle. The fantasy of the "mounted Aristotle" shaped the language of erotic violence in medieval French and English narratives so that a cultural notion of the scandal of female dominance could be cited visually or textually in equestrian images or metaphors. The erotic potential of such equestrian fantasies remains a recognizable feature of modern power erotics. The Circe chapter of James Joyce's *Ulysses*, for instance, includes Leopold Bloom's hallucinatory experience of being mounted by a woman brandishing a whip.[27] In contemporary dominatrix pornography, the whip has fetish status, and the erotic experience of performing as a horse is marketed by professional dominatrices as "pony-training."[28]

The Domestication of Violence

While the "mounted Aristotle" encodes a misogynist anxiety regarding female sexuality, it nonetheless designates sexual agency as separate from masculinity, and in the process it highlights the erotic value of sexual difference in medieval cultures. Despite the scandalous fantasy envisioned in the textual and visual traditions of the "mounted Aristotle," erotic violence in medieval cultures is most evident in marital violence, a form of intimate violence that enacts masculine dominance. The historical specificity of marital violence points to its erotic status and its emergence from the cultural constructions of desire. Marital violence is not much attested to in the ancient world; indeed violence first appears as a component of marriage in the late antique period in the Christian construction of the affective couple as the marital unit. As Amy Richlin summarizes the status of violence against women in classical Roman culture: "physical punishment of women at Rome was either extremely rare or extremely unmentionable. Although custom explicitly allowed a father, husband and sometimes male agnates the power of life and death over married women, very few cases, if any, are recorded in which adultery was punished by death. And Romans did not make jokes about wife-beating—though . . . the elegiac poets found fighting with their mistresses erotic."[29] Only three cases of husbands killing their wives survive from all of Roman history: two resulted from adultery, and the third was that of Metellius, who killed his wife for drinking wine—a case that takes on a mythical status in the *Wife of Bath's Prologue*, as we shall see. Otherwise, despite the legal restrictions on adultery enacted under Augustus, existing evidence suggests that Roman *matronae* seldom, if ever, suffered physical abuse at the hands of their husbands. An absence of violence in Roman marriage, however, does not mean an absence of erotic violence in Roman culture, and the status of violence against women in Rome must be understood in relation to the broader meanings of violence in the ancient world. Violence articulates a highly nuanced set of meanings in the hierarchical organization of position and identity in late Republican and Augustan Rome. Violence towards slaves—both male and female—was an everyday practice, but violence towards a Roman citizen was forbidden by law. Violence itself was a powerful cultural marker, as Moses Finley explains: "one fundamental distinction through much of antiquity was that corporal punishment, public or private, was restricted to slaves. Demosthenes said with a rhetorical flourish (22.55) that the greatest difference between the slave and the free man is that the former 'is answerable with his body for all offences.' "[30] The role of violence in determining and maintaining social divisions may explain the absence of records on wife-beating in Republican/Augustan Rome and the awareness of the erotic potential of violence against women in Latin love elegy. While elite Roman women shared none of the rights of citizenship enjoyed by their male relatives, they nonetheless belonged by association to a class of individuals who would not be appropriate objects of violence. The Roman matron was not situated as the object of desire since Roman marriage was not grounded on eros, and since she was not the object of desire, she was not the object of violence. Latin love elegy suggests that erotic violence arises within Roman heterosexual paradigms when the female does not belong to the "citizen" class but is rather a "freedwoman"—a somewhat ambiguous social position somewhere between slave and matron.[31] Latin love elegy is addressed to such freedwomen, and elegists are unabashed about describing how violence towards such women can be erotic, as we shall see in chapter 2.

By the end of the second century of the common era, the structures of marriage had undergone a transformation, from which emerges what Paul Veyne has identified as the "conjugal couple."[32] By contrast to marriage in the Republican/Augustan age, this new structure of marriage stresses the bond between husband and wife so that marriage takes on new expectations of affection and love, and new standards of conduct, including fidelity for both partners. By the time Christian marriage becomes hegemonic in Western culture in the fourth century—and divorce becomes more difficult to obtain than it was in the classical era—marriage becomes an institution intended to regulate desire as well as reproduction. And at this point, historical and literary allusions to wife-beating become more evident.[33] Augustine's description of his parents' marriage in *Confessions* 9.9 appeals to an ideal of fidelity on the part of both husband and wife, although Augustine notes that Monica had to endure her husband's infidelity until his conversion late in life. Augustine also tells us that Monica had to negotiate her husband's anger which could lead to violence, and that many married women in her circle were scarred from physical abuse: "plagarum vestigia, etiam dehonestata facie gererent" (9.9) ["they carried traces of blows even on their scarred faces"].[34] As marriage becomes an institution that structures eros, it simultaneously becomes an institution that both elicits and regulates violence.

Augustine presents his mother's conduct as exemplary: not only does she carefully negotiate her husband's anger and the violence it threatens, but she instructs the women of her community to know their place as *famulae* (domestic slaves) to their spouses, and to adopt conciliatory conduct that would soothe rather than aggravate their husbands. This attitude towards marital violence in the *Confessions* is elaborated as ideology elsewhere in the Augustine corpus. In the *De Civitate Dei*, Augustine describes the role of the *pater-familias*: "Si quis autem in domo per inobedientiam domesticae paci adversatur, corripitur, seu verbo, seu verbere, seu quolibet alio genere poenae justo atque licito, quantum societas humana concedit, pro ejus qui corripitur utilitate, ut paci unde dissiluerat coaptetur" (19.16)[35] ["So if anyone in the household through disobedience opposes the domestic peace, s/he is reproached, either by a word, or a blow, or some other form of just and lawful punishment, to the extent allowed by human society, for the sake of the one reproached, so that s/he may be joined to the peace from which s/he had broken away"]. The concept that the *paterfamilias* has a responsibility to verbally or physically "correct" all the members of his household—wives, children and slaves—puts violence at the heart of both marriage and family. Augustine sees violence as an expression of marital love, and he elsewhere comments that the gestures of discipline are gestures of affection. In the *Enarrationes in Psalmos 143*, he suggests that violence and love are mutually intertwined as in his version of domestic bliss:

> *Non enim contraria natura contra aliam naturam pugnat, sed tamquam in domo maritus et uxor. Si aduersus se dissentiant, molestus et periculosus labor; si maritus uincatur et uxor dominetur, pax peruersa; si autem uxor marito dominanti subiciatur, pax recta; non tamen aliud ex alia natura, quia ex homine facta mulier uiro. Caro tua, coniunx tua, famula tua."* *(118.6)*[36]

[For just as a contrary nature fights against another nature, just so in the home the husband and wife fight. If they disagree with each other, it is annoying and dangerous work; if the husband is conquered and the wife dominates, it is a perverse peace, if moreover the wife submits to be dominated by the husband, it is a proper peace, not however, something unnatural, because woman is made from man. Your flesh, your wife, your slave.]

The nature of marital affection that emerges in Christianity depends on the proper hierarchical arrangement within the household and the exemplary husband will perform his hierarchical role through violence and the threat of violence. Brent Shaw comments that the linguistic representation of domestic ideology in the term "*dominus* was integrally linked to *domus* (household) and to a whole host of terms signifying power, repression, and control—in short, domination: *domare* (to domesticate, to tame), *dominatio* (domination), *dominium* (control, ownership)."[37] In Augustine's vision of the marital bond, the potential violence of the husband as *dominus* is one manifestation of the emotional bond between husband and wife; with the emergence of Christian marriage, erotic violence has become domesticated.

Medieval discourse on sexuality and marriage assumes a conceptual link between eros and violence.[38] Legal texts, sermons, conduct literature, and literary texts all assume a certain level of violence to be normative in marriage. Medieval conduct books for women instruct their readers in the emotional responses they should adopt in response to the threat of violence. The *Livre du Chevalier de la Tour-Landry*, written by a late fourteenth-century knight for the education of his daughters and translated and printed by William Caxton in 1483, offers an example of a wife who would not keep her silence in obedience to her husband. As a consequence, the husband punishes her brutally: "And he, that was angri of her gouernaunce, smote her with his fiste downe to the erthe; And thanne with hys fote he stroke her in the uisage and brake her nose, and all her lyff after she had her nose croked . . . And therfor the wiff aught to suffre and lete the husbonde haue the wordes, and to be maister, for that is her worshippe."[39] The wife's responses to marital violence are a mark of gentility and breeding; the Chevalier concludes that the "gentil" woman internalizes the threat of violence so that it becomes the appropriate form of spousal love: "And thus pore men canne chaste her wyues with fere and strokes, but a gentille woman shulde chastise her selff with fairenesse. . . . And a gentille woman, the fairer that she is ferde with, the more ferdfulle she shulde be to displese or to disobeye her husbonde; for the good doutithe and louithe her husbondes" (28). In connecting the threat of violence to wifely devotion, the Chevalier articulates not only a cultural acceptance of marital violence but an assumption that violence and marital affection are interdependent. In a similar fashion, the late fourteenth-century conduct book composed by the *Menagier* of Paris for his young wife admonishes the wife to show patience in the face of a cruel husband. He initially proposes that the wife might deflate a husband's cruelty by her conduct: "Gardez que par bonne pacience et par la doulceur de voz paroles vous occiez l'orgueil de sa cruaulté" (112)[40] ["Take care to by good patience and by the sweetness of your words to destroy the pride of his cruelty"]. Should her demeanor fail to deflect the anger of her husband, he advises a pious acceptance: "Et se vous ne le pouez desmouvoir qu'il ne vous courrousse, gardez que vous ne vous en plaingniez a vos amis ne autre, dont il se puist apparcevoir; car il en tendroit moins de bien de vous, et luy en souvendroit autresfoiz. Mais alez en vostre chambre plourer bellement et coyement a basse voix, et vous en plaingniez at Dieu" (112) ["And if you cannot turn his anger away from you, be careful not to complain to your friends or to others which he might notice, for he would think less well of you for it and would remember it at another time. . . . But go into your chamber and weep gently and quietly in a low voice, and make your complaint to God"]. As we shall see in chapter 6, when Christine de Pizan composed a conduct book for women, she similarly advised a wife to strategically accept the violence of a cruel husband.[41] These approaches to the issue of marital violence echo the attitude of Augustine's mother a millennium earlier.

According to canon law, violence was legal in marriage as long as the violence did not exceed specific limits: practitioners and teachers of canon law routinely assert that a husband has the right to "correct" his wife, and many commentators consider physical punishment to be part of such correction. As James Brundage has recently shown, however, most commentators assume that there should be limits to a husband's right of correction. At one extreme is the author of the twelfth-century *Summa Parisiensis*, who would allow clerical husbands to beat their wives severely, as long as they avoided killing them.[42] Other twelfth-century commentators clarify that a husband is allowed to "correct" his wife, but not by beating or whipping her. Most commentators on canon law stress that a husband had to be temperate or moderate in disciplining his wife. A woman who experienced abuse that was unacceptably severe could sue in ecclesiastical court for separation from "bed and board," which would allow a wife to live apart from a violent husband, though neither could remarry.[43] In the various cases that historians have studied, sometimes the separation is granted, though just as often it would appear that a judge admonished or fined the violent husband and ruled that the couple remain under one roof, despite the violence.[44] Such restoration orders often required that the husband treat his wife with "marital affection" (*maritalis affectio*).[45] Assuming that cases that came to court were the tip of the iceberg, marital violence was accepted and routine, and a married woman would most likely endure violence and learn adaptive skills in marriage; appealing to ecclesiastical authorities would be a last resort.

Common law was likewise concerned with violence against wives only when it exceeded acceptable limits. As Pollock and Maitland summarize it: "The king's court would protect the life and limb of the married woman against her husband's savagery by punishing him if he killed or maimed her. If she went in fear of any violence exceeding a reasonable chastisement, he could be bound with sureties to keep the peace; but she had no action against him, nor had he against her. If she killed him, that was petty treason."[46] However, scholars have found that husbands were seldom prosecuted in royal courts for wife abuse: Margaret Kerr found no cases in the records she reviewed,[47] and Robert Palmer found one case in which wife-beating was mentioned, though it was only tangential to the case being tried.[48] Surviving cases suggest that when husbands killed their wives, such cases were treated as homicide.[49] Customary laws likewise assume that a husband may use physical force to punish his wife, although the limits to such violence may be articulated differently in different locales.[50] The customary laws of Beauvais offer one continental example:

> A man may beat his wife (although without loss of life or limb), when she offends against him, such as when she is committing adultery, or when she contradicts her husband or curses him, or when she will not obey his reasonable orders as an honest woman should: in such and similar cases a man should punish his wife moderately. But if they are chaste, wives must be excused of many other vices; and nevertheless, the husband should punish and correct his wife according to the vice, in any way he sees fit (excepting where it causes loss of life or limb) to rid her of this vice.[51]

On the local level, marital violence was less likely to be regulated by the court than by the community. Scattered throughout legal records are cases where neighbors and members of the community intervened in an incident of marital violence that was deemed excessive.[52] While medieval legal texts generally represent violence as a normative feature of marriage and assume that a husband had a right and even a responsibility to use violence to discipline his wife,[53] they also assume that such violence can be regulated and must be kept within "reasonable" limits so that the health or life of wives might not be unnecessarily endangered.[54]

Medieval hagiography and mystical texts frequently eroticize violence as a form of suffering, so that violence itself acquires what Sarah Kay terms a "sublime" quality.[55] Given the sacramental status of marriage, marital violence—within limits—would appear to serve a sacral function; indeed, women murdered by their husbands were occasionally venerated as saints.[56] Since an act of marital violence could be seen as either normative or deviant depending on the context, the local community standards invoked, and the amount of force involved, representations of intimate violence in medieval texts always invite the judgment of the reader, if only implicitly. Consequently, representations of erotic violence in medieval texts are unsettling even when such representations are in accordance with cultural norms regarding violence and sexual difference. The assumption that a husband had to observe specific limits in exercising his right to correct his wife required that he recognize her alterity as a bearer of rights despite the hierarchies of medieval marriage; such prohibitions on excessive violence thus conferred an ethical dimension on marital violence, and such prohibitions likewise structured *maritalis affectio* as a form of power erotics. If the pervasive cultural fantasy of the "mounted Aristotle" articulates the scandal that attaches to female erotic agency, the cultural norms for marital violence articulate an assumption that violence and erotic agency are inextricably linked.

CHAPTER 2

Ovid's *Ars amatoria*
and the Wounds of Love

> After millenniums of sex and centuries of poetry, the
> love poem . . . was invented in Rome in the first cen-
> tury before Christ.
>
> —Tom Stoppard

Towards the end of the *Wife of Bath's Prologue*,
the Wife bitterly complains about the codex that Jankyn, her fifth husband,
owned and from which he read aloud to her every night. As part of her
complaint, she catalogues the offending texts bound in Jankyn's volume, and
among them she lists "Ovides Art" (680), a version of the *Ars amatoria*.
Chaucer's reference to this classical Latin poem in the context of the *Prologue* is highly appropriate, since the discourse on erotic violence that animates the *Prologue* can be traced to the structures of desire initially articulated in the *Ars amatoria* and later appropriated by medieval vernacular poets
such as Jean de Meun. The *Ars* ironically proposed the notion that violence
was one effective option for heterosexual performance; that ironic proposition, however, acquired authority with the medieval reception, translation,
and adaptation of Ovid's *Ars*. As a result, one cannot fully engage with the
ethical dimensions of erotic violence in Ovidian poets such as Jean de Meun
or Geoffrey Chaucer without first considering how the categories of erotic
violence are formulated in the *Ars amatoria*.

Composed in 1–2 CE, Ovid's *Ars amatoria* ironically presents itself as a
handbook for heterosexual desire within a hierarchical dynamic. With excessive didacticism, it crudely proposes the sexual pursuit of women with
the goal of achieving dominance over them. Though at moments the text
insists that heterosexuality is natural, the extensive detail and exhortations

that constitute the rhetoric of the *Ars* ultimately present heterosexual performance as a skill that must be taught and learned. The *Ars* thereby acknowledges the performative basis of sexuality as it instructs the reader—designated as male in the first two books and female in the third book—in the gestures, mythology, attitudes, postures, and rhetoric that enable one to perform *amor*. Given such a pedagogical imperative, the narrator of the *Ars* presents himself as a teacher of love, a *praeceptor Amoris* (1.17), who must elaborate on the various tasks that the newly initiated lover must learn to perform.[1] The *Ars* was produced during the early years of imperial rule; as a tract on heterosexual desire, it parodically glances towards Augustus's legislation on marriage and reproduction, legislation intended to construct a moral ideology in an effort to reverse the declining birthrate. These laws, the Lex Julia of 18 BCE, and the Lex Papia of 9 BCE, were designed to require marriage and penalize adultery.[2] Since Roman expansion required a population that could meet the needs of the military, the work of empire required the production of legitimate offspring among Roman citizens.[3] Marital reproduction thus became a legal obligation in order to further the goals of Roman conquests and colonial occupation. By contrast to such official policy, the *Ars* defines *amor* as an experience that can only take place outside of marriage, and it is completely silent on the reproductive consequences of heterosexual performance. The *Ars* thereby mocks the assumptions of Augustus' marriage legislation that sexuality can be regulated by law. Augustus, however, apparently failed to appreciate the irony of the *Ars*, and the poem, along with another unknown transgression, resulted in Ovid's exile to the Black Sea.[4]

The irony of the *Ars amatoria* depends entirely on contemporary Roman politics. In the context of the imperial sexualities of Augustan Rome, the roles taught by the *praeceptor* are so excessively delineated that they call attention to the constructed and performative basis of desire; a constitutive component of that performance, as we shall see, is violence.[5] The first two books of the *Ars* catalogue the aggressive and dominant actions, occasionally punctuated by feigned gestures of submission, that will enable the male lover to acquire the female object of desire. The third book instructs the female in her heterosexual obligations. The heterosexual script as it develops in the course of the *Ars* emerges from the structures of imperialism so that the *praeceptor*'s discourse of sexual domination and conquest mimics the discourses of Roman coloniality. The irony and rhetorical excess of the *Ars amatoria* are relatively transparent to the reader able to situate the *Ars* in relation to Augustan poetics and imperial politics: read in that context, the *Ars* suggests that heteroerotics is one effect of imperialism. The medieval reception of the *Ars*, however, illustrates the contingent nature of literary irony: lacking much specific knowledge or information regarding the Augustan Age, medieval readers lacked the framework within which to appreciate the ironic texture of the poem. Instead, medieval readers treat the *Ars* as an ethical treatise on love and seduction. C. S. Lewis termed this reception of the *Ars* "Ovid misunderstood;"[6] that "misunderstanding" generated an influential discourse on erotic violence.

Ars amatoria 1 and 2: Desire and Imperial Spectacle

From the start of his lesson and throughout the text, the *praeceptor* employs military analogies; love is a kind of warfare, and the soldier a lover: "qui noua nunc primum miles in arma uenis" (1.36)[7] ["You who now come as a soldier into new battles for the first time"]. Such military analogies—a standard feature of Latin love elegy—illustrate the subversive values of amatory poetry in relation to Roman ideology. As Claude Nicolet points out, "the Roman, any Roman, is first and foremost a warrior, or rather a soldier . . . a disciplined citizen forming part of a machine whose redoubtable efficiency is the result of its coherence."[8] In the *Ars*, however, the lover as soldier pursues a personal goal that, in the face of Augustus' marriage legislation, works against the cohesion of both the family and the state. The *praeceptor*'s repetition of military analogies in the *Ars* ironically claims an imperial value for male conquest of women. In elaborating on heterosexual *amor*, the *praeceptor* negotiates a set of erotic norms structured by the distinctions of a slave-owning culture. A Roman citizen—who was by definition male—could select either women or boys as objects of desire. As Amy Richlin points out, for the male citizen, slave boys were legitimate objects of desire, but sexual intercourse with freeborn youths was forbidden by law.[9] The *praeceptor* sees little or no erotic potential in man-boy love, given its actual context as master-slave love, since the slave is always already available for use as a sex object: "odi concubitus, qui non utrumque resoluunt: / hoc est, cur pueri tangar amore minus" (2.683–84) ["I hate sexual unions which do not offer release on both sides. This is why I am less moved by the love of a boy"]. While slave boys were available as passive partners, same-sex desire between adult male citizens was highly questionable, if not transgressive, since a Roman citizen was expected to take the active role in intercourse—whether vaginal or anal.[10] The *praeceptor* thus articulates a cultural attitude in gendered terms when he comments that men who seek to please other men by excessive attention to physical desirability are comparable to women: "cetera lasciuae faciant concede puellae / et si quis male uir quaerit habere uirum" (1.523–24) ["Leave the remaining things for wanton girls to do and any man who ill-advisedly seeks to have a man"]. In order to address the specifics of these categories of heterosexual *amor*, the *praeceptor* offers detailed instructions for grooming and suggests that the heterosexual suitor should affect a slightly neglected look. Beyond attention to basic bodily cleanliness and clean clothes, clean teeth, and pared nails, the *praeceptor* is adamant that the lover should not preen: he should not curl his hair or depilate his legs. The male lover seeking to acquire and retain the love of women distinguishes himself by his behavior from "men seeking men." The *Ars* thereby identifies masculinity with the sexual pursuit of women.[11]

What is the social status of the woman whom the lover might pursue and whom Ovid addresses in his third book? Roman amatory poetry, like Greek erotic poetry, presumes the existence of a class of women who are sexually available yet relatively autonomous in that they have some degree of choice in selecting their partners. Married women were not perceived by their husbands to be objects of erotic desire, since marriage existed to fulfill the reproductive imperatives of family and empire, and the *praeceptor* does not offer advice on courtship leading to matrimony. Adulterous alliances, however, have definite erotic possibilities in the world of love elegy, but adultery was precisely the sort of sexual behavior criminalized by Augustus' marriage legislation, which would account for Ovid's specific claims that the *praeceptor* is not promoting the pursuit of matrons (3.615–16). At one point, the *praeceptor* describes a female as encumbered by a *vir*—a word that might denote husband, but as John Davis points out, could refer to a concubinate relationship as well.[12] Certainly, the female object of desire has to be elusive enough to allow for pursuit and jealousy and yet be hypothetically attainable. At the opposite end of the social spectrum from matrons were prostitutes—female slaves—who were readily available and required no erotic art to approach or obtain. In between prostitutes and respectable matrons there existed a cohort of freedwomen who were mistresses and courtesans, or matrons whose adulterous behavior classed them with freedwomen.[13] At *Ars* 1.435, Ovid refers to the female in question as a *meretrix*, which Saara Lilja defines as an elite, educated courtesan.[14] At other places, the female object of desire is called a *domina* (mistress), a *puella* (girl), and an *amica* (girlfriend), a range of terms which suggests that "her status is not consistent, for she is made to play out a variety of social and erotic roles in different situations," according to Alison Sharrock.[15] Like the women of amatory elegy in general, the desired female in the *Ars* is classed somewhere in between a prostitute and an unapproachable, respectable matron.[16] She behaves like a *meretrix* when she seeks some sort of financial gain, but her potential elusiveness classifies her with concubines or adulterous matrons. She is sexually available but potentially expensive to court, and a lover must have an *ars* if he is to successfully pursue her with minimum financial expenditure. While eros depends on the effort the lover must exert, the *praeceptor* fully expects his disciples to be successful in obtaining their pursuits.

As a category so carefully elaborated in the *Ars, amor* is both enabled by and implicitly enables Roman colonial power. The *Ars* suggests that heterosexual desire can be elicited by the spectacles central to public life in Augustan Rome, where vast amounts of public space were designed for the staging of urban spectacles such as gladiatorial shows, circuses, triumphs, or theatrical events. By the time of Augustus, these spectacles were mounted on a massive scale, so that the status of Rome as the center of imperial power was routinely enacted in public spaces in the display of exotic animals in the circus, in the combat of gladiators, in the parade of loot and conquered peoples in triumphs.[17] Such spectacles required the transport of objects, peoples and animals from distant territories at the periphery of the empire to be placed before the gaze of Romans, who would feast their eyes on scenes that by their very extravagance testified to the wealth, centrality, and power of Rome. The exotic difference of these animals, slaves, and goods visually confirmed the vast geographical expanse of imperial power.[18] Such imperial spectacles allowed the Roman citizen to feel placed at the center of the geopolitics of empire. In addition, during Augustus' reign, the act of attending a theatrical or gladiatorial show was explicitly an exercise in social hierarchies, since spectators were assigned seats according to their rank and marital status.[19] To participate in public life in Rome was not only to witness the wonderful products of peripheral territories on display at the center, but to be placed in a specific social niche in the process. All aspects of Roman dominion and power were enacted in these spectacles that were essentially colonial exhibits.

To the *praeceptor*, the imperialism of such performances is a potential aphrodisiac for his disciple, so that the spectacles of imperial conquest—especially triumphs—are evoked for their potential heteroerotic appeal. Early in *Ars amatoria* 1, in the midst of instructing his disciple about where to find a *puella*, the *praeceptor* abruptly shifts the topic from a discussion of Roman urban space to a send-off prayer—a *propempticon*—for Gaius Caesar, who was about to embark on a campaign to the East on behalf of Augustus to secure some disputed territories in Armenia: "ecce, parat Caesar domito quod defuit orbi / addere" (1.177–18) ["Behold, Caesar prepares to add to the conquered world that which was missing"]. For more than a dozen couplets, the *praeceptor* celebrates the possibilities of a Roman victory as though this particular campaign had much greater regional significance than it actually had.[20] Ovid's *praeceptor* indulges in a description of a future triumph—which actually never took place—but which, in its virtual detail, seems richly particular:

> *ergo erit illa dies, qua tu, pulcherrime rerum,*
> *quattuor in niueis aureus ibis equis;*
> *ibunt ante duces onerati colla catenis,*
> *ne possint tuti, qua prius, esse fuga.*
> *spectabunt laeti iuuenes mixtaeque puellae.*
>
> *(1.213–17)*

[Therefore that day will come when you, most beautiful among all, will go, clad in gold, behind four snow-white horses; leaders will go in front [of you], their necks weighed down by chains, so that they cannot be safe through flight, as before. Happy young men, joined by girls, will look on.]

This display of foreign leaders with shackles around their necks offers the would-be lover a scene of Roman domination that might effectively be employed in the seduction of women. The *praeceptor* advises his pupil that a woman in the crowded audience might inquire about the identity of subjugated peoples on view, and the *praeceptor* suggests that an astute lover would answer her with specifics, even if he had to invent them (1.227–28). Thus the act of viewing an extravagant procession of conquered peoples not only confirms Roman dominance, but that dominance encourages and enables heteroerotics in the way it situates its spectators. The power relations of coloniality offer a script for the power relations enacted in heterosexual desire.

The homoerotic spectacle of gladiators in combat might likewise enable heterosexual pursuit. Gladiatorial fighting staged a highly sexualized spectacle of glamorous male bodies—the bodies of slaves or condemned criminals—in a public display of blood and violence. The *praeceptor* suggests that in the gladiatorial shows in the Forum, for instance, the male spectator might be wounded by the God of Love ("Venus' boy") who functions in the *Ars* as a conduit for heterosexual desire:

> *illa saepe puer Veneris pugnauit harena*
> *et, qui spectauit uulnera, uulnus habet:*
> *dum loquitur tangitque manum poscitque libellum*
> *et quaerit posito pignore, uincat uter,*

saucius ingemuit telumque uolatile sensit
   et pars spectati muneris ipse fuit.
                    (1.165–70)

[Venus' boy often fought in that arena, and he who witnessed wounds
has a wound. While he speaks and touches her hand and requests the
program, and having placed a bet, inquires who will win, he moans,
wounded, and feels the flying arrow and is himself part of the enter-
tainment being watched.]

Keith Hopkins notes that "the victorious gladiator, or at least his image, was
sexually attractive."[21] The would-be lover who witnesses this homoerotic
spectacle of wounds becomes "wounded" as a consequence, and the *praeceptor*
offers him a strategy to regain his erotic agency through attending to a female
spectator who might subsequently become the object of desire. The homo-
eroticism of the gladiator show becomes a conduit for heterosexual desire
and thereby furthers the construction of the spectator as a heterosexual lover.

The *praeceptor* likewise narrates the rape of the Sabines to support his assertion that the theater is a potential locale in which the lover might seek his
prey (1.99–134). Ovid invented the narrative detail that the rape of the
Sabines took place in a theater, and his insertion of this foundation myth at
an early point in the first book of the *Ars* idealizes rape as a form of aggression that the more decadent Augustan lover would do well to emulate.[22] The
rape is nostalgically characterized as an activity befitting the rude and rustic
early Romans in a way that complemented the warrior state: "Romule, mil-
itibus scisti dare commoda solus: / haec mihi si dederis commoda, miles
ero" (1.131–32) ["Romulus, you alone knew to give rewards to soldiers: if
you will give me these kinds of rewards, I will be a soldier"]. The narrator
describes the fear of the women as they are carried off, and he notes in
voyeuristic appreciation the fact that they change color (1.120). While some
are silent, some shriek and wail; he adds pointedly: "ducuntur raptae, genialis
praeda, puellae, / et potuit multas ipse decere timor" (1.125–26) ["The ab-
ducted women, nuptial booty, are led off, and fear itself added grace to
many"]. This specular celebration of rape as Roman and heroic works programmatically in the *Ars* to eroticize violence and ironically promote heterosexual desire as a category central to the warrior ethos of Rome.

The relationship between colonial dominance and heterosexual seduction is established early in the *Ars*; likewise, the dominant role of the male
heterosexual lover is emphasized throughout, and throughout, this dominant status is articulated in violent metaphors and performed through vio-

lent gestures. *Amor*—the God of Love—is implicated in violence from the start of the *praeceptor's* lesson; as he initially explains:"quo me fixit Amor, quo me uiolentius ussit, / hoc melior facti uulneris ultor ero" (1.23–24) ["The more Amor pierced me, the more violently he inflamed me, the better I will avenge the wound he has made"]. Thus violence is a component of the *ars* preached by the *praeceptor*, and knowing how and when to use violence is a central lesson of the *Ars amatoria*. On the face of it, however, the *praeceptor* appears to contradict himself regarding the efficacy of violence. In the first book of the *Ars*, which addresses the topic of acquiring the *puella*, the *praeceptor* extends the lesson drawn from the rape of the Sabines to the lover's pursuit. He initially suggests that the lover use force:

> quis sapiens blandis non misceat oscula uerbis?
>   illa licet non det, non data sume tamen.
> pugnabit primo fortassis, et "improbe" dicet;
>   pugnando uinci se tamen illa uolet.
> tantum, ne noceant teneris male rapta labellis,
>   neue queri possit dura fuisse, caue.
>   (1.663–68)

[What wise man would not mingle kisses with flattering words? It is permitted, should she not give them [kisses] nevertheless to take them unoffered. Perhaps at first she will fight and cry, "Cruel one"; all the same, she will wish to be conquered in the fight. Only take care [the kisses] do not harm, being badly snatched from delicate lips, and that she not be able to complain that they were rough.]

Having provided this set of specific instructions for ignoring and overcoming the resistance of the *puella*, the *praeceptor* proceeds to explicitly authorize his disciple to rape her:[23]

> uim licet appelles: grata est uis ista puellis;
>   quod iuuat, inuitae saepe dedisse uolunt.
> quaecumque est Veneris subita uiolata rapina,
>   gaudet, et improbitas muneris instar habet.
> at quae, cum posset cogi, non tacta recessit,
>   ut simulet uultu gaudia, tristis erit.
>   (1. 673–78)

[It is permitted for you to use force: such force is pleasing to girls; that which delights they often wish to have given unwillingly. Whoever is

violated by a sudden theft of love, rejoices, and considers the impro-
bity a kind of gift. And she who departed untouched when she could
have been forced, though she simulate pleasure in her countenance,
she will be sad.]

Later in *Ars amatoria* 2, the book that addresses how a lover might make love
endure, the *praeceptor* relates an anecdote that appears to question the lover's
prerogatives when it comes to violence:

> me memini iratum dominae turbasse capillos;
>   haec mihi quam multos abstulit ira dies!
> nec puto nec sensi tunicam laniasse, sed ipsa
>   dixerat, et pretio est illa redempta meo.
> at uos, si sapitis, uestri peccata magistri
>   effugite et culpae damna timete meae.
> proelia cum Parthis, cum culta pax sit amica
>   et iocus et causas quicquid amoris habet.
>
>   (2.169–76)

[I remember that enraged, I disturbed the hair of my *domina*; how
many days did this anger take from me! I do not think nor did I perceive that I had torn her tunic, but she said so, and it was paid for by
my money. But you, if you have any sense, avoid the sins of your master and fear the losses of my errors. Let there be battles with the
Parthians, but with a refined girlfriend, let there be peace and play, and
whatever are the pretexts of love.]

This anecdote closely resembles the situation described by Ovid in *Amores*
1.7,[24] when the narrator rehearses his belated remorse for his physical violence towards his *puella*, a violence he simultaneously describes and dis-
avows: "nam furor in dominam temeraria bracchia mouit; / flet mea uesana
laesa puella manu" (3–4) ["For a fury moved rash arms against my *domina*,
the girl, injured by my frenzied hand, weeps"]. Throughout *Amores* 1.7 the
narrator describes his violent agency with a rhetorical detachment: "at nunc
sustinui raptis a fronte capillis / ferreus ingenuas ungue notare genas" (1.7.
49–50) ["And now, hair having been torn from her head, I, hard-hearted,
have managed to mark her noble (freeborn) cheeks with my nails"]. Both
couplets suggest that these violent acts occurred without the poet's volition.

The poem is structured around the narrator's expression of remorse; in a
virtuoso moment of Ovidian overstatement, the narrator/lover opens the
poem with the request that he be restrained: "Adde manus in uincla meas"

(1.7.1) ["Put my hands in chains"]. By the middle of the poem, however, these power-relations are reversed as the narrator mockingly depicts his violence in terms of an imperial triumph in which his *puella* is paraded as human booty and the poet's conquest celebrated:

> *i nunc, magnificos uictor molire triumphos,*
> *cinge comam lauro uotaque redde Ioui,*
> *quaeque tuos currus comitantum turba sequetur,*
> *clamet "io, forti uicta puella uiro est!"*
> *ante eat effuso tristis captiua capillo,*
> *si sinerent laesae, candida tota, genae.*
>
> *(1.7.35–40)*

[Go now, victor, undertake magnificent triumphs, circle your hair with laurel and render votive offerings to Jove, and let whatever crowd that follows, thronging around your chariot, call out: "Io, a girl was conquered by a strong man." Let her go in front [of you], a sad captive with disheveled hair; completely white except for her wounded cheeks.]

The narrator emphasizes the erotic pleasure afforded by the sight of Corinna, his radiant *puella*, as a *tristis captiva*. The subjugated woman is thereby eroticized—whether she be the captive foreigner brought to Rome to be enslaved or the freedwoman rendered abject by her position as object of desire, a position that has resulted in her being the object of violence. The invocation of an imperial triumph cuts in two directions simultaneously: its erotic content mocks the high cultural value assigned to the triumph as a staged event.[25] Yet this imaginary triumph represents heterosexual male dominance in imperial terms when the narrator states that the violent lover might feel like a triumphant general. In *Amores* 1.7, the masculinities elicited in heterosexual performance and imperial conquest are equally mocked for their excess.

The narrator's remorse in this poem seems excessive, especially in light of its contradictory impulses. While the lover professes to have been too violent, he nonetheless notes that his violence renders his *puella* attractive: "ergo ego digestos potui laniare capillos? / nec dominam motae dedecuere comae: / sic formosa fuit" (1.7.11–13) ["Then was I able to tear her coiffed hair? Disheveled locks were not unbecoming to my *domina*: she was beautiful thus"]. The lover/narrator of the *Amores* 1.7 categorizes his violence by its

impact: though violence might enhance his sense of erotic agency, its efficacy is diminished when it reduces his *puella* to a fearful and unresponsive
object "pauido est lingua retenta metu" (1.7.20) ["Her tongue was restrained by quaking fear"]. Instead of brute violence that pushes her into
mute resistance, he notes that violence could have been effectively deployed: "aptius impressis fuerat liuere labellis / et collum blandi dentis
habere notam" (1.7.41–42) ["It would be more fitting if she had been
bruised by pressing lips, and for her neck to have the marks of white teeth"].
Indeed, the lover explicitly defines the limits to his aggressive behavior towards his *domina*:

> *nonne satis fuerat timidae inclamasse puellae*
> *nec nimium rigidas intonuisse minas*
> *aut tunicam a summa diducere turpiter ora*
> *ad mediam (mediae zona tulisset opem)?*
> *1.7.45–48*

[Was it not enough to have scolded the timid girl, and not to have
thundered very harsh threats, or to have shamefully split her tunic
from the top to the waist (the belt had protected the waist)?"]

When the *praeceptor* instructs his disciple in the use of violence in *Ars amatoria* 2, he comments specifically on the event narrated in *Amores* 1.7: the *praeceptor's* reference to an incident when he unwittingly grabbed the hair of his
puella or tore her dress echoes the language of *Amores* 1.7 when the lover
suggests that erotic violence occurs without his volition. Based on the *praeceptor's* experience that his *puella* keeps him at a distance when she is angry,
he advises the lover to cultivate peace and play (*iocus*) rather than violence.
The passage in *Ars amatoria* 2 thus sets the limits to the levels of force recommended in the first book of the *Ars*: to be erotically efficacious, force and
violence must be deployed sparingly and knowingly. In addition, Ovid
specifically identifies violence as a marker of the social status of Corinna in
Amores 1.7: "an, si pulsassem minimum de plebe Quiritem, / plecterer, in
dominam ius mihi maius erit?" (29–30) ["But if I had struck the lowest
Roman citizen of the common people, I would be punished; shall have I a
greater right over my domina?"] Latin love elegy suggests that violence has
the potential to be erotic only when the female is a "freedwoman." Unlike a
slave, she has a right to resist violence and is debased by being struck, though
such resistance only enhances her erotic appeal. Unlike a matron, she is not

in a social position which would be irrevocably compromised by being the object of violence, though the sense of transgression the violent lover experiences when he abuses his *puella* is heightened by her liminal status; as Ovid notes in *Amores* 1.7, it is Corinna's freeborn status that violence throws into relief. When the *praeceptor* recommends erotic violence to the male lover in book 2 of the *Ars amatoria*, he develops the pedagogical implications of the scene described in *Amores* 1.7.

The *praeceptor* also suggests that the male lover might occasionally debase himself, even to the point of enduring mild physical abuse or humiliation at the hands of his *domina*: "nec maledicta puta nec uerbera ferre puellae / turpe nec ad teneros oscula ferre pedes" (2.533–34) ["Do not think it an insult to bear the lash of your girl, nor disgraceful to give kisses to her delicate feet"]. This voluntary subjugation—which the *praeceptor* offers as a theatrical role the lover might effectively adopt—is derived from the topos of the *servitium amoris*. In Latin amatory poetry, the metaphor of the lover as *servus* to an all-powerful *domina* provided a rhetorical formula for expressing the emotional agency of the *puella*—an agency which amounted to her ability to withhold affection and sexual favors from the lover; her ability to exercise any control over her own sexuality, that is, made her all-powerful. As a rhetorical topos, *servitium amoris* had acquired a recognizable currency by Ovid's day, a currency that owed much to the terminology of a slave-owning culture. The term *domina*, as Judith Hallett notes, means a "woman in command of household slaves."[26] Like a slave, the lover might be expected to be abused by his *domina*, but such momentary debasement allows for a position of recovery as the *praeceptor* suggests that the lover move from a scene of anger to a sexual caress: "cum bene saeuierit, cum certa uidebitur hostis, / tum pete concubitus foedera: mitis erit" (2.461–62) ["When she will have raged fully, when she will seem a definite enemy, then seek the bonds of sexual union: she will be gentle"]. The *praeceptor* only suggests the pose of the *servitium amoris* as a means for the lover to consolidate his power over his *puella*.

The *praeceptor* sees violence as an integral component of eros, the deft performance of which should enable the lover to maximize his access to and hold over his *puella*. In this respect, the *praeceptor* suggests that violence is a skill, like rhetoric, to be learned and used towards a specific end. "Disce bonas artes" (1.459) ["Learn the good arts"], the *praeceptor* advises, though he proceeds to recommend epistolary rhetoric in the place of declamation for amatory pursuits. In suggesting that violence as an *ars* must be equally subtle, the *praeceptor* parodically offers a theatrical model of heterosexual agency for the would-be lover.

Ars amatoria 3 and the Performance of Femininity

Just as the first two books of the *Ars* tutor the male reader in the pleasures of effectively deployed dominance and submission, the third and last book of the *Ars* instructs the female in the erotics of submission, a power play she may be able to manipulate to her advantage, according to the *praeceptor*. While the third book purports to arm women against men, it does not situate the woman reader in a symmetrical subject position to the male lover. The *praeceptor* tutors the woman reader in the art of being the object of male desire; to that end, he instructs his *discipula* in grooming and cosmetics, demeanor and manners, as well as personal hygiene.[27] While the *praeceptor* encourages his female disciple to cultivate a rustic look, he nonetheless notes that the urbane woman of his day may consume goods from any corner of the empire, since "nunc aurea Roma est / et domiti magnas possidet orbis opes" (3.113–14) ["Now Rome is golden and holds the great wealth of a conquered world"]. Roman colonial dominance thereby facilitates the tasks assigned to the female intent on attracting a male lover, since the colonial economy makes available the commodities needed for a particular standard of grooming required to enhance her attractiveness. The *Roman de la Rose* and Chaucer's depiction of the Wife of Bath in the *General Prologue* develop more fully the notion that exotic commodities—particularly clothing—increase the erotic appeal of women. The *praeceptor* also discusses appropriate sexual responses for the female lover, who is encouraged to discipline her appetite for food and drink, as well as her emotions, and to respond in a calculated fashion to male advances, even to the extent of faking orgasms: "tu quoque, cui Veneris sensum natura negauit, / dulcia mendaci gaudia finge sono" (3.797–98) ["and you to whom nature has denied the feeling of sexual love, feign sweet joy with counterfeit sounds"]. The coy and calculating female—if she learns the lessons of the *praeceptor*—might be able to manipulate her male suitors; her *ars*, however, depends entirely on her responses to sexual advances made by men. As the *praeceptor* puts it: "efficite (et facile est) ut nos credamus amari" (3.673) ["make us believe we are loved—and it is easy"]. In addressing itself to women, *Ars amatoria 3* becomes more insistently concerned with the mechanics of seduction and sexual performance; the final section of the book offers explicit instructions on sexual positions and admonishes the female reader to strike the most appropriate pose for her body type. As Holt Parker has shown, this aspect of *Ars 3* parodies the genre of sex manuals, Hellenistic texts whose self-conscious concern with the mechanics of heterosexuality exposes a shift in cultural values "from a predominantly aristocratic and homoerotic code to a bourgeois and heteroerotic code."[28] This parodic discourse on sexual mechanics sets off by contrast the *praeceptor's* advice on psychological manipulation: he insists that the male suitor will respond warmly to rebuffs and some calculated resistance from the object of desire. Indeed, the *praeceptor* presents his own psyche as the norm: "en ego, confiteor, non nisi laesus amo" (3.598) ["And I, I confess, do not love unless wounded"]. Thus he encourages the female reader to allow the male lover the gestures of submission appropriate to an elegiac lover: in elegy, the male lover can be found reclining, excluded outside the closed door of the beloved, fearing rivals, and so forth. However, the *praeceptor* insists that this domineering behavior be followed by passionate submission on the part of the *puella*.

In the context of instructing the *puella*, the *praeceptor* notes the efficacy of wine for female eroticism. Having commented on the aesthetics of moderate eating, the *praeceptor* instructs:

> *aptius est deceatque magis potare puellas:*
>   *cum Veneris puero non male, Bacche, facis.*
> *hoc quoque, qua patiens caput est animusque pedesque*
>   *constant nec, quae sunt singula, bina uide.*
> *turpe iacens mulier multo madefacta Lyaeo:*
>   *digna est concubitus quoslibet illa pati.*
>
>   (3. 761–66)

[It is more suitable and more fitting for girls to drink: Bacchus— you do not perform badly with the son of Venus. This is so as long as the head holds up, and the mind and feet stand firm, and you do not see double things that are single. A woman lying soaked with much wine is repulsive: that one deserves to suffer any sexual union.]

This passage has a parallel in *Ars* 1 when the *praeceptor* suggests that the male lover consider the value of wine for setting a seductive mood: "uina parant animos faciuntque caloribus aptos" (1.237) ["Wines prepare the spirit and make it suitable for passion"]. While the *praeceptor* comments that wine makes a male lover more vulnerable to the attractions of women (1.237–40), the risks of wine for the *puella* are far greater; nonetheless, the *praeceptor* insists on the erotic potential of wine in moderation. Roman culture explicitly associated wine-drinking and female sexuality.[29] Valerius Maximus, Ovid's near contemporary who recorded the received wisdom of Roman declamatory discourse as a paradigm for contemporary ethics,[30] asserts that it is transgressive, at least for a wife, to consume wine, since wine activates female libido: "Vini usus olim Romanis feminis ignotus fuit, ne scilicet in aliquod dedecus prolaberentur, quia proximus a Libero patre intemperantiae gradus ad inconcessam uenerem esse consueuit"[31] (2.1.5) ["The use of wine was formerly unknown to Roman women, undoubtedly lest they slipped into some disgrace, because the next step for the intemperate was accustomed to be from Father Bacchus to forbidden love"]. So strong was this prohibition that Valerius Maximus cites an exemplary case of uxoricide as punishment for wine-drinking:

Magno scelere horum seueritas ad exigendam uindictam concitata est, Egnati autem Mecenni longe minore de causa, qui uxorem, quod uinum bibisset, fusti percussam interemit, idque factum non accusatore tantum sed etiam reprehensore caruit, uno quoque existimante optimo illam exemplo uiolatae sobrietati poenas pependisse. et sane quaecumque femina uini usum immoderate appetit, omnibus et uirtutibus ianuam claudit et delictis aperit. (6.3.9)

[Their severity was urged to enforce punishment for a great crime, but the severity of Egnatius Mecennius was provoked by a far more minor cause: he killed his wife, striking her with a club because she had drunk wine, and this deed was exempt not only from prosecution but from blame: indeed, this one was considered an excellent example because she had paid the penalty for violating sobriety, and doubtless every woman who tries the immoderate use of wine closes the door on all virtues and opens it to transgressions.]

Valerius includes this anecdote in a list of cases that illustrates "severity" (*severitas*). This graphic description of a wife being clubbed to death for drinking wine is intended to illustrate the crude rustic virtues of ancient Romans who knew how to control wives, an exemplum designed to expose, by contrast, the decadence of imperial Rome. While the *puella* addressed in *Ars* 3 is categorically not a wife, and the consumption of wine is recommended in a context of nonmarital erotics, the suggestion that a *puella* might drink runs counter to the high-minded ethical program encouraged by early imperial morality and codified by Valerius Maximus. As we shall see in chapter 5, Chaucer's Wife of Bath refers to this exemplum in a boast about her own licentiousness.

Throughout *Ars* 3, the *puella* is encouraged to acquire the *ars* needed to attract and retain a male lover. However, the *praeceptor* prescribes limits to the claims a *puella* might reasonably have regarding her lover. Most significantly, the *praeceptor* insists that, despite the erotic possibilities of submissive gestures

on the part of the male lover, the *puella* should not expect his exclusive devotion; indeed, she is not to expect anything: "sed te, quaecumque est, moderate iniuria turbet, / nec sis audita paelice mentis inops" (3.683–84) ["But
whatever wrongs (you suffer), let them trouble you slightly, nor, hearing
about a mistress, think yourself bereft"]. As support for the precept that the
puella should not employ her skills to track the infidelities of her lover or
identify possible rivals, the *praeceptor* narrates the mythic example of Procris
whose gruesome death embodies submissive femininity. As told in *Ars* 3,
Procris hears rumors that her husband, Cephalus, has a mistress because he is
overheard calling on "Aura"—Breeze—to come to him when he rests in
the forest after hunting. Procris hides in the woods to spy on Cephalus and
her supposed rival *Aura*. When she hears him call on *Aura* and realizes her
mistake, she starts from her place and Cephalus, thinking she is a wild ani-
mal, throws his javelin at her and mortally wounds her. The *praeceptor* vividly
narrates her death:

> *ille sinu dominae morientia corpora maesto*
>   *sustinet et lacrimis uulnera saeua lauat;*
> *exit et incauto paulatim pectore lapsus*
>   *excipitur miseri spiritus ore uiri.*
>   *(3.743–46)*

[He supports the dying body of his *domina* on his sad bosom, and he
bathes the cruel wound with tears. Her spirit, slipping gradually from
her heedless breast, escapes and is intercepted by the mouth of her
wretched husband.]

The *praeceptor* portrays Procris as a loyal and devoted wife whose only error
was to believe reports that she had a rival. Her wound characterizes the sexual meanings of her death; as she says in her final speech, her wound signifies that Cephalus loves her exclusively: "'ei mihi,' conclamat 'fixisti pectus
amicum: / hic locus a Cephalo uulnera semper habet. / ante diem morior
sed nulla paelice laesa'" (3. 737–39) ["'Alas,' she cries out, 'you have pierced
my loving heart: this place will always have the wounds from Cephalus. I die
before my day but wronged by no mistress'"]. Latin love elegy often refers
to wounds as sexual metaphors, and as Cephalus embraces the dying body of
Procris and weeps over the wound he has inflicted, the *praeceptor* operatically
draws out the convention of the sexual wound to its overdramatic conclusion, and as she lies dying on Cephalus' bosom, Procris is referred to as his
domina (3.743), his mistress. When Ovid tells the Cephalus-Procris myth

later in the *Metamorphoses*, the narrative emphasizes the rashness of Cephalus; in the *Ars* he draws on the didactic potential of the myth to further the erotics of female mastery through submission. Just as the rape of the Sabines programmatically points to the violence of the *ars* professed by the *praeceptor*, the death of Procris offers an eroticized spectacle of female submission. All three books of the *Ars* use the category of erotic violence to script the performative possibilities of heterosexual *amor*.

The *Ars amatoria* as Ethical Treatise

When Augustus sent Ovid into exile, he had copies of the *Ars amatoria* removed from public libraries.[32] Given the notoriety of Ovid's poetic career and the offence of the *Ars* itself, Ovid's texts—unlike Virgil's—did not become central texts in the ancient or early medieval curriculum. Consequently, no ancient or late antique scholia developed around the text of any of Ovid's poems.[33] The twelfth century, however, marks a dramatic shift in attitudes towards Ovid in general and to the *Ars amatoria* in particular. With the expansion of education both within and beyond the monastery and the cathedral schools, the classrooms of the high Middle Ages required texts that could be appropriated into contemporary value systems and simultaneously offer possibilities for instruction in Latin grammar and syntax. Ovid's poetry, including the *Ars amatoria*, met this requirement, and from that point on, for centuries Ovidian texts exerted an immeasurable influence on Western cultures.[34] In the medieval classroom, the Latin text of the *Ars amatoria* was taught as a poem about *amor*, both *magister* and *discipulus* seem to have accepted its didactic rhetoric without attending to its irony. Testimony to this reception of the *Ars* as a serious treatise on love comes from the various versions of the academic prologues known as the *accessus ad auctores*—short introductory comments in Latin prose that accompany Latin texts and offer an interpretive framework for the reader. The surviving *accessus* to the *Ars amatoria* state that Ovid intended to instruct his reader in the ways of love:

> *Videns ouidius ex amoris ignorancia iuuenes deuiare, quasi eis conpaciens opus istud tractare proposuit in quo Materia ipsius est amor, Intencio instruere iuuenes et puellas, Vtilitas, quantum ad auctorem, delectacio, quantum ad legentes, amoris cognitio.*[35]

[Ovid, seeing that young men, out of ignorance of love, strayed from the straight path, as if out of concern for them, he proposed to treat that in a work, the Matter of which is love, the Intention to instruct young men and girls, the Utility for the author is pleasure, for the readers knowledge of love.]

After briefly cataloguing the Matter, Intention, and Utility of a text, the *accessus* conventionally assigns the text to a branch of philosophy. The *Ars amatoria*, like poetry generally, pertains to ethics: "Ethice supponitur liber iste quia loquitur de moribus iuvenum et puellarum[36] ["that book pertains to ethics because it speaks about the customs of young men and girls"]. In suggesting that the poem be read as a philosophical treatise, the *accessus* encourages the medieval Latin student to read the excessive rhetoric of Ovid's *Ars amatoria* as a philosophical exploration of the ethics of erotic violence.

Ovid's *Ars amatoria* was exceptionally well suited to the complex pedagogical needs of the twelfth century. Its elegiac couplets contain a single syntactic idea within two lines, making its Latin particularly accessible to the beginning student. In addition, the didactic discourse of the *Ars* offered a sustained lesson in heterosexual desire and performance. While Ovid's *praeceptor* ironically elaborates on the mechanics of seduction and intercourse in order to parody Augustus's marriage legislation, the excessive detail and overblown rhetoric that made the *Ars* ironic in its original Roman context made it pedagogically efficacious within the discourses of the twelfth century church. Existing commentaries on the *Ars* suggest that it was considered an appropriate school text: since line-by-line commentaries attend to the demands of Latin grammar and syntax, the didactic rhetoric on sexual desire did not go unnoticed. Ralph Hexter has examined several medieval Latin commentaries on the *Ars*; regarding one in particular, he notes: "near the end of both books 2 and 3 Ovid discusses sexual intercourse very openly. The commentator makes no protests or condemnations. That the comments continue through these passages shows that he did not expurgate them: he expected his students to study them, and with the same aid he gave them throughout the poem."[37] Reading the *Ars* within the context of ethics might render it a rather banal conduct book on sexual performance; such a message was highly suited to the homosocial culture developing in twelfth-century educational institutions designed to prepare students for lives of clerical celibacy in which they would have been expected to uphold heterosexual ideals but not to participate in marital sexuality and to simultaneously shun same-sex desire. Indeed, the *Ars* was pedagogically appropriate not in spite of its explicit approach to sexual conduct, but because of it.

While the monastic ideals of the twelfth century ultimately could not accommodate *amor* unless it was directed towards divine love, Ovid's *Ars amatoria* could also provide a treatise on earthy love against which to mea-

sure divine love. To this end, William of St. Thierry—designated by his bi-
ographer as an "anti-Ovid"—initiates his meditation on the nature of love,
De natura et dignitate amoris, with an echo from Ovid: "Ars est artium ars
amoris" ["the art of arts is the art of love"].[38] He describes Ovid's poetic
achievement:

> qui in amoris incentiva vel vetera quasi per quemdam pruritum excitanda, vel
> in nova invenienda toto se effuderat ingenio . . . sed naturalem ejus vim indis-
> ciplinatis quibusdam disciplinis in quamdam erudiebat lasciviam, et super-
> vacuis quibusdam fomentis luxuriae in quamdam perurgebat insaniam (381).

[He (lavished all his talents) on incentives to love, either by stirring up
old ones enticingly or by inventing new ones . . . he earnestly applied
himself to change its natural power into a kind of insane licentiousness
by some undisciplined approaches and urged it towards a licentious
insanity by superfluous incitements to lust.][39]

William St. Thierry characterizes Ovid's *Ars amatoria* as a serious treatise on
desire and sexuality. Such readings of the *Ars* had tremendous implications
for the vernacular reception of Ovid's text.

Given its presence in the twelfth-century curriculum, the *Ars* became in-
creasingly important in vernacular literary culture. In the opening lines of
Cligés (1170's) Chrétien de Troyes presents himself as the author of *Erec et
Enide* and translator of Ovid's *Ars amatoria* and *Remedia amoris*; these translations, however, have not survived.[40] A few lines later he claims that as a consequence of *translatio studii*, chivalry and learning have passed from Greece
to Rome to France. Such rhetoric claims Ovidian authority for *Cligés*, the
first of Chrétien's romances to dramatize desire, courtship, and the suffering
of lovers.[41] In addition, *Cligés* juxtaposes the heterosexual plot of courtship
and desire to the demands of empire and dominance, an imperial thematics
that nods towards the *Ars amatoria* as the originary exploration of colonialism and desire. Chrétien's lost translation of the *Ars* testifies to a vernacular
audience for this text as early as the middle of the twelfth century, and the
following century produced four verse adaptations of the *Ars* and one prose
translation that included both text and commentary. These vernacular versions of the *Ars*—along with the elaborate rendering of Ovid's *Metamorphoses* in the *Ovide moralisé*—suggest a rapid expansion in readership for
Ovid's texts from the elite Latin reader to a wider vernacular audience in
the thirteenth century.[42] As readings of the *Ars*, these translations adopt a serious tone in keeping with the spirit of the *accessus* to the Latin text of the
Ars; the vernacular versions of the *Ars* show an obsessive interest in elabo-

rating on the mechanics of heterosexual performance, as we shall see in chapter 4. The *Roman de la Rose* is the most elaborate cultural production to emerge from this vernacular engagement with the *Ars amatoria*. Vernacular poets characterized Ovid primarily as the author of the *Ars amatoria*: when Chaucer depicts Ovid in the *House of Fame*, it is Ovid in his poetic persona as *praeceptor amoris* from the *Ars amatoria*: "Venus clerk Ovide, / That hath ysowen wonder wide / The grete god of Loves name"(1487–89). Christine de Pizan likewise thought of Ovid the poet as the teacher of Love—as *praeceptor amoris*. While she relied extensively on the *Ovide moralisé*, she excoriated Ovid the poet.[43] From the classroom to the court, over the course of two centuries, the *Ars* was read as a treatise on the heterosexual ethic.

CHAPTER 3

Dominus/Ancilla
Epistolary Rhetoric and Erotic Violence in the
Letters of Abelard and Heloise

> The lover's discourse is usually a smooth envelope
> which encases the Image, a very gentle glove around
> the loved being.
>
> —Roland Barthes

> A letter does not *always arrive* at its destination, and
> from the moment that this possibility belongs to its
> structure one can say that it never truly arrives, that
> when it does arrive its capacity not to arrive torments
> it with an internal drifting.
>
> —Jacques Derrida

In *Ars amatoria* 1, the *praeceptor* extols the erotic
potential of letters in the early stages of amatory pursuit, and he recommends epistolary endeavors to the prospective lover: "ergo eat et blandis
peraretur littera uerbis, / exploretque animos primaque temptet iter" (1.
455–56) ["Then let a letter composed of flattering words go before and test
her spirit and try the way first"]. The *praeceptor* distinguishes amatory rhetoric from declamation; instead of persuasion, the erotic epistle should employ
flattering language in a familiar tone (1.467–48). Throughout the *Ars*, the
praeceptor identifies the exchange of letters as the rhetorical performance of
amor, so that epistolary discourse becomes identified with erotic discourse.
Several centuries later, the exchange of letters between Abelard and Heloise
enacts the precepts of the *Ars amatoria*, particularly in terms of the erotic
value of letters. In the *Historia calamitatum* (1131–32), Abelard identifies the
epistolary possibilities of his incipient affair when he praises Heloise's learning, not only because it would make her more responsive to his advances,
but also because it would enable the epistolary eroticism that he considers a
significant component of a sexual relationship: "nosque etiam absentes
scriptis internuntiis invicem liceret presentare et pleraque audacius scribere
quam colloqui" (71)[1] ["and even when apart, we could be present to each
other through written mediators and write many things more audaciously

than we could speak them"]. Abelard proposes that their textual selves could express and enact desire more boldly than their corporeal selves; he does not consider their textual relationship to be secondary to their physical relationship. The exchange of letters starts at the beginning of their affair and persists intermittently throughout their lives. The letters that survive under Heloise's signature, however, all date from a period long after Abelard's castration and the physical separation mandated by their entry into religious life.[2] These letters represent a rhetorical shaping of desire that enacts a textual eros; this textual desire may have been a supplement to their physical performance at the beginning of their relationship but functions as a sexual performance after Abelard's castration.

The construction of a letter in Latin prose in the twelfth century was determined by the rhetorical prescriptions of the *ars dictaminis*, the art of letter writing.[3] Based on classical rhetoric, the *ars dictaminis* offered formulae for various components of a letter: the *salutatio*, the *captatio benevolentiae* (the appeal to the goodwill of the addressee), the *narratio, petitio*, and *conclusio*.[4] As a rhetorical exercise, the composition of a letter fixed the status of the sender in relation to the addressee and thereby encoded and enacted social hierarchy.[5] The conventions of epistolary discourse required the sender to explicitly request that the addressee recognize the identity of the sender; in this respect, epistolary structure replicates the structures of desire. The promise and potential of epistolary rhetoric often go unachieved, just as desire often goes unrequited. The *locus classicus* for such epistolary desire is Ovid's *Heroides*, fictive letters in elegiac meter supposedly written by the abandoned women of myth and epic, such as Medea, Dido, and Phyllis.[6] Since each of the *Heroides* is addressed to the hero who has already abandoned the sender, the *Heroides* effectively illustrate Jacques Derrida's dictum that the letter does not always arrive at its destination; in a typically Ovidian display of rhetorical excess, the *Heroides* offer an intensive meditation on unrequited love. Ovid's *Heroides* were widely read and imitated in the medieval West as though they offered a formulary for epistolary desire, however unrequited. When Abelard and Heloise employ the rhetorical conventions prescribed by the medieval *ars dictaminis* to enact the forms of desire prescribed by the *Ars amatoria*, their erotic script shows traces of several Ovidian traditions on the practice of *amor*.

The *ars dictaminis* prescribed learned discourse, and by all accounts, Heloise was an extremely learned woman: throughout the *Historia calamitatum* and the epistles signed by Heloise, we find significant traces of her extensive reading in classical Latin texts.[7] Heloise's extraordinary level of schooling and skill enabled Abelard's erotic enterprise; as he himself notes:

"Tanto autem facilius hanc mihi puellam consensuram credidi, quanto amplius eam litterarum scientiam et habere et diligere noveram"(71) ["Moreover, I believed that this girl would consent all the more easily to me as much as she was known to have and to esteem knowledge of letters"]. Abelard here assumes that erudition in a woman is less likely to shape her as an autonomous, independent subject than to make her submissive to the advances of her *magister*. Both Abelard and Heloise were schooled in Ovidian texts, especially in the *Ars amatoria*. As *magister*, Abelard would have known the *Ars*, given its centrality in the twelfth-century Latin curriculum.[8] While Peter Dronke has demonstrated the significance of the *Heroides* to Heloise's epistolary performance of desire, he also identifies Heloise's wide-ranging use of Ovid.[9] In a discussion of the "literary and intellectual partnership" of Abelard and Heloise, Peter Dronke places Ovid "among those texts that both he and she cite oftenest, and cite at times in such unexpected contexts that it gives the impression of spontaneous recollection."[10] Heloise, for instance, cites the *Ars amatoria* in her third letter to Abelard which discusses the adaptation of the Benedictine rule for women. In this passage, she quotes three separate couplets from book 1 (233–34; 239–40; 243–44) to illustrate her anxiety regarding wine-drinking as a potential temptation to fornication for her nuns, a highly synthetic citation of the association Ovid makes between wine and libido in the *Ars amatoria*, as we saw in the last chapter. Such a highly incongruous citation of a secular Latin authority in a discussion of the religious life of women points to the sort of spontaneous recall posited by Dronke: Heloise would appear to know her *Ars* almost by heart. Heloise's literacy and extensive experience with the Latin amatory tradition represented by the Ovidian *corpus* developed her awareness of her part in this erotic encounter with her *magister*.

The female reader of *Ars amatoria* 3 who disregards the irony of Ovid's didactic discourse would find herself situated as the object of eroticized violence in an elaborate power play in which she could only acquire recognition through submission. As he initiates his affair with his young pupil, Abelard expresses his desire through the violent eros of pedagogy, and ultimately he claims the erotic possibilities of violence as outlined by Ovid. For a learned woman such as Heloise, the rhetorical eros of classical Latin poetry was easily transferred into the eroticized violence of her affair with her *magister*. In his *Historia calamitatum*, Abelard describes the terms set by Fulbert when he entrusted his niece, Heloise, to Abelard's pedagogical guidance: "ut quotiens mihi a scolis reverso vaccaret, tam in die quam in nocte ei docende operam darem, et eam si neglegentem sentirem vehementer constringerem" (72) ["That whatever time I had left, having returned from the schools, I should devote to her instruction by day or by night, and that if I found her to be careless, I should constrain her severely"]. A violent pedagogy suits Abelard's construction of his sexual desire for Heloise:

> *Qui cum eam mihi non solum docendam, verum etiam vehementer constringendam traderet, quid aliud agebat quam ut votis meis licentiam penitus daret, et occasionem, etiam si nollemus, offerret, ut quam videlicet blanditiis non possem, minis et verberibus facilius flecterem. . . . Apertis itaque libris, plura de amore quam de lectione verba se ingerebant, plura erant oscula quam sententie; sepius ad sinus quam ad libros reducebantur manus, crebrius oculos amor in se reflectebat quam lectio in scripturam dirigebat. Quoque minus suspicionis haberemus, verbera quandoque dabat amor, non furor, gratia, non ira, que omnium ungentorum suavitatem transcenderent. (72–73)*

[When he entrusted her to me not only to be taught, but also to be constrained severely, what else was he doing but giving license to my deep longings, and offering an opportunity, even if we did not wish it, that if I could not persuade her through flattery, I might persuade her more easily through threats and blows? And so, though books lay open, there were more words about love than about reading, there were more kisses than theses for discussion. Hands were drawn more often to bosoms than to books, love drew our eyes towards each other more frequently than it directed them towards the text for reading. Indeed, to attract less suspicion, I sometimes gave her blows, but out of love, not fury, out of kindness, not anger—blows that surpassed the sweetness of all ointment.]

Abelard reports that his role as *magister* authorizes his violence towards Heloise, which increases his pleasure as her lover. Such a construction of desire links the erotic and the violent traditions of pedagogy in Western culture: the eros of pedagogy was a given in the classical Mediterranean classroom, but it also had a particular currency within twelfth-century Platonism. As Leonard Barkan observes, such erotic humanism animated the twelfth-century classroom: "Not only is the student-teacher relationship reinvestigated (and perhaps re-experienced) in its potential for Socratic pederasty, but homosexuality is itself understood as homologous to new practices of rhetoric, grammar, and poetic innovation."[11] In addition, the *magister/discipulus* relationship in the medieval classroom was structured around the threat of corporal punishment, since the *magister* was given full authority to discipline his *discipulus*.[12] Desire was elicited as part of the educational experience and shaped by the erotic violence of traditional pedagogies.[13] While the same-sex composition of the medieval classroom determined the homoerotic circulation of institutional eros, Abelard's situation as a domestic tutor to a female enabled him to develop a pedagogy that eroticized sexual difference.

Abelard would appear to have learned his Ovidian lessons quite well: in this passage he connects rhetoric *(blanditia)* and violence *(minae* and *verbera)* as the constitutive features of eros. In the *Ars*, the *praeceptor* speaks of *blanditia* as the basic skill that a male lover might effectively employ to initiate his affair: "cera tuae primum conscia mentis eat; / blanditias ferat illa tuas imitataque amantem/ uerba" (1.438–40) ["Let a wax tablet go forth as a witness to your thinking; it would bear your flatteries and words that imitate a lover"]. As we saw in chapter 2, the *praeceptor amoris* authorizes his disciple to use force—indeed to rape—his *puella*; in his statement that he might deploy *blanditia* followed by force, Abelard as *magister* echoes the erotic and pedagogic authority of the Ovidian *praeceptor*. This passage enacts an eroticized violence that situated Heloise as the object of desire precisely because she is the object of violence.[14] Though Abelard reports a mutual pleasure in this sexual performance, he particularly notes his own pleasure: "Et quo me amplius hec voluptas occupaverat, minus philosophie vaccare poteram . . ." (73) ["And the more these pleasures occupied me, the less time I was able to have for philosophy"]. Thus Heloise as a pupil encounters a *magister* armed with an Ovidian amatory arsenal—both the rhetoric and the violence associated with erotic dominance. As a reader of Ovid herself, she had absorbed the disciplinary lessons of the amatory treatise: for the woman reader as object of desire, violence and forced sex are erotic and that eros is rhetorically constructed. Later, in his second letter addressed to Heloise, Abelard suggests that their sexual performances were frequently marked by violence: "Sed et te nolentem et, prout poteras, relunctantem et dissuadentem, quae natura infirmior eras, saepius minis ac flagellis ad consensum trahebam" (89) ["But even when you refused, dissuading me as much as you were able in your weaker nature, I would drag you to consent with threats and lashes"]. Abelard's depiction of his violent sexual performance in these passages is complemented by the submissive subjectivity that animates Heloise's *epistulae*, in which she willingly submits to Abelard's rhetorical violence as it textually reenacts this initial erotic encounter between *magister* and *discipula*.

Heloise's pregnancy and Abelard's castration illustrate the limits of the Ovidian script in the ambient world of twelfth-century Paris. The pregnancy exposes their actions and initiates the sequence of events that brings their private, sexual activities under the scrutiny of social authority and eventually leads to Abelard's castration and their entrance into religious life.[15] Heloise's pregnancy also exposes an aporia in the *Ars* for these two Ovidian lovers—that for women, the performance of heterosexual desire carries reproductive consequences and the resulting biological risks of childbirth. As their experience forcefully demonstrates to Abelard and Heloise, reproduction is a social act under the surveillance of a patrilineal regime, so that Fulbert, Heloise's uncle, owns the reproductive rights of his unmarried niece. Since the *Ars* scripts desire without mentioning reproduction, their readerly experiences with Ovidian desire as an entirely private intersubjective experience did not provide them with effective rhetorical responses to the public consequences of Heloise's pregnancy. In the *Historia calamitatum*, Abelard expresses dismay at their predicament "quanta contritione super afflictione puelle sum afflictus!" (74) ["How greatly I was agitated with grief over the suffering of the girl!"] Abelard reports that Heloise rejoices to be pregnant; Heloise, however, never mentions her pregnancy nor their child in her letters to Abelard, a silence that perhaps reflects the Ovidian silence regarding reproduction.

In addition, Heloise's pregnancy makes public their private desires, and their secret marriage fails to legitimize it. The process of subjecting their private world to public scrutiny results in further violence for both Abelard and Heloise. As Abelard relates in the *Historia*, Fulbert publicizes the "secret" marriage of Abelard and Heloise. When Heloise denies the marriage and attempts to privatize her desire, Fulbert becomes violent towards her: "Unde vehementer ille commotus crebris eam contumeliis afficiebat" (79) ["Then in his violent agitation he repeatedly hurled abuse at her"]. Abelard intervenes to remove Heloise from Fulbert's power, and once Heloise has been installed in the convent, Abelard becomes an object of violence in her place when Fulbert has him castrated as a punishment that publicly marks him as abject. Abelard's castration thus occurs as the result of this circulation of violence intended to police private desires so that they serve the reproductive goals of a patrilineal social order. Women are the conventional targets of such violence, and Abelard becomes a target through substitution; once the object of such patriarchal violence, Abelard considers himself to have undergone a change in his gendered identity. He calls himself a "monstrous spectacle" (omnibus monstruosum spectaculum futurus [80]) and comments that the Old Testament forbids eunuchs to enter churches, since they are considered unclean—*immundi* (80)—the same term used to describe menstruating women excluded from the temple in the pollution laws of Leviticus 15.20. Abelard claims that castration frees him from sexual desire and thereby releases him from fleshly temptations and the attractions of the world; though rendered abject and monstrous, as a eunuch he ultimately acquires greater potential for spiritual transcendence.[16] In renouncing his previous position as subject of desire, Abelard assumes that his status depends on the phallic authority conferred on him through his possession of a penis and testicles.[17] Deprived of these "parts of his body" and their fetish value, he renounces claims to the particular form of phallic sexuality. While Abelard sees his castration as an event that reconfigures his phallic authority and accords him greater spiritual mastery by altering his anatomy, Heloise's desire is not constructed solely around Abelard's anatomy and his castration does not substantially reconfigure her desire for him. The rhetorical structure of their epistolary desire exemplifies their conflicting views of his masculinity.

In his seminar on the "Purloined Letter," Jacques Lacan emphasizes the phallic potential of the letter in signifying the "castrated" status of the female letter writer. Derrida furthers this notion: "The letter alone . . . carries the necessary ideality or power of idealization that can safeguard (in any event this is what it means) the indivisible, singular, living, non-fragmentable integrity of the phallus."[18] The epistolary exchange between Abelard and Heloise vividly illustrates the phallic potential of letters in the face of castration. Abelard's castration resituates the desire of both letter writers, and the physical violence of their early sexual encounter is later reenacted in the rhetorical violence Heloise reads in Abelard's epistles. Though scholars such as Barbara Newman and Martin Irvine among others have read Heloise as a repressed woman,[19] her epistles point to a sustained eroticism that is repeatedly expressed and thereby performed rather than repressed. Heloise's letters testify to her persistent desire for an eroticized relationship with Abelard despite his castration, and her letters eventually function to recognize Abelard's phallic authority in spiritual matters as a consequence of his anatomical lack. In her unwavering recognition of Abelard as phallic and powerful, Heloise anticipates the conventional role of the female heterosexual subject in the libidinal economy of Western culture. As Kaja Silverman argues, the female subject is historically expected to deny the psychic reality of male castration and thereby uphold a construction of masculinity that supports the "dominant fiction." Silverman asserts: "the 'ideal' female subject refuses to recognize male lack, and that disavowal and fetishism provide important mechanisms for effecting this refusal. Indeed, traditional masculinity emerges there as a fetish for covering over the castration upon which male subjectivity is grounded."[20]

In her letters, Heloise sees Abelard with her "imagination rather than her eyes," as Silverman defines the task of the female in the heterosexual matrix. Language is the conventional mechanism for maintaining phallic identification, and Heloise finds in the rhetorical formulas of the *ars dictaminis* the linguistic fetish for her imaginative refusal of Abelard's castration. Her first letter to Abelard scripts her subject position in the rhetorical paradigms of the salutation, in keeping with the precepts of the *ars dictaminis*, which recognize rank in the grammatical placement of names: "Domino suo immo patri, coniugi suo immo fratri, ancilla sua immo filia, ipsius uxor immo soror, Abaelardo Heloisa" (68) ["To her master, indeed her father, to her husband, indeed her brother, from his slave/servant, indeed his daughter, the wife of him, indeed sister, to Abelard, Heloise"]. The rhetorical structure of the *epistula* shapes desire around the *dominus/ancilla* hierarchy, which subsumes the other hierarchical relationships acknowledged here: father/daughter, husband/wife, brother/sister.[21] The father/daughter pair of the first clause is expanded in the second. Within this context, the initial category of the salutation—*dominus*—inscribes Abelard's phallic masculinity; the phrase of the salutation offers the alternatives of *coniunx* and *frater* as substitutes that vary the role of the dominant term and yet maintain the inherent inequality, since brother and sister, like husband and wife, represent a gendered hierarchy. Heloise's epistolary eroticism rehearses—indeed, by its repetition, fetishizes—a rhetoric of dominance and submission in which the masculine term occupies the position of power. Within this context, the initial category of the salutation—*dominus*—inscribes Abelard's phallic masculinity, and its counterpart, *ancilla*, rhetorically performs Heloise's submission. Heloise later insists on the rhetoric of hierarchy as part of a proper salutation, as we shall see.

This narrative of masochism in the correspondence follows the script articulated for the female lover in *Ars amatoria* 3. In addition, the prescriptive tradition of the *ars dictaminis* provided a rhetorical script for the power relations of amatory discourse. The intertextual theatrics of this epistolary performance of dominance and submission suggest that the ultimate meanings of Heloise's submissive eroticism are rooted in the gendered traditions of learning and rhetoric as well as in the power erotics of Ovidian discourse. The performance of submissive desire is grounded in a desire for recognition;[22] Jessica Benjamin, for instance, notes that the "fantasy of erotic domination embodies both the desire for independence and the desire for recognition . . . voluntary submission to erotic domination is a paradox in which the individual tries to achieve freedom through slavery, release through submission to control."[23] Heloise's first letter to Abelard directly equates letter writing and desire: the entire letter develops her complaint that Abelard has not written to her since his castration, thirteen years earlier, though he did compose a long *epistula consolationis* to a male friend. Heloise's complaint is designed to claim Abelard's attention for the desire her letter enacts in opposition to the homosocial world rhetorically figured in the *Historia*. She complains bitterly throughout the letter: "non . . . fluctuantem me et iam diutino moerore confectam vel sermone praesentem vel epistola absentem consolari tentaveris" (70) ["nor . . . did you try to console me, wavering and already consumed with a long lasting sorrow, either with a word in your presence nor a letter in your absence"]. In this passage, she invokes their marriage bond (nuptialis foedere sacramenti) and expresses the status of her enduring desire: "immoderato amore complexa sum" ["I have been embraced by an excessive love"].

This letter is aimed at provoking an epistolary response from Abelard. Heloise reminds him that before his castration, he wrote frequent letters to her at the start of their affair, and she insists on the efficacy of letters by citing an authoritative passage from Seneca regarding the potential of letters to bring separated people together. Heloise's letter demands that Abelard address a letter to her and thereby provide the erotic recognition that marked her submissive role in their relationship. Heloise directly equates Abelard's epistolary silence with his castration, which marked the end of his desire, and she begs him to send her a letter:

> *Concupiscentia te mihi potius quam amicitia sociavit, libidinis ardor potius quam amor. Ubi igitur quod desiderabas cessavit quicquid propter hoc exhibebas pariter evanuit. . . . Dum tui praesentia fraudor verborum saltem votis quorum tibi copia est tuae mihi imaginis praesenta dulcedinem. (72)*

[Lust rather than friendship joined you to me, the ardor of desire rather than love. Thus when what you desired ceased, whatever you displayed disappeared as well. . . . While I am cheated of your presence, at least promise me through your words, of which you have plenty, the sweet presence of your image.]

Heloise's appeal acknowledges that the performance of desire is textual as much as physical, and letters as a transcription of language appear to be one option for her erotic experience. In a similar vein, she asserts that Abelard's poetic gifts and his ability to compose love songs are one significant component of her attraction to him.

Heloise describes Abelard's sweeping power as though her identity depends entirely on her emotional submission to him: "Solus quippe es qui me contristare, qui me laetificare seu consolari valeas" (70) ["In fact, it is you alone who have the power to sadden me, to cheer me, or console me"]. In this first letter, she constructs Abelard as her *dominus* in her declaration that if Augustus as emperor offered her the magnificence of an imperial marriage, she would rather be a *meretrix* than an *imperatrix*: "carius mihi et dignius videretur tua dici meretrix quam illius imperatrix" (71) "[more dear and more worthy would it seem to be called your *meretrix* than the empress of that one"]. The word *meretrix* evokes the erotic world of amatory adventures outside of marriage—the world of courtesans, mistresses, and concubines of Ovid's amatory poetry. Ovid uses the term with some frequency in his amatory poetry, and the female addressee of the *Ars* is implicitly a *meretrix*.[24] The juxtaposition of *imperatrix/meretrix* also evokes the imperial categories of desire that emerge from the *Ars amatoria*: in the *Ars*, as we have seen, Roman imperial power enables the male pursuit of women. In rhetorically rejecting the status of *imperatrix* for that of *meretrix*, Heloise revels in an Ovidian language that eroticizes subject positions in terms of an imperial framework. When Heloise states that she prefers the status of *meretrix* to Abelard rather than empress to Augustus, she claims the only subject position within the Ovidian libidinal economy in which the female subject might be sexually recognized. Heloise further clarifies how abjection enables her erotic identity when she rhetorically embellishes *meretrix* with the terms *concubina* and *scortum*. Heloise takes linguistic and erotic pleasure in the epistolary contract since it allows her to rehearse her subject position as *ancilla* to Abelard's *dominus*: she exists only through Abelard, and she has denied herself all pleasure in accordance with his will (Omnes denique mihi voluptates interdixi ut tuae parerem voluntati [73]). Yet she revels in the power she attains through such submissive gestures; as Claire Nouvet comments concerning this passage: "this apparent self-humiliation in fact reverses the master/slave relation, for it puts the master in the position of the debtor. . . . the whore is the true master of a master who precisely could not be a master without her."[25]

Heloise composed her first letter after Abelard's castration had transformed his desire into indifference. In the face of such indifference, she asks for recognition in the form of a letter addressed to her as his *ancilla*, a letter that would acknowledge that her letter has indeed arrived at its destination. Her subject position as *ancilla* in her letter textualizes her status as an abject or discarded lover who has relinquished her entire self into the control of her *dominus*: "Non enim mecum animus sed tecum erat. Sed et nunc maxime si tecum non est, nusquam est" (73) ["My heart was not with me but with you. But especially even now, if it is not with you, it is nowhere"]. Her submissive desires in the face of Abelard's rhetorical silence after his castration are an attempt to sustain the submissive pleasure she found in the violent eros of their affair before Abelard's castration. The rhetorical scripting of desire made possible by the *artes*—the *Ars amatoria* and the *ars dictaminis*—creates and sustains an intersubjectivity in which Heloise seeks recognition through submission. This initial letter characterizes Abelard's epistolary indifference as a form of rhetorical violence, an abusive gesture of psychic denial as damaging as physical abuse and one which causes her to suffer exceedingly.[26] Both Abelard and Heloise consider verbal abuse and rhetorical violence to be more painful than physical abuse. As Abelard says in the *Historia*, the inquisition over his treatise on the Trinity—and the judgment that he was to burn the book—was more painful than his castration. For Heloise, the rhetoric of Abelard's *Historia* situates her as a discarded and even abject lover; her exquisite descriptions of suffering in her first letter create a space in which she might pleasure in this pain. Like the physical violence she experienced from Abelard as his student lover, the rhetorical violence of his *Historia* allows her to experience identity through suffering his indifference. In response to the implicit violence of Abelard's rhetorical indifference, and as a dedicated reader of Ovid, Heloise cultivates a language of suffering and pain that is rhetorically self-conscious of its status as performance.

Abelard responds to Heloise by sending her an *epistula*, yet he implicitly refuses her desire for submission in his salutation, in which he refuses the role of *dominus*: "Heloisae, dilectissimae sorori suae in Christo, Abaelardus, frater eius in ipso" (73) ["To Heloise, his most beloved sister in Christ; from Abelard, her brother in Christ"]. This refusal elicits Heloise's extensive critique of his deviation from the rhetorical expectations of the *Ars*:

> *Miror, unice meus, quod praeter consuetudinem epistolarum, immo contra ipsum ordinem naturalem rerum, in ipsa fronte salutationis epistolaris me tibi praeponere praesumpsisti, feminam videlicet viro, uxorem marito, ancillam domino, monialem monacho et sacerdoti diaconissam, abbati abbatissam. Rectus quippe ordo est et honestus, ut qui [ad] superiores vel ad pares scribunt, eorum quibus scribunt nomina suis anteponant. Sin autem ad inferiores, praecedunt scriptionis ordine qui praecedunt rerum dignitate. (77)*

[I am astonished, my one and only, that contravening the custom of letters, or rather against the natural order itself, you have presumed to place me before you at the front of the salutation of the letter, that is, the woman before the man, the wife before the husband, the servant before the lord, nun before monk, deaconess before priest, and abbess before abbot. It is the correct and proper order that they who write to their superiors or equals place the names of those they address before

their own names. But if they write to inferiors, they who go before in
dignity go before in the order of writing.]

In her desire to be rhetorically situated as Abelard's inferior, Heloise reiterates in her second letter her need for recognition as the submissive partner
in their relationship. Thus she asserts that Abelard should not praise her
(Quiesce, obsecro, a laude mea [82]). Heloise appeals to the conventions of
the *ars dictaminis*, which reflects the "natural order," to justify the terms of
her desire: rhetoric and nature script her subject position and her desire.

Heloise's second letter is structured by her complaint that the language of
Abelard's letter has caused her—and her community of nuns—considerable
pain and anxiety; his intimations of mortality are experienced as violence
and described as such in Heloise's metaphorical prose: "Parce unicae saltem
tuae huiusmodi scilicet supersedendo verbis quibus tamquam gladiis mortis
nostras transverberas animas ut quod mortem praevenit ipsa morte gravius
sit" (78) ["At least spare your one and only by omitting words of this sort,
for with them, as with lethal swords, you thrust through our souls, so that
what comes before death is worse than death itself"]. She depicts her suffering in graphic language drawn from the classical idiom of her textual training when she describes Fortune's blows: "Plenam in me pharetram exhausit
ut frustra iam alii bella eius formident. Nec, si ei adhuc telum aliquod superesset, locum in me vulneris inveniret. Unum inter tot vulnera metuit ne
morte supplicia finiam" (78) ["She has emptied a full quiver into me so that
others fear the hostilities of that one in vain. If she had one spear left, she
would not find a place in me for a wound. She only fears that among so
many wounds, I might end my sufferings in death"]. As the Cephalus and
Procris exemplum in *Ars amatoria* 3 demonstrates, Ovidian eroticism is often
expressed in terms of wounds. Heloise's exuberant use of the metaphor of
wounds and the personification of Fortune to express the painful experience of reading Abelard's letter suggests a readerly pleasure in his rhetorical
violence. She engages in an animated response to the discourse that she finds
painful, since that very discourse offers her a recognition that acknowledges
an identity formed from desire.

Although Heloise's first letter was shaped by her insistent pleas for a response from Abelard that would simultaneously recognize her as *ancilla*, her
second letter exquisitely expresses her erotic desires: "Hoc autem in me
stimulos carnis haec incentiva libidinis ipse iuvenilis fervor aetatis, et iucundissimarum experientia voluptatum plurimum accendunt" (81) ["The
same youthful fervor and the experience of the most delightful pleasures
kindle greatly in me the goading of the flesh and the incentives of desire"].

She claims to be the cause of Abelard's sufferings and insistently expresses her desire to be the one who suffers. The rhetoric of this second letter of Heloise's is a sustained expression of pain and pleasure as well as of the painful memory of pleasure:

> *In tantum vero illae, quas pariter exercuimus, amantium voluptates dulces mihi fuerunt ut nec displicere mihi, nec vix a memoria labi possint. Quocumque loco me vertam, semper se oculis meis cum suis ingerunt desideriis. Nec etiam dormienti suis illusionibus parcunt. . . . Nec solum quae egimus, sed loca pariter et tempora in quibus haec egimus, ita tecum nostro infixa sunt animo, ut in ipsis omnia tecum agam, nec dormiens etiam ab his quiescam. (80–81)*

[Truly, so sweet were the pleasures of lovers to me that they cannot displease me nor be loosened from memory. To whatever place I turn, always they put themselves before my eyes with their desires nor do they spare me their illusions in sleep. . . . Not only the things we did but the places and times in which we did them are fixed in our heart with you, so that I do all things in those places with you, nor in sleeping am I spared these things.]

In describing her autoerotic experiences, Heloise paradoxically notes that the *voluptates* of lovers never fail to please her, yet she uses a biblical citation to lament the misery of her corporeal captivity (Romans 7:24: "Infelix ego homo . . ."). In this passage Heloise suggests that the autoerotic performance of desire is as substantial as her previous sexual experiences with Abelard, an interpretation that is consistent with the "ethic of intention." As Heloise defines the ethic of intention in her first letter, the spirit in which deeds are performed constitutes their meaning; Abelard elaborates explicitly on this premise in his *Ethica*: "Non itaque concupiscere mulierum sed concupiscentiae consentire peccatum est, nec uoluntas concubitus sed uoluntatis consensus dampnabilis est" ["So sin is not lusting for a woman but consenting to lust; the consent of the will is damnable, but not the will for intercourse"].[27] Although this passage is often considered proof of Heloise's repression, Heloise describes a powerful autoerotic experience, not a repression of sexual desire. The passage depicts her persistent performance of sexual desire in intense and fulfilling terms: "ut in ipsis omnia tecum agam." Indeed, Heloise's sexuality causes her dismay precisely because it is not repressed and thereby constitutes a transgression of *castitas* and *virtus*, the privileged categories of Christian doctrine.[28] She categorizes her autoerotic sexual experiences as sex acts to which she continues to consent:

Quo modo etiam poenitentia peccatorum dicitur, quantacumque sit corporis af-
flictio, si mens adhuc ipsam peccandi retinet voluntatem, et pristinis aestuat
desideriis? Facile quidem est quemlibet confitendo peccata seipsum accusare, aut
etiam in exteriori satisfactione corpus affligere. Difficillimum vero est a
desideriis maximarum voluptatum avellere animum. (80)

[How is it called repentance for sins, however much it is an affliction
of the body, if the mind retains the very will toward sinning, and burns
with former desires? It is an easy thing for anyone to accuse oneself of
sins in confession, or even to strike the body in order to make exterior
satisfaction; but it is most difficult to turn the mind away from the desire for the greatest of pleasures.]

Heloise's powerful conviction that she should repent for these "greatest of
pleasures" demonstrates her assumption that these sexual experiences are
erotic performances, not fantasies.

Heloise's letters inscribe and enact a sexuality defined by the submissive
subjectivity of her relationship with Abelard, a dynamic that persists long
after his castration, their separation, and her entry into a religious life. The
pedagogical and religious institutions as well as the rhetorical practices of
her day likewise required of the learned woman a passionate submission to
authority, however violent. The relationship of Abelard and Heloise as it
emerges from their letters demonstrates the cultural contexts for the engen-
dering of rhetoric and rhetorical structuring of gender. As a woman learned
in elite Latin textual cultures who employed the prescriptive rhetoric of the
ars dictaminis, Heloise was capable of performing within a phallic economy.
Abelard's masculine privilege as a powerful *magister* is initially compromised
by his castration, but paradoxically, the less "masculine" he is on a corporeal
level, the more authority he gains in spiritual stature, so that he interprets his
castration as his salvation. Heloise and Abelard enact a rhetoric of dominance and submission in their correspondence that is ultimately structured
by the social inequities of the ecclesiastical and secular institutions of their
day: no matter how learned, Heloise can never earn the status or privileges
of masculinity, yet Abelard's compromised "masculinity" only increases his
claim on privilege, authority, and power. Heloise's letters achieve a rhetorical play of dominance and submission within the erotic script suggested by
Ovid's *Ars amatoria*: Heloise's extraordinary skill in Latin prose and her bril-
liant reputation in Latin scholarship enabled her subjugation within this
Ovidian paradigm.

FIGURE 12.   Abelard and Heloise. *Roman de la Rose*, BnF, fr. 1560, fol. 58r. By permission of the Bibliothèque nationale de France.

Heloise as Author

The letters exchanged between Abelard and Heloise appear to have been gathered into a collection at the Paraclete by Heloise or under her direction; as a textual compilation that was in circulation by the middle of the twelfth century, the letters reified Heloise's affair with Abelard as a textual event.[29] The letters sustained a readership throughout the medieval period and be-

yond;[30] the Latin text survives in nine manuscript copies, four of which date
to the thirteenth century, and medieval inventories of books suggest that a
number of other manuscripts have been lost. Read as a collection, the letters
offered an erotic and amatory narrative that made Abelard and Heloise into
literary figures identified by the nature of their love. After having completed
his section of the *Roman de la Rose*, Jean de Meun undertook the translation
of five Latin texts into French prose, among them the letters of Abelard and
Heloise. The only surviving version in French is found in an early fifteenth-
century manuscript; the first seven letters in this collection are French translations of seven of the eight that constitute the Latin manuscript tradition.[31]
Three additional letters—two by Abelard and one by Peter the Venerable—
are added to the manuscript in order to provide a more resounding conclusion than the initial collection offered. This manuscript is transcribed in the
hand of Gontier Col, secretary to Charles VI and a participant in the early
fifteenth-century *Querelle de la Rose*, as we shall see in chapter 6.[32] The
translations of the three additional letters have been tentatively attributed to
Gontier Col.[33] Translated by Jean de Meun, copied by Gontier Col—the
fortunes of the letters of Abelard and Heloise in thirteenth- and fourteenth-
century French literary cultures testify to the attraction of this epistolary
collection as a literary text, especially among readers of the *Rose*.

Jean de Meun's version of the letters follows the Latin text precisely in
order to render a highly accurate French prose translation. Nonetheless, he
occasionally makes assertions that emphasize Heloise's wisdom and intellectual agency in the course of the exchange.[34] The French prose is more parat-
actic than the Latin text, but Jean de Meun overall captures the rhetorical
gravity of the correspondence. For instance, when Heloise characterizes her
argument against marriage, she frames her position, as we have seen, with
the assertion that she would prefer to be Abelard's *meretrix* than *imperatrix* of
the whole world. This passage loses none of its sharpness in translation, despite the fact that French does not allow for the word play of the Latin:

> [J]e appelay Dieu a tesmoing que se li emperierres Augustes, sire de
> tout le monde, me daignast prandre par honnour de mariaige et me
> confermast tout le monde a tenir pardurablement, si me sembleroit il
> plus chiere chose et plus digne d'estre appellee ta putain que seue em-
> pereris. (49–50)

The Latin term, *meretrix*, given its roots in Roman social hierarchy, refers to
"courtesan" as well as "prostitute"; the French term *putain* signifies "prostitute" exclusively. The choice of *putain* as a rendering of *meretrix* actually intensifies the rhetorical effect of Heloise's rejection of imperial honor in her

performance of erotic submission to Abelard. The French text often shifts the register of the Latin: Heloise's juxtaposition of *dominus/ancilla* in the salutation of her first letter becomes *seigneur/chamberiere* (45) in translation. The term *chamberiere*, chambermaid, is not inverse to the term *seigneur* with its feudal connotations. In translating the castration scene in Abelard's *Historia calamitatum*, Jean de Meun renders the term *genitalis* as *coillons*,(18) a word that evokes the argument between Raison and Ami in the *Roman de la Rose* over the appropriate use of language to describe genitalia. Often the French represents the power relations between Abelard and Heloise more starkly than does the Latin. In the *Historia calamitatum*, for instance, Abelard describes the terms by which Fulbert entrusts Heloise to him: "eam videlicet totam nostro magisterio committens." (72) Jean de Meun's version reads: "quant il bailla sa niepce du tout a nostre mestrie." (11) In translating *magisterium*, tutorship, by *mestrie*, Jean de Meun brings out the language of mastery in Abelard's Latin. Jean de Meun's version of these epistles sustains the erotic dynamics of the Latin text and at times heightens them.

By contrast, the *Roman de la Rose*—as the most extensive exploration of the *Ars amatoria* in the medieval vernacular—subsumes Heloise's discourse of subjection as part of the larger Ovidian project of allegorically staging the violence of eros. In Jean de Meun's section of the *Roman de la Rose*, Heloise is praised for her articulate antimatrimonial arguments as we shall see in chapter 4; it is Heloise rather than Abelard who emerges from the *Rose* as a figure of authority, a learned woman as well as an author. Likewise, in Jean Le Fèvre's allusion to her in his fourteenth-century *Livre de Leesce*, he identifies her as a philosopher:

> *Feüst Heloïs, l'abeesse*
> *Du Paraclit, qui tant fu sage*
> *Du droit de coustume et d'usage;*
> *Et si estoit philosofesse,*
> *Combien que elle fut professe.*
> (1132–36)

[There was Heloise, the abbess of the Paraclete, who was very learned about the law of customs and ways. And she was also a philosophess, although she was professed.]

Despite her language of abjection and her performance of submission, Heloise is known here for her intellectual mastery. Likewise, in Chaucer's *Wife of Bath's Prologue*, Heloise, "That was abbesse nat fer fro Parys" (678), is one of the "authors" listed in Jankyn's "book of wikked wyves," as we shall see in chapter 5. In a Tudor manuscript produced in 1500 she is even credited with the authorship of a treatise on the "art d'Amours," a French translation of Andreas Capellanus's *De amore*.[35] Through her mastery of the *ars dictaminis*, Heloise gained recognition as an author and even an authority on love.

✎ CHAPTER 4

Tote Enclose
The *Roman de la Rose* and the Heterophallic Ethic

Nothing is more violent than the fury of human love.

—Justinian

Guillaume de Lorris' narrator identifies the *Roman de la Rose* as a vernacular version of the *Ars amatoria*: "ce est li *Romanz de la Rose*, / ou l'art d'Amors est tote enclose"[1] (37–38) ["It is the *Roman de la Rose*, in which the whole art of love is contained"]. While Ovid's *praeceptor* proclaims in *Ars* 3 that love is a form of warfare ("militiae species amor est" [2.233]), the *Rose* poets stage this precept through the elaborate allegory of siege warfare. The pedagogical urgency of the *Ars* becomes an insistent lesson in seduction for the untutored lover/dreamer of the *Rose*. The most striking Ovidian trace in the *Rose* is the adaptation of the imperial ethos of Augustan Rome—which so thoroughly structures desire in the *Ars*—to the mercantile economic cultures of the late medieval world evoked in the *Rose* texts. The *Rose* is saturated with commodity fetishism, evident in the relentless detail regarding exotic fabrics, jewels, minerals, and ornaments, all of which enhance and enable desire within the allegory.[2] While the *Ars* evokes the performative spaces of the triumph and the games as markers of Rome's colonial centrality, the emphasis throughout both texts of the *Rose* on artifacts—especially textiles and minerals—situates northern French culture at the center of a vast network of trade and exchange. The mercantilism of the *Rose* replaces the imperialism of the *Ars* in eliciting and structuring desire.

Throughout the *Rose*, erotic desire is allegorized in violent terms; when he first looks into the Mirror Perilous, Amant experiences desire as a violent seizure ("Quant cele rage m'ot si pris [1621]); his subsequent encounter with Amor leaves him wounded and suffering. The allegorical level of the text is structured around violence as an erotic mechanism: Dangier threatens and beats Paour and Pitie, and later Franchise; Bel Acueil is forcefully imprisoned, Malebouche is murdered, and so on. The narrative—as narrative—is predicated on violence: characters attack, beat, or threaten each other endlessly, and the climax of the narrative occurs when the castle is besieged and then eventually falls as a result of Venus' incendiary attack. As an allegory of erotic subjectivity, the *Rose* depends on violence for agency: violence, pain, and suffering are the medium through which *amor* is shaped and through which desire achieves visibility. Genius' reactionary sermon, delivered towards the end of Jean de Meun's text, exemplifies the violent tenor of the allegory;[3] with characteristic rhetorical fervor, Genius urges his barons to aggressively and even violently pursue the heteronormative and reproductive goal he metaphorically calls "plowing":

> *Arez, por Dieu, baron, arez,*
> *et voz lignages reparez.*
> *Se ne pansez formant d'arer,*
> *n'est riens qui les puist reparer.*
> . . . .
>   *et du soc bouter vos penez*
> *raidemant en la droite voie,*
> *por mieuz affonder en la roie;*
> *et les chevaus devant alanz,*
> *por Dieu, ne les lessiez ja lanz*
> *aspremant les esperonez*
> *et les plus granz cos leur donez*
> *que vos onques doner porroiz,*
> *quant plus parfont arer vorroiz.*
>   *(19671–90)*

[Plough barons, plough for God's sake, and restore your lineage. Nothing can restore it if you do not put your minds to ploughing vigorously . . . and make an effort to thrust the ploughshare straight along the right path, the better to penetrate the furrow. As for the horses in front, for God's sake do not let them slow down, but spur them on harshly and give them the most violent blows you possibly can, if you want to plough deeply.]

Genius situates sexual difference as a foundational discourse: in this description, derived as it is from Alain de Lille's *De Planctu Naturae*, heterosexual performance assures gender difference so that male heterosexual performance establishes masculinity.[4] Genius also represents male sexual performance in violent metaphors, so that erotic violence secures masculinity in this heterophallic paradigm. Genius' exuberant exhortation to his barons to goad the horses in the plow is emblematic of the violent register in which heteroerotics is represented in both sections of the *Rose*.

The *Ars amatoria* in Medieval French

The discourse on erotic violence as it emerges from the *Roman de la Rose* is consistent with the status of the *Ars amatoria* in thirteenth-century French literary cultures. At the point that Guillaume composed the *Roman de la Rose* in the early part of the thirteenth century, Ovid's *Ars amatoria* was frequently the object of vernacular translation, imitation, and appropriation. Although Chrétien de Troyes' twelfth-century translation of the *Ars* has been lost, five translations from the thirteenth century survive, four in verse and one in prose. These five vernacular versions of the *Ars amatoria* are not all complete translations of the entire three books of the *Ars*; they nonetheless collectively attest to the authority ascribed to Ovid's *Ars amatoria* at the time. All of these thirteenth-century translations discuss the mechanics of seduction as though that were the focus of Ovid's *Ars amatoria*; consequently, the translators adapt the didactic claims of Ovid's *praeceptor* without importing the elaborate ironies that Ovid's mythological and contemporary allusions make possible. Seen in this cultural context of translation and assimilation, the *Roman de la Rose* appears to be part of a larger cultural engagement with Ovid's Latin text. Both Guillaume de Lorris' and Jean de Meun's portions of the *Roman de la Rose* share general features with these French translations of the *Ars amatoria*, yet the nature of these intertextual relationships is difficult to trace precisely since several of the verse translations cannot be dated exactly, though they were probably all produced before Jean de Meun composed his section of the *Rose* in the 1270's.[5] While the *Rose* poets produce much more elaborate versions of the *Ars*, they share with these translators the purpose of adapting Ovid's discourse on desire and *amor* to a vernacular audience, however loosely and however digressively.[6]

The single prose version of the *Ars*, the anonymous *Art d'amours*, best illustrates the literary status of Ovid's *Ars* as an authoritative Latin text.[7] The first two books of the *Ars* appeared in this French prose version between 1214 and 1233; the translation of *Ars* 3 was undertaken later by another translator between 1260 and 1290. The text of the *Ars* is denoted by the rubric *texte* (text), and each text segment is followed by an explanatory passage marked *glose* (gloss). The glosses frequently draw on Ovid's *Metamorphoses* or *Heroides* to explain allusions to mythological figures or events. These glosses emphasize the alterity of the world depicted in the *Ars amatoria*: several references to Rome as a colonial power are glossed; for instance, Ovid's evocation of a Roman triumph (1.177–228) is provided with a historical context. The translator likewise comments that if the rape of the Sabine women had taken place in his own time, it would have started a war. In addition, the glosses contain aphoristic or proverbial sayings intended to illustrate or reinforce the wisdom of the *Ars*. This arrangement of text followed by gloss sets off the translated portions of the *Ars* as an authoritative text, full of mythological references that must be contextualized by reference to Ovid's other works, and full of the sort of ethical wisdom thought to be found in ancient texts.

This process of authorizing the text as a repository of wisdom identifies the author with the narrator, so that the rhetorical framework provided by Ovid's *praeceptor* disappears, and the gloss treats the *Ars* as the product of Ovid's experience. This transformation of the *Ars* into an authoritative text flattens out the irony of Ovid's *Ars* and offers in its place an exercise in ancient wisdom. However, it was in this prose vernacular version that many late medieval readers knew Ovid's text. The prose *Art d'amours* circulated widely and probably shaped the reception of Ovid's Latin text; indeed, it may have influenced the later verse translations of the *Ars*. Copies of the *Art d'amours* are found in the inventories of the French royal library, as well as the libraries of the dukes of Berry and Burgundy. Jean de Meun appears to have consulted the *Art d'amours* (before the third book of the *Ars* was added to it),[8] and for Christine de Pizan and Chaucer, the *Art d'amours* was almost certainly their source for Ovid's *Ars amatoria*.

The verse translations of the *Ars* include the anonymous *Clef d'amors*, a translation of all three books of the *Ars amatoria* produced in Normandy at some point during the thirteenth century.[9] Although it shows similarities to Guillaume de Lorris' section of the *Rose*, the *Clef d'amors* cannot be dated with any certainty; thus it is impossible to determine whether its author borrowed from the *Rose* or the other way around.[10] The text opens with a dream vision in which the God of Love appears to the narrator and instructs him in the commandments of love; the dreamer then awakens and dictates the instructions from the three books of the *Ars amatoria*. This rhetorical structure erases the role of the *praeceptor* and instead refers repeatedly to Ovid as an authority on love. Most of the references to Roman life and cul-

ture are changed to reflect medieval customs, and many—though not all—
of Ovid's mythological references are removed. Despite these differences,
the *Clef d'amors* follows the sequence of Ovid's poem relatively closely; in
the process, the ironic pedantry of the *praeceptor*'s performance is transformed into a set of instructions on love and desire delivered in a serious
tone. At times the register of the poem is courtly, at times pragmatic; consequently, the *Clef d'amors* not only lacks the irony of Ovid's *Ars* but renders
the text of Ovid's *Ars* as purely didactic discourse.

The short verse text under the signature of Guiart ("qui l'art d'amours
vost en romanz traitier" [5]) exemplifies the rhetorical resistance Ovid's *Ars
amatoria* posed for a medieval vernacular translator.[11] Though Guiart attempts to render only a small portion of Ovid's *Ars amatoria*, and an even
smaller section of the *Remedia amoris*, the contortions of his *Art d'amors* result in a text that only crudely imitates its classical pre-text. In his prologue,
Guiart casts his translation as an effort at exposing the falseness of worldly
vanity; such an effort, he says, is similar to Aristotle's efforts at unmasking the
textual treachery of clerks:

> *Aristote en son livre nos aprent a savoir*
> *Qu' un clerc puet par fallace son amie decevoir,*
> *En cel mëisme livre aprent a parcevoir*
> *De cele fausseté a conoistre le voir.*
>
> *(21–24)*

[Aristotle in his book teaches us that a clerk is able through trickery to
deceive his love, and in the same book he teaches us to perceive this
trickery and to recognize the truth.]

The single surviving copy of Guiart's *Art d'amors* is preserved in a manuscript alongside Henri d'Andeli's *Lai d'Aristote*, a narrative that describes the
tale of Aristotle's erotic humiliation, as we saw in chapter 1. This reference to
the cultural authority of Aristotle (and his unnamed book) must be read
against the anecdote of the mounted Aristotle in Henri d'Andeli's tale: Aristotle's textual dominance in Guiart's text counters his sexual submission in
the *Lai d'Aristote*. In this discourse of dominance, Ovid's suggestion (1.673–
76) that force might be useful becomes a mechanical set of instructions for
rape; Guiart advises the lover: "A une main li lieve la chemise et les dras, /
L'autre main met au con, ainsi comme par gas" (95–96) ["With one hand,
lift up her dress and chemise, put the other hand on her cunt, as if for a
joke"]. But according to Guiart, such a rape should lead to marriage, if the

woman is worthy of marriage, and after a few nods towards the *Remedia amoris*, Guiart subsumes his entire project under a Marian religious ideology by inserting a prayer to the Virgin at the end of his text. Such a range of discourses takes the Ovidian play with context and contingency to an absurd level. Guiart's effort at integrating such disparate codes demonstrates the difficulty of rehearsing Ovid's model of erotic violence in the absence of Ovidian irony.

The early thirteenth-century verse translation by "Maistre Elie" is an adaptation of *Ars amatoria* 1 and sections of *Ars amatoria* 2.[12] Maistre Elie revises the references to the Roman locations of Ovid's text to make it legible within the context of medieval Paris, and he casts Ovid's military discourse in the language of chivalry. In some respects, this brief, schematic rendering of Ovid's text in a medieval context results in a vernacular text that effectively preserves the register of the *Ars amatoria*. While none of the references to Roman coloniality in Ovid's text survives, Maistre Elie substitutes in its place a discourse that equates love and warfare in chivalric terms:

> *Cheualerie amors resanble*
> *Si ont pris compaignie ensanble;*
> *Hardiz couient estre ameor*
> *Ausi com le combateor.*
>> *(1142–45)*

[Chivalry resembles love thus they keep company together; courage is appropriate to love, just as to the warrior.]

In following the discourse of the *Ars amatoria*, Maistre Elie says that the lover must suffer, but he likewise encourages the lover to gain dominance. At one point he urges the lover, when faced with a recalcitrant woman, to assail her, and he adds: "Bien est droiz que il auant prit / Et cele enuers lui s'umelit" (618–20) ["It is right that he take her, and that she humble herself towards him"]. Maistre Elie's verses on the art of love represent desire and *amor* in stark terms, but the starkness of these terms captures some of the contradictions of Ovid's eroticism.

A verse translation of several thousand lines, produced in the thirteenth century by a translator who identifies himself at the end of his text as Jacques d'Amiens,[13] includes material form all three books of the *Ars*, though only 28 lines from book 3 are included. Jacques d'Amiens was interested in the rhetorical demands of courtship and seduction, and his translation adapts Ovid's text to this purpose. After a long disquisition on how and when to address a woman and how to court her, he offers hundreds of lines of sample speeches a lover might use, a sort of rhetorical handbook that might function as a script for seduction. He also discusses the mechanics of how and when to kiss a woman, and he spends 160 lines discussing Ovid's assertion that women want to be raped (1139–1294). In this extensive amplification on the Ovidian comment that force might be useful, Jacques d'Amiens offers a detailed set of guidelines about how to judge a woman's responses and when a suitor should use force despite a woman's resistance to his advances. He concludes this discussion by ventriloquizing a speech a suitor should make when he perceives that a woman is weeping after having been raped.

All five of these French translations of Ovid's *Ars amatoria* specifically address the issue of force and violence; a similar discourse becomes an elaborate ethics of erotic violence in the course of the *Roman de la Rose*. When Guillaume de Lorris states that his project encloses the *Art d'amours*, he claims the identity of Ovidian translator in a rhetorical move almost identical to these translators of the *Ars amatoria*. Structuring this Ovidian project around the allegory of the quest for the rose offers an expandable structure for examining every aspect of the mechanics of seduction.[14] When Jean de Meun undertook the expansion of Guillaume's text, he took his cue from Guillaume's Ovidianism. Precisely because Guillaume's text was recognizable as an Ovidian project structured according to the *Ars amatoria*, Jean de Meun could look to the *Ars* as a means of generating his sequel to the allegory of the *Rose*. Thus the enclosure of the *Ars amatoria* forms the poetic crux of the conjoined *Rose* texts. As Sylvia Huot has shown, several medieval manuscripts testify to medieval readers' awareness of the intertextual relationship between the *Rose* and the *Ars*.[15] There also exists a fourteenth-century manuscript of the *Ars* which contains glosses drawn from the *Roman de la Rose*,[16] and several florilegia include material from both poems.[17] Such manuscripts testify to the extent to which Ovid's *Ars amatoria*—in both the classical and medieval versions—underpins the textual as well as the allegorical structures of the *Rose* as a single poetic unit.[18] The *Roman de la Rose* almost literally encapsulates Ovid's *Ars amatoria*.

Ami and the Jaloux

As the precursor text that drives and animates Jean de Meun's *Rose*,[19] the *Ars amatoria* emerges as the most important classical text in the allegory, although several of Ovid's other poems are also significant.[20] Two figures in particular—Ami and the Vieille—are derived from the *Ars amatoria*.[21] Since

Ami is adapted from *Ars* 1 and 2, and the Vieille from *Ars* 3, their appearance in the *Rose* follows the sequence of the *praeceptor*'s instruction in the *Ars*. In addition to Ovid's Latin text, the vernacular versions of the *Ars amatoria*, particularly the prose *Art d'amours*, contributed significantly to the profiles of Ami and the Vieille as critical interlocutors for Amant in his training in Ovidian eroticism. Both Ami and the Vieille see erotic violence as efficacious and both see such violence in ethical terms. When Ami takes over from Raison early in Jean de Meun's section of the allegory, Ovidian rhetoric comes forward to counteract the Boethian discourse of Raison, and Amant turns out to be a better student of Ovid's than of Boethius'. For almost a thousand lines (7401–8325), Ami speaks as a learned practitioner who considers the seduction of the rose to be an art or skill. Using details imported directly from *Ars amatoria* 1 and 2, Ami instructs Amant in the skills needed to pluck the rose. As part of this lesson in Ovidian eroticism, which Ami refers to as open warfare ("aperte guerre" [7790]), Ami renders Ovid's couplet on force ("uim licet appelles: grata est uis ista puellis; / quod iuuat, inuitae saepe dedisse uolunt" [1.673–74]) in the following terms:

> *cuillez la rose tout a force*
> *et moutrez que vos estes hon,*
> *quant leus iert et tens et seson,*
> *car riens ne leur porroit tant plere*
> *con tel force, qui la set fere;*
> *car maintes genz sunt coustumieres*
> *d'avoir si diverses manieres*
> *qu'il veulent par force doner*
> *ce qu'il n'osent abandoner,*
> *et faignent qu'il leur soit tolu*
> *ce qu'il ont soffert et volu.*
>
> 7660–70

[Pluck the rose by force and show that you are a man, when the place and time and season are right, for nothing could please them so well as that force, applied by one who understands it. For many people are accustomed to behave so strangely that they want to be forced to give something that they dare not give freely, and pretend that it has been stolen from them when they have allowed and wished it to be taken.]

In the allegorical context of siege warfare that structures the *Roman de la Rose*, this advice appears highly appropriate. The passage from the *Ars*, however, only suggests that force might be effective; in Jean de Meun's terms, force becomes constitutive of masculine identity: "et moutrez que vos estes hon."[22] The erotic violence that Ovid's *praeceptor* recommended as a skill is characterized by Ami as an action through which masculinity might be achieved and maintained. But Ami stresses that the critical issue for such masculinity is to properly assess the signal from Bel Acueil so that such force does not actually become rape, at least as Ami understands it:

> *Mes se par paroles apertes*
> *les sentez corrociez a certes*
> *et viguereusement deffendre,*
> *vos n'i devez ja la main tendre,*
> *(7677–80)*

[But if they speak clearly and you feel that they are really angry and defending themselves vigorously, you must not stretch out your hand.]

Ami categorically states that this level of judgment is necessary for Amant to conduct himself if he wishes to act as a worthy, valiant and wise man ("Ainsinc vers eus vos contenez / com preuz et vaillanz et senez" [7687–88]).

Jacques d'Amiens makes a similar suggestion in his translation of the *Ars*. As part of his amplification on the suggestion from the *Ars* that force might be effective, he takes pains to distinguish between different levels of resistance from the female object of desire:

> *Et telle i a qui de son gré*
> *T'otroiera ta volenté,*
> *Que faire vaura cortoisie,*
> *Ne force faire n'aime mie,*
> *Mais durement se desfendroit,*
> *C'outre son gré l'enforceroit.*
> *(1211–16)*

[And there is the sort of woman who will willingly grant your wish, and because she considers it to be courtly, though she does not like force and she will hardly defend herself if forced against her will.]

Nevertheless, he suggests that in almost all cases, the would-be seducer or lover needs to consider female resistance as part of an erotic dynamic. Like Jacques d'Amiens, Ami refines Ovid's ironic advice into a code of masculine heterosexual conduct. A large portion of Ami's speech is given over to the long, ventriloquized speech of the Jaloux,[23] which vigorously rehearses a performance of verbal abuse that is crude and offensive. Ami cites the Jaloux to illustrate the decline from the Golden Age, before marriage, property, or civilization, a concept derived from Ovid's *Ars Amatoria* 2.472–80.[24] Despite the explicit transition from the ideal represented by the Golden Age that motivates the negative exemplum of the Jaloux, the vicious speech and behavior of the Jaloux seem highly out of place in Ami's lessons on the erotic skills that Amant might acquire. Indeed, Huot has identified one manuscript in which the entire exemplum of the Jaloux has been cut.[25]

The figure of the Jaloux does not derive from Ovid's *Ars amatoria*, but the glosses in the *Art d'amours* frequently take up the topic of jealousy as well as the topic of domestic violence. The gloss to 1.491–93, for instance, appeals to Ovid to develop the concept of jealousy: "Et c'est ailleurs prouvé la ou il dit ou je vois ay parlé de jalousie, car je di que jalousie vient d'amours et nulz ne puet estre jalous s'il n'aime, et qui plus aime, plus est jaloux, et d'amours viennent les maulx que jaloux sentent" (1604–8) ["This is proved elsewhere where he has spoken about jealousy, for he says that jealousy comes from love, and no one can be jealous if he does not love. He who loves more, is jealous more, and from love comes the evil that the jealous feel"]. The *Art d'amours* also comments expansively on violence in marriage. Ovid's *Ars amatoria* only elliptically mentions marital quarrels by way of illustrating the opposite of the *dulcia verba* appropriate to love: "lite fugent nuptaeque uiros nuptasque mariti / inque uicem credant res sibi semper agi" (2.153–54) ["Let married women pursue their husbands with disputes, and married men their wives, and let them believe that they always do these things, in turn, to each other"]. The *Art d'amours* greatly elaborates on this passage. Under the rubric *texte* it offers a translation: "Par paroles tencheresses chastie le mari sa femme et la femme son mari, et cuide li uns et l'autre tousiours bien faire par ce faisant" (2481–83) ["The husband chastises his wife and the wife her husband with quarrelsome words, and each one always thinks that he is doing well in this"]. This topic is picked up again in the gloss to a passage a few lines later; just before the section in the *Ars* when the *praeceptor* states that he tore his mistress' tunic, the gloss offers a long disquisition on marital violence:

> *Ce dit li proverbes: «Bien se chastie, qui par autruy se chastie». Et si vois di: ne li faictes nul mal, car se vous le fectes, elle se fera malade et dira, ja si petit de mal ne li ferez qu'elle ne die que ce soit la mort. . . . Aucun dient, que nous avons oy de voir, que homme n'amera ja femme s'il ne la bat, car quant il la bat, il convient qu'il en face l'amende . . . et la femme se prent garde com-*

ment il se paine de l'amender. Et selon que elle voit sa repentance, selon ce elle l'ayme. (2517–26)

[The proverbs say this: "He chastises himself well who is chastised by others." So he says to you, do not do her any harm, for if you do, she will become ill. Furthermore, he says that you must never hurt her even a little, for that is death. . . . Some say what we have truly heard, that a man will never love a woman if he does not beat her, for when he beats her, it is proper for him to apologize for it . . . The woman notices how he troubles himself to apologize for it. By virtue of this, she sees his repentance, and by virtue of this, she loves him.]

The contradictions in this passage result partially from the fact that Ovid's text makes a clear distinction between married women and mistresses that the French translator does not observe. But in *Ars 2*, Ovid also suggests that violence against a mistress might be erotic, while he suggests that reciprocal conflict for a married couple is nothing more than the tiresome reality of marriage. The translator, however, appeals to proverbial wisdom to gloss this passage by suggesting that violence enables love because it sets up a cycle of beating, repentance, and forgiveness that fosters love. This notion evokes Ovid's advice (2.457–60) that a lover attempt to soothe an angry woman by sexual caress, which the translator offers as: "Quant tu verras qu'elle sera plus esragié et forsenee, lors li queur plus seure et la solace et la mignote du jeu d'amours: elle devenra aussitost debonnaire. Ilec remaint toute ire et tout mautalent" (3105–7) ["When you see that she is very angry and enraged, seek her more firmly and console her and caress her with the game of love. She will soon become agreeable. This stops all anger and bad feelings"]. This advice resonates with the Vieille's attitude towards violence, as we shall see.

These glosses in the *Art d'amours* form the source for Ami's long digression on the Jaloux as a negative exemplum. An affluent merchant, the Jaloux dwells obsessively on his wife's elegant dress and accessories: he worries that his wife's finery makes her a spectacle, and that such display could lead to infidelity—indeed, in his terms, his wife's making a spectacle of herself is itself a form of infidelity. The Jaloux speaks of his wife and her clothing as though both were his property, a graphic illustration of Ami's argument that marriage and property are both symptoms of decline from the rustic values of the mythic Golden Age. The desire and anxiety of the Jaloux are elicited by the luxurious commodities he provides his wife: her elaborate attire testifies to his mercantile success but potentially makes her attractive to others. While commodities represented the imperial possibilities of eros in the *Ars*, the Jaloux articulates an anxiety regarding the erotic possibilities of specific commodities such as textiles and cloth whose presence in northern Europe testifies to the region's centrality in trade and networks of exchange. The Jaloux's argument—like many misogamous arguments—propels itself along through a catalogue of mythic or legendary women whose stories illustrate unattainable ideals of marital conduct for women. Lucretia and Penelope initiate the Jaloux's list, but into this predictable litany of "good" women the Jaloux inserts an exemplum about Heloise, whose antimatrimonial arguments earn her recognition as an exemplary woman. This reference to Heloise and her affair with Abelard is the first vernacular literary reference to the letters of Abelard and Heloise.[26] While Jean de Meun later translated the letters of Abelard and Heloise into French several decades after composing the *Roman de la Rose*, his long-standing interest in these letters is evident in the detailed description of Heloise's discourse provided by the Jaloux in this seventy-two-line exemplum. Indeed, some of the phrases and lines from the *Rose* reappear later in his prose translation, which suggests that Jean de Meun already had a command of the text when he composed the *Rose*. The exemplum offers a synthesis of Heloise's arguments against marriage in the *Historia calamitatum*, a brief account of Abelard's castration, as well as a brief comment on the salutation of Heloise's first letter to Abelard.[27]

The Jaloux refers to Heloise's wisdom and learning in her attempt to persuade Abelard not to marry:

> *ainz li fesoit la jenne dame,*
> *bien antendanz et bien letree*
> *et bien amanz et bien amee,*
> *argumenz a lui chastier.*
> > (8734–37)

[Instead the intelligent and well-read young woman, who loved truly and was truly loved, reasoned with him.]

Heloise is praised for her ability to construct arguments drawn on textual authority to "chastier" or correct Abelard. The Jaloux rehearses Heloise's request for a union with Abelard "sanz seigneurie et sanz mestrise" (8750), then he adds that Abelard married her despite her warning:

> *car puis qu'el fu, si con moi semble,*
> *par l'acort d'ambedeus ensemble,*
> *d'Argentuell nonain revestue,*

fu la coille a Pierre tolue
a Paris en son lit de nuiz,
don mout ot travauz et enuiz.
            (8763–68)

[For after she had, I think, taken the habit of a nun at Argenteuil, as
they had both agreed, Peter's testicles were removed as he lay in bed
one night in Paris, which caused him great suffering and anguish.]

In such a condensed version of the events from the *Historia calamitatum*,
Abelard's castration appears to result directly from his marriage to Heloise
and her entrance into the convent at Argenteuil.[28] According to the *Historia*
calamitatum, however, Fulbert had Abelard castrated because Abelard removed Heloise from his home after he publicized their secret marriage. Not
surprisingly, the Jaloux's version does not implicate Abelard beyond his de-
cision to marry Heloise, so that Abelard's castration appears to be an unfortunate result of his marriage alone, not the result of a sequence of events following from his deception of Fulbert and his seduction of Heloise.

While the Jaloux praises Heloise for her learning and wisdom in arguing
against marriage, he extends the exemplum a further twenty lines to include
a description of Heloise's discourse of abjection; this final segment is not
necessary for the rhetorical purposes of his misogamous tirade. The Jaloux
expresses some surprise at the salutation in her first letter to Abelard:

Ele meïsmes le raconte
et escrit, et n'en a pas honte,
a son ami, que tant amoit
que pere et seigneur le clamoit,
une merveilleuse parole,
que mout de genz tendront a fole.
            (8777–82)

[She herself was not ashamed to write in her letters to her beloved,
whom she loved so well that she called him father and lord, strange
words that many people would think absurd.]

Through these comments of the Jaloux, Jean de Meun astutely identifies the
abject subjectivity that Heloise's salutation is intended to convey in her first
letter. The Jaloux quotes her famous speech as Abelard had reported it in the
Historia calamitatum:

> "Se li empereres de Rome,
> souz cui doivent estre tuit home,
> me daignet volair prendre a fame
> et fere moi du monde dame,
> si vodroie je mieuz, fet ele,
> et Dieu a tesmoign en apele,
> estre ta putain apelee
> que empereriz coronee."
>
> (8787–94)

["If the emperor of Rome, to whom all men should be subject, deigned to want to marry me and make me mistress of the world, I call God to witness that I would rather," she said, "be called your whore than be crowned empress."]

The rhetorical brilliance of Heloise's Latin prose is quite effectively rendered in these eight octosyllabic lines that close with the word "coronee" in stark contrast to the implications of the phrase "estre ta putain apelee" in the previous line. In a poem so invested in the nominal potentials of language, this version of Heloise's speech rhetorically performs an erotics of submission that is beyond the understanding or purpose of the Jaloux, if not of Ami, who rehearses this speech of the Jaloux for Amant. For Amant, however, Heloise's exemplum works as part of a larger discourse on erotics and violence in the development of the narrative; if its pedagogical implications escape the narrow purposes of the Jaloux's speech, the exemplum contributes to Amant's overall development as a disciple of Amor.

The speech of the Jaloux is frequently illustrated in fourteenth- and fifteenth-century manuscripts. Such illustration participates in the larger visuality of the *Rose* as a supremely visual text, one that engages directly with issues of optics[29] and the role of visuality in the construction of subjectivities and identities. Manuscripts of the *Roman de la Rose* are often highly decorated; of almost three hundred manuscripts of the *Rose* that survive, at least two hundred contain illustration of some form.[30] The visual programs in *Rose* manuscripts vary widely over the course of two centuries of production: some manuscripts contain only a frontispiece, while the most lavish exemplars contain over one hundred miniatures. Almost all programs of illustration that go beyond a single frontispiece include images clustered around the first few folios of Guillaume de Lorris' section in order to illustrate the figures on the outside of the garden wall. As illustrations of personifications of anti-courtly "vices"—Avarice, Envy, Poverty, Sadness, Old Age, etc.—

these images rely on highly iconic cues in order to express abstract values as persons.[31] This initial set of images programmatically structures the text/image relationship in an iconic register that invites the viewer to read later images in either section of the *Rose* for their iconicity, whether those images illustrate the mythological references or the allegorical level of the text. In addition, the interpretive implications of the *ordinatio* of *Rose* manuscripts generally go beyond illustration: as Sylvia Huot has convincingly demonstrated, *Rose* manuscripts frequently exhibit rubrics, decorated initials, marginal notations, and marginal decoration that shape the reading process and that make each and every manuscript of the *Rose* a distinct reading experience.[32]

Most manuscripts that extend illustration into Jean de Meun's portion of the *Rose* offer some image to accompany the speech of the Jaloux, though the illustration may be at the allegorical level (the Jaloux's abuse of his wife), or at the mythological level (the suicide of Lucretia, for instance). No manuscript better exemplifies the range of potential illustrations for the Jaloux than the Valencia manuscript (ms. 387), made in Paris in the first decade of the fifteenth-century and known to Christine de Pizan.[33] The 130 images in the Valencia *Rose* are a vivid witness to the interpretive possibilities in the violent tenor of the allegory, since the manuscript consistently illustrates the violent moments or references in the *Rose*, often in gruesome detail.[34] In addition, the visual program in the Valencia *Rose* is an exceedingly literal interpretation of the text: every detail in every image is a visual illustration of a textual detail. Nonetheless, even such a "literal" visual program enters into a dynamic play with the text, and the illustrations in the Valencia manuscript frequently subvert the poetic discourse of the *Rose*. In its literalness, the visual program of the Valencia manuscript often contributes to a parodic register in the discourse of the allegory.

The speech of the Jaloux in the Valencia manuscript is illustrated by eight images, which makes it the most densely illustrated portion of Ami's speech. The topic of jealousy in marriage is introduced with an elaborate, two column image of the Golden Age (Fig. 13). This miniature depicts a scene of early rustic life: simply clad figures harvest nuts, grains, fruits, and vegetables in the wild; they drink from a spring; and they wait out a storm under a rock or in the trunk of an oak tree—all details taken directly from Ami's description. To the right of the image, a couple is shown in two stages of an embrace that situates them as equals in terms of height, size, and implicitly, value.[35] By contrast, in the initial image that depicts the Jaloux at the start of his tirade at line 8425 (Fig. 14), the husband stands facing his wife and holds his hands in a set of speaking gestures that visualize the aggressive thrust of

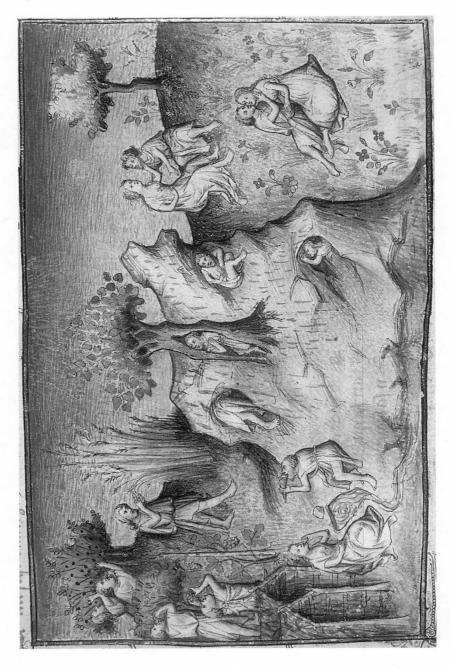

Figure 13. The Golden Age. *Roman de la Rose*, BUV, MS 387, fol. 59v. By permission of the Biblioteca Històrica, Universitat de València.

FIGURE 14. The Jaloux speaks to his wife. *Roman de la Rose*, BUV, MS 387, fol. 60v. By permission of the Biblioteca Històrica, Universitat de València.

his words. Her posture signals her status as a recipient of this barrage: she stands balanced on both feet and holds her left hand up, either in concession or in agreement. On the next folio, the artist punctuates the Jaloux's speech with two images on one page (Fig. 15). In the first, Lucretia falls on a large sword and blood spurts from the wound in her chest. The second image somewhat incongruously illustrates the Jaloux's brief comment at lines 8637–47 that no one would buy a horse without examining it and trying it out, but no one tries out a woman before marriage. Two men hold a large horse by its bridle and tail, while a rider sits perched on its bare back. Though this image illustrates the briefest of comments on the part of the Jaloux, the artist interprets this fantasy of equestrian mastery as an iconic statement regarding just how much agency and skill are actually required to control a horse, and by implication, a wife. When the Jaloux refers to the exemplum of Abelard and Heloise (Fig. 16), that exemplum is punctuated with a distressing image of a nude and vulnerable Abelard, leaping out of bed just as he is about to be castrated by two men, both armed with large swords, while Heloise in a nun's habit gestures in dismay at his side. This discom-

FIGURE 15. Lucretia's suicide; trying out a horse. *Roman de la Rose*, BUV, MS 387, fol. 61v. By permission of the Biblioteca Històrica, Universitat de València.

forting scene is followed by a two-column miniature depicting the labors of Hercules (Fig. 17). While the Jaloux alludes only generically to Hercules' twelve labors and his demise through the trick of the poisoned shirt, the artist employed the expansive possibilities of the two-column miniature to depict eight of Hercules' twelve labors, a vision of extraordinary strength

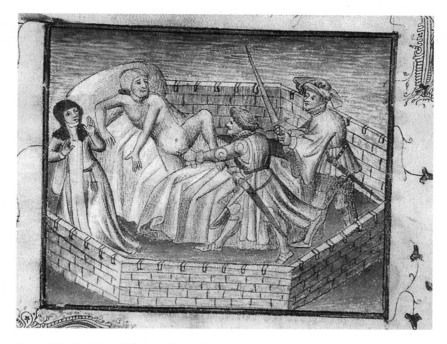

FIGURE 16.   Castration of Abelard. *Roman de la Rose*, BUV, MS 387, fol. 62v. By permission of the Biblioteca Històrica, Universitat de València.

and force. The Jaloux also mentions that Samson, like Hercules, was overcome by a woman, and the artist obligingly inserts a miniature at this point that depicts a wily Delilah cutting Samson's locks (Fig. 18). This mythological exemplum is actually narrated in some detail later in Genius' response to Nature (lines 1647–58), and Genius' description provides the details used in the execution of this image. Genius notes that Delilah held Samson close as he slept on her lap and cut his hair with her scissors, details appropriate to the rhetorical excesses of Genius' speech later in the allegory. Though this sequence of images is closely cued to the narrative and allegory of the *Rose*, the images do not neatly or consistently emphasize the Jaloux's misogamous points. Taken together, these images actually emphasize the vulnerability of male heterosexual performance: from the shocked onlookers at Lucretia's suicide to Hercules consumed by flames and Samson's recumbent figure, the images do not visualize the possibilities of achieving heterosexual mastery. Though these images closely illustrate the words of the Jaloux, they underscore Ami's overall advice that Amant should avoid attempting the sort of mastery that the husband seeks, given the uncertainty and the risk involved

Figure 17. Labors of Hercules. *Roman de la Rose*, BUV, MS 387, fol. 65r. By permission of the Biblioteca Històrica, Universitat de València.

FIGURE 18. Samson and Delilah. *Roman de la Rose*, BUV, MS 387, fol. 65v. By permission of the Biblioteca Històrica, Universitat de València.

in such attempts. By contrast to the images, the violence of the Jaloux appears all the more excessive and impotent.

The final image of the Jaloux, placed above line 9331, illustrates the physical abuse that occurs at the end of the Jaloux's speech (Fig. 19). When he has finished quoting the verbal abuse of the Jaloux, Ami details a scene of domestic violence:

> *Lors la prent espoir de venue*
> *cil qui de mautalant tressue*
> *par les treces et sache et tire,*
> *ront li les cheveus et descire*
> *li jalous, et seur li s'aourse,*
> *por noiant fust lions seur ourse,*
> *et par tout l'ostel la traïne*

FIGURE 19. The Jaloux beats his wife. *Roman de la Rose*, BUV, MS 387, fol. 66v. By permission of the Biblioteca Històrica, Universitat de València.

> *par corrouz et par ataïne,*
> *et la ledange malement.*
> > *(9331–39)*

[Then perhaps, boiling with rage, he takes her there and then by the hair and pulls her and tugs her, tearing and rending her locks in his jealousy, setting upon her (a lion attacking a bear is nothing in comparison), dragging her all through the house in his anger and fury and insulting her cruelly.]

Eventually the neighbors arrive and separate the Jaloux from the wife once he has exhausted himself in beating her. In the image in the Valencia manuscript, the Jaloux stands over the wife who has fallen under his attack: she writhes on the ground while he pulls her hair with one hand and raises a staff to strike her with the other. This image achieves an iconic value in its composition: by contrast to the rich costumes worn by the Jaloux and his wife in the initial miniature (Fig. 14) the figures in this image are all simply depicted in grisaille, so that they do not take on any distinguishing features; they starkly represent the status of husband and wife as they enact a generic—and recognizable—scene of domestic violence.

At least thirty manuscripts contain an illustration of the Jaloux beating his wife. It first appears in early manuscripts and remains a frequent scene of illustration throughout the fourteenth and fifteenth centuries (Figs. 20–23). In many versions, the wife has fallen as a result of a blow. The Jaloux often pulls her by the hair and usually wields a club—both specific details mentioned in the text. This weapon, however, semiotically connects the husband with the allegorical figure of Dangier, who is usually depicted wielding a club at Amant (Fig. 24). Amant, however, is never depicted crumbling under the attack of Dangier the way the wife collapses under the club of the husband. In some versions of the Jaloux's abuse, the wife kneels and holds up her hands in a prayer gesture reminiscent of hagiographic iconography where martyrs are depicted as piously enduring physical abuse (Fig. 25). Sometimes the neighbors pull the husband back from the fallen wife (Fig. 26), which also visualizes a detail from the text. Ami describes this physical abuse as the final consequence of the Jaloux verbal abuse; in manuscripts that illustrate this scene, the entire speech of the Jaloux is visually summed up in the image of domestic violence; in manuscripts in which the Jaloux is first depicted talking to his wife and then beating her after he has finished his speech (Figs. 27 and 28), the scene of physical abuse retrospectively borrows its violent tenor from the initial scene of verbal abuse, thereby exposing the linguistic component of violence, and the violent potential of language. Jody Enders has demonstrated how medieval rhetoric assumed that violence intensifies memory.[36] The depiction of this violence makes the anecdote of the Jaloux especially memorable, and the vivid and arresting quality of this image in illustrated *Rose* manuscripts casts a long shadow over the remainder of the allegory.

The Jaloux, however, is rhetorically bracketed by Ami as a negative exemplum: Ami asserts that such an abusive husband will only alienate his wife, who might even plot to have him poisoned. The behavior of the Jaloux is so vividly described in order for Ami to satirize him as a brute whose strategy will destroy eros. The textual and the visual codes work against each other in this context: in manuscripts that contain a single illustration of the Jaloux beating his wife, the iconic image has a memorable quality despite highly critical terms of the text. Since the visual program of the *Rose* offers mnemonic placeholders for portions of the text, this scene of wife-beating

FIGURE 20. The Jaloux beats his wife. *Roman de la Rose*, MS M 48, fol. 68v. By permission of the Pierpont Morgan Library, New York,

might visually override Ami's satiric representation of the Jaloux as a brute. Once he has dismissed the Jaloux, Ami proceeds to tutor Amant in the more subtle approaches to erotic success in the quest for the rose. Ami concludes as he began, by juxtaposing the behavior of the Jaloux to love and sexuality in the ancient mythological location of the Golden Age, before gold was used for economic exchange, before pilgrimages, and before seas were conquered by mariners, before women were sold on the marriage market, or sold themselves—before desire was structured along a mercantile ethos.[37] Ami specifically warns against jealousy and aggression, and he tells the lover not to scold or rebuke his beloved, but to "correct her kindly" ("mes amiablement reprendre [9664]), even if she is seeking another lover. Ami also warns against domestic violence: "Ja ses vices ne li reproche / ne ne la bate ne ne touche" (9703–4) ["He should never reproach her for her vices, nor should he beat or touch her"]. Like Ovid's *praeceptor*, Ami suggests that a man or husband might even find it effective to submit to abuse on occasion, and indeed, throughout the *Rose*, Amant is threatened with abuse. However,

FIGURE 21.   The Jaloux beats his wife. *Roman de la Rose*, BnF, fr. 19156, fol. 61r. By permission of the Bibliothèque nationale de France.

like the contradictions in the *Art d'amours*, the topic of violence and love leads Ami into a discussion of how a male lover might eroticize violence when it occurs:

> *Et s'il avient que il la fiere,*
> *por ce qu'el li semble trop fiere*
> *et qu'ele l'a trop corroucié,*
> *tant a forment vers lui groucié,*
> *ou le veust espoir menacier,*
> *tantost, por sa pez porchacier,*
> *gart que le geu d'amors li face*
> *ainz qu'el se parte de la place.*
> *(9725–32)*

FIGURE 22. The Jaloux beats his wife. *Roman de la Rose,* BnF, fr. 1565, fol. 62v. By permission of the Bibliothèque nationale de France.

[And if he should happen to strike her because she seems too aggressive or has angered him too much with the violence of her complaints, or perhaps because she wants to threaten him, he should immediately make sure, in order to secure his peace, that he makes love to her before she leaves.]

Ami here reproduces the suggestion from the gloss in the *Art d'amours* that the husband who beats his wife should immediately, then and there, seek her forgiveness: Ami specifies that the husband apologize, through a play of love, "geu d'amors," a term used throughout the *Roman de la Rose* as a euphe-

FIGURE 23. The Jaloux beats his wife. *Roman de la Rose*, MS M 132, fol. 66r. By permission of the Pierpont Morgan Library, New York.

mism for sexual intercourse. The gloss in the *Art d'amours* thus becomes one of Ami's precepts for eroticizing violence.

The Vieille

Several hundred lines after Ami has dismissed the behavior of the Jaloux as ineffective, the discourse of the Vieille indirectly invokes this scene of erotic violence.[38] The Vieille makes a long speech addressed to Bel Acueil on the

FIGURE 24.   Dangier threatens Amant *Roman de la Rose*, MS M 132, fol. 109v. By permission of the Pierpont Morgan Library, New York.

ways in which women might pursue and manipulate men with maximum financial gain and minimum emotional risk. The rhetorical complications of the Vieille's speech are enormous: Amant perceives that Bel Acueil is frightened of "la pute vielle" (12540), and he says that Bel Acueil reports the speech of the Vieille to Amant so that Amant becomes the implicit student of the lessons of the Vieille:

> Lors a reconmencié sa verve
> et dist, con fausse vielle et serve,
> qui me cuida par ses doctrines
> fere lechier miel sus espines
> quant vost que fusse amis clamez

FIGURE 25.   The Jaloux beats his wife. *Roman de la Rose*, BnF, fr. 802, fol. 62v. By permission of the Bibliothèque nationale de France.

sanz estre par amors amez,
si con cil puis me raconta
qui tout retenu le conte a;
car s'il fust tex qu'il la creüst,
certainement trahi m'eüst;
mes por riens nule qu'el deïst
tel traïson ne me feïst:
ce me fiançoit et juroit,
autrement ne m'aseüroit.
                    (12957–70)

[Then she resumed her speech, the false and servile crone, imagining that through her teaching she could make me lick honey from thorns, for according to Fair Welcome, who remembered everything she said

FIGURE 26.   The Jaloux beats his wife. *Roman de la Rose*. MS. e Mus. 65, fol. 72v. By permission of the Bodleian Library, University of Oxford.

and recounted it to me afterwards, she wanted him to call me his lover without loving me *par amour*. If he had been the kind of person to believe her, he would certainly have betrayed me, but he pledged me his word, and this was the only assurance he gave me, that nothing she said could have made him commit such treason.]

Bel Acueil personifies the female's responses to Amant, yet the grammatical gender of the noun *accueil* requires that the personification be male. At the beginning of *Ars* 3, Ovid suggests that the grammatical gender of personified abstract nouns has semantic value when he states that it is appropriate that Virtue be a feminine noun (3.23). The male gender of Bel Acueil in the *Rose* demands the reader's recognition of the significance of grammatical gender,

FIGURE 27. The Jaloux speaks to his wife. *Roman de la Rose*, BnF, fr. 12595, fol. 63v. By permission of the Bibliothèque nationale de France.

and Bel Acueil's masculine identity offers a queer commentary on the circulation of desire in the poem, as Simon Gaunt has shown.[39] The instructions of the Vieille are all explicitly delivered to the masculine Bel Acueil, yet they just as explicitly address the performance of the ostensibly "female" rose. Such rhetorical gender bending becomes even more complex when Amant states that Bel Acueil recounts the discourse of the Vieille to Amant, who is emphatically not the audience the Vieille is ostensibly attempting to reach.

A similar rhetorical complexity animates the text of the Vieille's advice as an adaptation from Ovid's *Ars amatoria* 3. The Vieille insists that her instructions to Bel Acueil are based, not on learning, but on experience:

n'onc ne fui d'Amors a escole
ou l'en leüst la theorique,
mes je sai tout par la practique.
Experimenz m'en ont fet sage,
que j'ai hantez tout mon aage.
                    (12772–76)

[I have never been to the school of Love, where they teach the theory, but I know it all through practice. Experience, which I have pursued throughout my life, has made me wise in love's ways.]

A few lines later she comments that in old age, "la treuve l'en sen et usage" (12790) ["sense and experience are to be found there"], so much so that she could offer a sermon on the knowledge she has gained from "usage" or experience.[40] Several hundred lines further on, she asserts that her advice will acquire pedagogical authority: "car bien sai que ceste parole / sera leüe an mainte escole" (13467–68) ["I know that these words will be taught in many schools"].[41] In the *Ars amatoria*, it is the *praeceptor* who early on in book 1 dismisses literary learning and claims his pedagogy to be inspired instead by experience: "Vsus opus mouet hoc," (1.29) he states. However, when it comes to advising his female audience in book 3 of the *Ars*, his "experience" is somewhat removed from the topic of the lessons, and he speaks as a male lover who has received certain treatment at the hands of his female lovers. Jean de Meun, by contrast, put the discourse of *Ars* 3 in the mouth of an old woman instead of a male poet; in order to do this, he adapted the discourse of *Ars* 3 for the figure of the Vieille, an allegorical figure modeled on Dipsas, the old woman in Ovid's *Amores* 1.8[42] The personification of the Vieille is also indebted to the Old woman depicted in the pseudo-Ovidian poem the *de Vetula*. Both *Amores* 1.8 and the *de Vetula* offer portraits of old women who are deceptive and manipulative, and both texts assert that old women by their nature acquire an uncanny ability with magical arts.[43] Seen against this cultural construction of the extraordinary—and frightening—power that age and sexual experience confer on women, the claims of the Vieille to the authority that comes from experience enhance her presence as a personification; her speech appeals to her experience as though experience were an exemplum that could be called upon as proof. Thus the Vieille in the *Rose* makes the same claim to authority that the *praeceptor* makes in *Ars* 1, and in the process, she simultaneously performs femininity both as an art and as a "natural" gender. When Amant later comments on his methodology, "onc riens n'en dis . . . qui ne soit en escrit trové / et par experimant prové" (15263–66) ["I have never . . . said anything that was not found in

FIGURE 28. The Jaloux beats his wife. *Roman de la Rose*, BnF, fr. 12595, fol. 69v. By permission of the Bibliothèque nationale de France.

writing and proved by experience"], he indirectly confirms the authority of the Vieille, whose discourse appeals only to experience, while Amant uses experience to test textual authority.

The visual apparatus of *Rose* manuscripts often presents the Vieille as an authoritative interlocutor. Although Amant initially refers to her as an old whore and dismisses her as a crone, Amant eventually acknowledges that she

FIGURE 29.   The Vieille gives the chaplet to Bel Acueil. *Roman de la Rose*, BUV, MS 387, fol. 87v. By permission of the Biblioteca Històrica, Universitat de València.

is instrumental in his progress because, despite her cynical advice to Bel Acueil, she delivers Amant's chaplet to him, and she also unlocks the door to the castle so that Amant can enter and approach Bel Acueil after she leaves. The status of the Vieille in the visual program of the Valencia manuscript emphasizes her agency in the progress of the allegory. In the image that illustrates her presentation of the chaplet (Fig. 29), she and Bel Acueil face each other in front of the tower. Her slightly stooped posture (compared to Bel Acueil's erect pose) signals her age, yet it also conveys a sense of entreaty, and even earnestness. Later, the artists depict two scenes side by side (Fig. 30) when the Vieille directs Amant to the castle and opens the door. In both frames her body claims the central space in the image, in both she is situated to look slightly taller than Amant, and in both images he gestures towards her in deference and gratitude. Likewise, many manuscripts offer very pre-

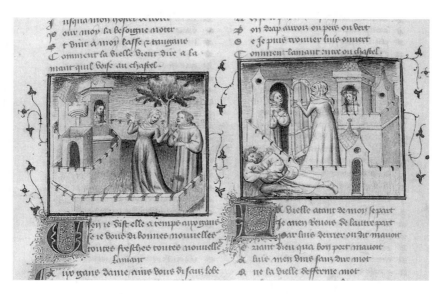

FIGURE 30. The Vieille directs Amant to the castle; the Vieille lets Amant enter. *Roman de la Rose*, BUV, MS 387, fol. 101v. By permission of the Biblioteca Històrica, Universitat de València.

cise rubrication in the Vielle's sermon, marking off parts and often breaking her sermon down into topics. The rubric in one manuscript even identifies her as an authority on the art of love when it introduces her speech, "Comment la vieille ensegne a bel acueil de art d'amours" ["How the Vieille teaches Bel Acueil the art of love"].[44] Since the Vieille draws her discourse from *Ars 3*, her speech extends and revises the advice of Ami, whose speech is based on *Ars* 1 and 2; the Vieille's lesson, in particular, offers a gloss on the tirade of the Jaloux. This juxtaposition is often made evident in the visual programs of *Rose* manuscripts: while the Jaloux invokes Lucretia, who commits suicide to reclaim her honor (Fig. 15), the Vieille cites the suicide of Dido, a woman whose passion and abandonment led her to fall on a sword (Fig. 31). The images of Lucretia's and Dido's suicides are often very similar; in the Valencia manuscript, for example, both are depicted slumping over a large sword; only the context distinguishes the two deaths.[45] The Vieille adds Phyllis and Medea to her list of abandoned women (Fig. 32), and all three exempla are meant to illustrate her advice that women should not put their trust in one man alone. These exempla, however, juxtapose the erotic deaths of three highly passionate women who loved and lost to the chaste Lucretia, whose death to avoid dishonor pales by contrast. This visual program underscores the ways in which the discourse of the Vieille evokes and complicates

FIGURE 31.   Suicide of Dido. *Roman de la Rose*, BUV, MS 387, fol. 91v. By permission of the Biblioteca Històrica, Universitat de València.

the discourse of Ami and the Jaloux. Perhaps for that reason, the Vieille, like the Jaloux, has been a troubling figure for readers of the *Rose*; Huot notes two manuscripts of the *Rose* that omit or abbreviate the Vieille's speech.[46]

The speech of the Vieille closely paraphrases in places the Latin text of the third book of the *Ars amatoria*. Since the *Art d'amours* did not include the third book of the *Ars* until after Jean de Meun had completed the *Roman de la Rose*, and since the four verse translations include relatively little material from *Ars* 3, the Vieille's speech was drawn directly from the Latin text of the *Ars amatoria* without an intermediary French text.[47] The Vieille endorses the basic assumptions of the *Ars*, that female sexual desire—like male sexual desire—is a performance that must be taught and learned, and a good performance can be manipulative and manipulated. The Vieille repeats—sometimes verbatim—the *praeceptor's* advice on cosmetics, hygiene, and how to wear clothes. She also repeats the *praeceptor's* assertions that a

FIGURE 32. Suicide of Phyllis; Jason and the Golden Fleece; Medea killing her children. *Roman de la Rose*, BUV, MS 387, fol. 92r. By permission of the Biblioteca Històrica, Universitat de València.

woman should seek love while she is young, and she offers general advice on conduct, such as table manners. In this context, she warns more strongly against drunkenness than does Ovid's *praeceptor*. While the latter suggests that wine in moderation can be erotically efficacious (3.761–69) the Vieille firmly addresses the risks of intoxication (13419–26). The Vieille otherwise follows Ovid's text rather closely when she advises on the mechanics of heterosexual performance and when she comments specifically on sexual positions and even sexual responses. In *Ars* 3, Ovid parodies ancient sex manuals that had begun to circulate in the Hellenistic period, as we saw in chapter 2;

the Vieille's sermon reproduces Ovid's parodic discourse as advice. The Vieille greatly expands on the *praeceptor*'s elliptical suggestion in *Ars 3* that heterosexual intercourse should please both partners, "et ex aequo res iuuet illa duos" (3.794); the Vieille glosses this notion with explicit advice drawn from *Ars amatoria* 2.725–28 about the simultaneous orgasm: "et s'antredoivent entr'atendre / por ansamble a leur bonne tendre" (14269–70) ["they should wait for each other so that they may come to a climax together"]. The Vieille then goes on to repeat the detailed advice from *Ars 3* that a woman who does not enjoy heterosexual intercourse ought to fake orgasms (*Ars* 3.797–98 and *Rose* 14275–80).

In following Ovid's *praeceptor*, the Vieille advises Bel Acueil to feign desire, so that the long lesson she offers Bel Acueil addresses female heterosexual performance as a means of manipulating male desires rather than an exploration of female subjectivity and its relation to desire. Despite this cynical context, the Vieille concludes her long speech in an altogether different register when she shifts to a confessional tone and offers a much less cynical comment about sexuality and desire in direct contrast to her advice to Bel Acueil:

> *Onc n'amoi home qui m'amast;*
> *mes se cil ribauz m'antamast*
> *l'espaule, ou ma teste eüst quasse,*
> *sachiez que je l'en merciasse.*
> *Il ne me seüst ja tant batre*
> *que seur moi nou feïsse enbatre,*
> *qu'il savoit trop bien sa pes fere,*
> *ja tant ne m'eüst fet contrere.*
> *Ja tant ne m'eüst maumenee*
> *ne batue ne trahinee,*
> *ne mon vis blecié ne nerci,*
> *qu'ainceis ne me criast merci*
> *que de la place se meüst;*
> *ja tant dit honte ne m'eüst*
> *que de pes ne m'amonetast*
> *et que lors ne me rafetast :*
> *si ravions pes et concorde.*
>
> (14461–77)

[I never loved a man who loved me, but if this wretch had hurt my shoulder or cracked my skull, I tell you I would have thanked him for it. However much he beat me, I would still have had him fall upon me, for he was so good at making peace, whatever hurt he might have done me. However badly he treated me, beating me and dragging me about, hurting my face and bruising it, he would always beg my forgiveness before he left. However humiliating his language to me, he would always sue for peace and then take me to bed, and so there was peace and harmony between us once more.]

Since the Vieille has claimed authority for her own experience, this personal anecdote punctuates her advice with a compelling account of erotic violence, and these comments explicitly demonstrate the efficacy of Ami's advice that the lover follow violence with the "geu d'amor." This confessional moment in the Vieille's speech also glosses the earlier representation of violence as brutish when deployed by the Jaloux: although the Vieille describes actions that are remarkably close to the violence perpetrated by the Jaloux, she interprets this violence as desire when she concludes with the assertion that a good lover can effectively deploy violence as part of eros. While the violent scene described by the Vieille is never illustrated, the Vieille's description of being beaten would evoke the reader's visual memory of the image of the Jaloux in any one of the more than three dozen manuscripts that contain that illustration.

Given the theatricality of the Vieille's discourse, this portion of her speech actually purports to express desire and to offer a glimpse into an authentic female subjectivity by contrast to the Ovidian discourse that precedes it. This narrative of her "experience," however, undermines her overall instructions for Bel Acueil, since she advises him to remain aloof from desire as a way of retaining control. Yet, on another level, this is a powerful performance of the erotics of submission that the *praeceptor* delineates for his female disciple in *Ars* 3, and in that sense, the Vieille has outdone her own Ovidian discourse. The most notable feature of this passage is the role of violence in the definition of desire from the female perspective. The Vieille categorically links violence—which she itemizes here—with *amor* and eros. According to the Vieille, being the object of violence defines the female as the object of desire. Her speech—one performance among many competing performances in the *Rose*—claims that erotic violence is foundational to female heterosexual desire. Thus the advice of Ami is glossed by the advice of the Vieille, which is then glossed by Nature, and so forth. In such a context, the text of the *Rose* develops a cumulative lesson on erotic violence. The Vieille, in tutoring Bel Acueil, normalizes erotic violence when she instructs the lover on the effective use of violence to enthrall rather than alienate the object of his desire. By her account, the lover can best achieve his erotic dominance through a more disinterested use of violence than that exhibited by the Jaloux.

Amant and the Rose

The teachings of Ami and the Vieille anticipate the conclusion of the poem which explores the allegorical potential of siege warfare and conquest and thereby thematizes the connection between violence and eros. When Genius has finished his speech and stirred up the host, the final task of seduction is described in military language: "Lors se sunt tuit an piez levé, / prest de continuer la guerre, / por tout prandre et metre par terre" (20678–80) ["Then all rose to their feet, ready to continue the war until everything should be captured and razed to the ground"]. After a lengthy digression on Pygmalion and Myrrha, Amant undertakes to pluck the rose; however, the virginity of the rose makes that feat difficult, and Amant describes his efforts as heroic:

> Et je, qui ci tant me travaill
> que tretouz an tressu d'angoisse
> quant ce paliz tantost ne froisse,
> sui bien, ce cuit, autant lassez
> conme Herculés, ou plus assez.
> > (21598–602).

[As for me, when I could not immediately break the barrier, I struggled so hard and with such violence that I was drenched in sweat, and I was, I believe, quite as weary as Hercules, or even more so.]

Amant's allusion to Hercules' three attempts on Cacus mythologizes the erotic agency required for the deflowering of a virgin. The Valencia manuscript includes an image of Hercules at this point (Fig. 33) placed between two graphic images of Amant thrusting his staff into the statue that represents the rose;[48] while Amant appears to effortlessly insert his staff, Hercules throws his entire body into the blow on the gate. This visual reference to Hercules evokes the elaborate two-column miniature of Hercules from the speech of the Jaloux (Fig. 17) who emphasized Hercules's vulnerability to Deianeira and his consequent death. This frantic depiction of Hercules's brute, hypermasculine strength makes the heroic rhetoric of Amant appear as a form of hyperheterosexual discourse.

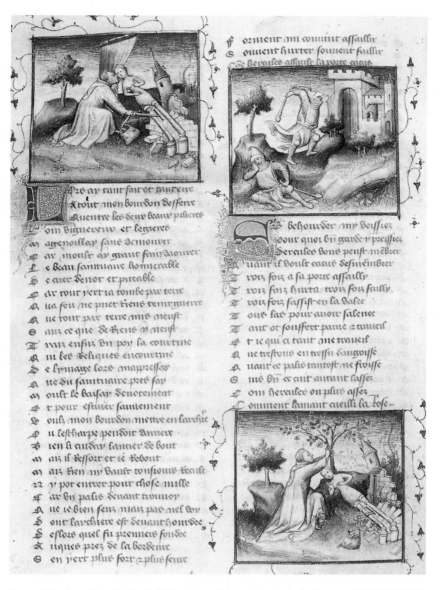

Figure 33. Amant inserts his staff; Hercules and Cacus; Amant plucks the rose. BUV, MS 387, fol. 147v. By permission of the Biblioteca Històrica, Universitat de València.

The metaphor of the rose reifies female desire as a genital response to Amant's heterophallic agency. By contrast to the agency of Amant, the object of desire, the rose, is represented solely through the personification of Bel Acueil:

> *Bel Acueill por Dieu me priait*
> *que nul outrage fet n'i ait;*
> *et je li mis mout en couvant,*
> *por ce qu'il m'an priait souvant,*
> *que ja nule riens ne feroie*
> *for sa volanté et la moie.*
> > *(21669–74).*

[Fair Welcome begged me in God's name to do nothing violent, and I promised him solemnly, in response to his repeated prayers, to do nothing that was not both his will and my own.]

Amant's shift in focus—from describing his heroic use of force to acknowledging the responses of Bel Acueil—enacts the earlier precepts of Ami that force is both efficacious and constitutive of masculine identity, but only if deployed in the context of some "implied" consent; that is, only if Bel Acueil does not become angry and defend himself vigorously. Amant's performance proceeds in precisely these terms when he notes the response of the rose and the response of Bel Acueil. When Amant scatters his seed, he mingles it with seed from the rose:

> *Si fis lors si meller les greines*
> *qu'el se desmellassent a peines,*
> *si que tout le boutonet tandre*
> *an fis ellargir et estandre.*
> > *(21697–700)*

[I thus mingled the seeds in such a way that it would have been hard to disentangle them, with the result that all the rose-bud swelled and expanded.]

Among the competing medical theories of sexuality in the thirteenth century, one paradigm assumed that women ejaculated during orgasm;[49] when Amant offers this detail about the response of the rosebud, he interprets the presence of seed in the rose as a sign of consent and pleasure on its part, personified by the responses of Bel Acueil:

Si m'apele il de couvenant,
et li faz grant desavenant,
et suis trop outrageus, ce dit.
Mes il n'i met nul contredit
que ne preigne et debaille et cueille
rosier et rains et fleur et fueille.
               (21707–12).

[Of course, he reminded me of my promise, and told me that my be-
haviour was outrageously improper. But he did nothing to oppose my
taking and caressing and plucking the rose-bush, with all its branches,
flowers, and leaves.]

Kathryn Gravdal sees the violent conclusion of the allegory as a form of
sexual assault rather than erotic violence: "The 'seduction' of the Rose, the
courtly lady, is depicted blatantly as the rape of a virgin."[50] According to medieval theories of female sexual response, however, the emission of seed on
the part of the rose precludes any possibility of rape. Indeed, the ending
would seem to exemplify the precept asserted in the *Art d'amours*, that
women cannot be raped: "il leur plaist a estre efforciés, ja soit ce que on ne
puisse nulle femme efforcer oultre sa volenté" (1992–94) ["It pleases them
to be forced, even though one cannot force any woman against her will"].
The conclusion to the *Rose* is emblematic of the Ovidian discourse of eros
that depends on the erotics of violence as a means of rendering heterosexual
desire legible.

    When Venus leads the charge against the castle, she predicts to Honte that
Bel Acueil will sometimes sell his roses and rosebuds, and sometimes give
them away ("une heure en vante, autre heure an don" [20710]), an assertion
that suggests that Bel Acueil has learned the lessons taught by the Vieille. In
the course of the allegory of the *Rose*, the Ovidian language of the Vieille
claims an expansive space for a performance of female desire, however cynical. The Vieille lives on in the *Wife of Bath's Prologue;* not only is the Wife of
Bath a disciple of the Vieille, but Chaucer's construction of the Wife effectively embodies the gendered discourse of desire derived from the *Ars amatoria* and assigned to the Vieille in the *Roman de la Rose.*

↩ Chapter 5

The *Vieille Daunce*
The Wife of Bath and the Politics of Experience

> Cunning lingua is, properly speaking, an erotics-
> poetics whose fictional dialogues and sexual dialects
> perform a blasphemous act of seductive illocution.
>
> —Dianne Chisholm

Chaucer's *Wife of Bath's Prologue* opens with the Wife's famous claim: "Experience, though noon auctoritee / Were in this world, is right ynogh for me" (1–2)[1] With this spontaneous-sounding assertion, the narrator of the *Prologue* rejects textual authority and claims personal experience as the basis for an "authentic" subjectivity that authorizes her to speak. Despite the rhetorical force of her pronouncement, the Wife's discourse does not originate in experience but in the text of the *Roman de la Rose*, specifically in the speech of the Vieille who also claims experience as the source of her authority: "Experimenz m'en ont fet sage, / que j'ai hantez tout mon aage" (12775–76) ["Experience, which I have pursued throughout my life, has made me wise in love's ways"]. The Vieille, as we saw in the last chapter, speaks not from experience but from Ovid, since her discourse is largely compiled from the third book of the *Ars amatoria*. The Wife of Bath's "experience" thus derives ultimately from the *Ars amatoria*, so that Ovid's text and its discourse on erotic violence form the basis of the female subjectivity constructed in the *Prologue*. Readers, however, often fail to recognize the discursive quality of the Wife's experience; modern readers frequently take Alisoun of Bath for a recognizable version of a woman—sometimes even to the point of implicitly mistaking her for a historical figure. Of course, readers seldom do this explicitly; almost a set piece of Chaucerian scholarship on the *Wife of Bath's Prologue* is the initial acknowledgment that the text of the *Prologue* is male-authored, which makes the Wife, as Arlyn Diamond pointed out over twenty-five years ago, a "figure compounded of masculine insecurities and female vices as seen by misogynists."[2] Nonetheless, critics often express some version of this standard disclaimer and then proceed to discuss the *Prologue* as a text that might testify to female consciousness and desire in historically contingent terms.[3] This response to the Wife results in part from the juxtaposition of the *Wife of Bath's Prologue* to her tale, a rhetorical framework that situates the Wife as a speaker whose subject positions are so thoroughly explored in her *Prologue* that the reader is thereby invited to take the speaker of the *Prologue* as the honorary author of the tale.

This modern response to the Wife has antecedents in the Chaucerian corpus as well as in the reception of Chaucer's texts. The Canterbury pilgrims themselves refer to the Wife as an honorary author when the Clerk refers to the Wife of Bath as a spokeswoman for "al hire secte" (1171), and the Merchant cites her as an authority on marriage, about which she "Declared hath ful wel in litel space" (1687). Chaucer reinforces the concept of the Wife as an author in *Lenvoy de Chaucer a Bukton*, when, in an attempt to dissuade Bukton from marriage, Chaucer suggests to him: "The Wyf of Bathe I pray yow that ye rede" (29). In the reception of Chaucer's *Canterbury Tales*, the character of the Wife of Bath stands out as a figure of extraordinary authority. Fifteenth-century poets cite the Wife as an expert witness on marriage as though she were a figure separate from Chaucer, her creator. In the *Dialogus cum Amico*, Thomas Hoccleve invokes the Wife of Bath's *Prologue*: "The wyf of Bathe, take I for auctrice / þat wommen han no ioie ne deyntee / œat men sholde vp-on hem putte any vice." (694–96)[4] Lydgate occasionally cites the Wife of Bath as an authority on marriage,[5] and in his short poem, the *Pain and Sorrow of Evil Marriage*, he offers a portrait of marriage as a "tempest of deedly violence" (5)[6] that derives from the *Wife of Bath's Prologue*. When John Skelton's *Phyllyp Sparowe* evokes the *Canterbury Tales*, the *Wife of Bath's Tale* is completely overshadowed by the supposed life-writing of the *Prologue* and its pedagogic potential:

And of the wyfe of Bath,
That worketh moch scath
Whan her tale is tolde
Amonge huswyves bolde,
How she controlde
Her husbandes as she wolde,
And them to despyse
In the homylyest wyse,

Brynge other wyves in thought
Their husbandes to set at nought.
                (618–27)[7]

The didactic confidence of the *Wife of Bath's Prologue* gives the Wife of Bath unusual stature as a literary character; she is the only pilgrim in the *Canterbury Tales* to compete with Chaucer for the authority of authorship.

Mistaken for an author, Chaucer's Wife of Bath consequently appears to be a female speaker whose subjectivity is compellingly accessible. Despite its discursive texture as an appropriation of Ovid's *Ars amatoria*, mediated through the *Roman de la Rose*, the *Prologue* seems to exert a visceral appeal as a text that purports to embody the lived experience of a married woman. One critic, for instance, observed that to him, the *Wife of Bath's Prologue* and the *Wife of Bath's Tale* suggest that "Chaucer knew a lot about women."[8] Such readerly transference has occasionally resulted in highly empathetic connections to the Wife. Lee Patterson finds in the *Wife of Bath's Prologue* a "titillating ambivalence of eroticism," and he clarifies the quality of his response to the speaker of the *Prologue*: "The very intimacy of her revelations assures us that *we* are not old and foolish, that we might even be one of those with whom she has shared 'many a myrthe.'"[9] A similar empathy between the reader and the Wife of Bath sometimes leads feminists to read Chaucer's *Prologue* as the autobiographical discourse of a historical figure, which would make the *Prologue* a text similar to the *Book of Margery Kempe*.[10] In such a reading, the empathy elicited by the *Wife of Bath's Prologue* implicitly claims validity for the personal anecdotes narrated by the Wife. Such an approach takes a textual representation of a cultural construct of "woman" for a transparent witness to the "experience" of women. The figure of the Wife of Bath illustrates how the hermeneutics of experience in a fictional text places specific demands on the modern scholar. While the interpretive nature of experience in a fictional text would seem obvious,[11] the referential nature of the *Prologue* nonetheless records various discourses of marriage and sexuality in medieval cultures. As Satya Mohanty has argued, experience, even in a fictional text, "has a cognitive component," and Sonia Kruks emphasizes that experience also has a social element.[12] When medieval and modern readers recognize the fictional widow of Bath as an authority on the lived experience of marriage, they acknowledge the powerful potential of a literary character to represent the ethical dimensions of a cultural ideology. The performance of the Wife of Bath achieves authenticity to the degree that it is consistent with marriage as an institution that elicits and disciplines sexual desire. If this medieval literary figure seems familiar to the modern reader, that familiarity suggests the extent to which modern heterosexualities are haunted by medieval discourses on sexuality, including medieval marital ideology. The modern reader's recognition of the Wife of Bath initiates an ethical engagement with the representations of erotic violence in her text.

The Wife and the Whip

Chaucer's Wife of Bath acquires her unique authority from the first-person discourse of the *Prologue* that situates her as a teller of a purportedly autobiographical narrative that precedes an explicitly fictional tale. But her vivid, compelling presence in the *Canterbury Tales* derives as well from her portrait in the *General Prologue* where she is characterized by her equestrian abilities and accoutrements:

> Upon an amblere esily she sat,
> Ywympled wel, and on hir heed an hat
> As brood as is a bokeler or a targe;
> A foot-mantel aboute her hipes large,
> And on hir feet a paire of spores sharpe.
>
> *(469–73)*

Richly enveloped in textiles that denote her "estaat," the Wife rides comfortably among the Canterbury pilgrims: her voluminous wimple and hat denote her social status as a wife.[13] Her easy mastery of a saddle horse interprets her marital expertise in equestrian terms consistent with her later self-presentation in the *Prologue*, where she characterizes herself as the scourge of her husbands.

The two surviving illustrations of the Wife of Bath from early fifteenth-century manuscripts of the *Canterbury Tales* draw on the discourse of horsemanship from the language in the *General Prologue* and the *Wife of Bath's Prologue*. While the Canterbury pilgrims are all depicted on horseback, the images of the Wife of Bath employ an equestrian portrait in order to visualize her discourse of dominance; these images interpret the Wife of Bath as a woman on top. The Ellesmere artist (Fig. 34) depicts her riding astride, like the male pilgrims, according to the standard practice of the day and in contrast to the portraits of other female pilgrims in the Ellesmere manuscript, the Second Nun and the Prioress, who ride sidesaddle. In her left hand, the Wife grasps the reins and in her right she wields a riding whip consisting of a long handle from which hang two straps with tips at the end. Her easy control of the horse is visually rendered by her relaxed, confident posture. The whip in her right hand functions as her attribute, a visual clue to her

FIGURE 34. The Wife of Bath. *Canterbury Tales*, Ellesmere 26C9, fol. 72r. By permission of the Huntington Library, San Marino, California.

FIGURE 35.   The Wife of Bath. *Canterbury Tales*, Cambridge, Gg.4.27. fol. 222r. By permission of the Syndics of Cambridge University Library.

social status and occupation as a wife in the same manner that the urinal functions as an attribute for the vocation of the Physician or the meat hook for the Cook in the Ellesmere portraits. The illustration of the Wife of Bath in MS. Cambridge Gg.4.27 likewise depicts a heavily garbed woman, swathed in an enormous amount of blue and scarlet material; she holds aloft a sizeable riding crop with visible metal studs (Fig. 35). In this image, the

Wife rides sidesaddle and her large frame appears to almost overpower her well-accoutred horse; her nearly frontal posture reinforces the vision of agency and power suggested by the oversized whip. These two images offer a visual interpretation of the Wife's sexual skills precisely as she describes them in the *Prologue* when she characterizes her dominance of her first three husbands with the words, "myself have been the whippe" (175). She later uses an equestrian metaphor to describe her negotiations with her fifth husband: "He yaf me al the bridel in myn hond" (813).[14]

When the artists who produced these illustrations of the Wife envision the equestrian details such as the bridle and the whip, they cite the visual tradition of the "mounted Aristotle." As we saw in chapter 1, in images of the "mounted Aristotle" the riding whip represents the erotic agency of the female rider (Figs. 1–4, 8–10). Indeed, both the visual and the textual traditions of the "mounted Aristotle" form important intertexts for Chaucer's Wife of Bath. A textual account of the "mounted Aristotle" was known to Chaucer in Jean le Fèvre's *Livre de Leesce*, a fourteenth-century French text that also provided several rhetorical structures or phrases found in the *Wife of Bath's Prologue*.[15] The *Livre de Leesce*, for instance, provided the source for the Wife's comment: "if wommen hadde writen stories, / As clerkes han withinne hire oratories, / They wolde han writen of men moore wikkednesse" (693–95)[16] Even the argumentative texture of Chaucer's *Wife of Bath's Prologue* owes something to the structure of the *Livre de Leesce*, which stages a critique of misogyny by recording the arguments Leesce offers in response to Matheolus' *Lamentations:* Jean le Fèvre, who had initially translated the *Lamentations*, later composed the *Livre de Leesce* in order to refute, point by point, its misogynist arguments. In the *Livre de Leesce*, the narrator, Leesce, notes that Matheolus had cited Aristotle as an example of a learned and wise man humiliated by a woman:

> *Et qu'Aristote, le grant maistre,*
> *Ot en son chief frain et chevestre*
> *Et que femme le chevaucha*
> *Et par dessus luy se haucha.*
> *(819–22)*[17]

[And . . . Aristotle, the great master, had on his head bridle and a halter, and a woman rode him, mounted on his back.]

Leesce responds by suggesting that sexual desire in humans was created by God to further the race through propagation (823–46). Leesce reads the exemplum of the mounted Aristotle as an example of the power of *amor:*

Et s'il se laissa chevauchier,
Ce fu par joye et par deduit;
Amour a ce faire le duist
Par sa grant debonnaireté.
(888–91)

[And if he let himself be ridden, this was for joy and pleasure. *Amor* made him do this by his great nobility.]

Leesce's gloss on the Aristotle exemplum from Matheolus specifies the erotic value of Aristotle's ride, suggesting by extension the erotic attraction of the woman rider. As we saw in chapter 1, when the Vieille in the *Roman de la Rose* refers to the "tender mouth" of her violent lover, she makes a veiled reference to the "mounted Aristotle." The *Wife of Bath's Prologue* likewise evokes the "mounted Aristotle" in the equestrian metaphors the Wife uses in her celebration of female erotic mastery.

The pilgrim portraits in the Ellesmere manuscript are placed at the margin of the text; the Cambridge miniatures appear in the column of text. Both illustrations of the Wife of Bath follow the *Prologue* and introduce the *Wife of Bath's Tale*, and both consequently represent Alison of Bath as the young wife described there.[18] Both illustrations also emphasize the dramatic and rhetorical framework of the *General Prologue* that supplies the details for the portraits, even though the images are not situated as illustrations of the *General Prologue*. In addition, the *General Prologue* emphasizes the Wife's achievements as a pilgrim who has been to Jerusalem, Rome, Compostela, and Cologne. Only the Knight—who has campaigned extensively in the East, in Spain, and in North Africa—has traveled more widely than the Wife of Bath. The Wife's itinerary along well-known pilgrimage routes anticipates the more expansionist engagement beyond Western Europe represented by the Knight. Both pilgrimage to the Middle East and the crusades reflect the orientalist visions of Western Europe represented by the Knight, and both presage the colonial efforts of the early modern era.[19] In addition, the well-traveled Wife is also well-garbed:

Hir coverchiefs ful fyne weren of ground;
I dorste swere they weyeden ten pound
That on a Sonday weren upon hir heed.
Hir hosen weren of fyn scarlet reed,
Ful streite yteyd, and shoes ful moyste and newe.
(453–57)

The *General Prologue* follows the *Roman de la Rose* in detailing the commodity fetishism of medieval trade and economic exchange. The fine quality of the Wife's head scarves and the suppleness of her boots attest to her economic achievements in cloth making, an activity in which "She passed hem of Ypres and of Gaunt" (448). Cloth was the wealth of the wool-producing region around Bath, and the Wife's heavily draped figure metaphorically suggests her economic dominance in a highly competitive international market.[20] While the *General Prologue*, like the *Roman de la Rose*, details the qualities and origins of silk or gold as the most desirable commodities, the textiles that the Wife of Bath displays on her body represent English wealth and power. The overall portrait of the Wife collates her sexual and economic power in a gendered fantasy of sexual and even imperial dominance.

The concluding lines to the portrait of the Wife of Bath go beyond her economic and social stature in order to hint at her erotic skills: "Of remedies of love she knew per chaunce, / For she koude of that art the olde daunce" (475–76). In assigning to the Wife a knowledge of the "remedies of love," Chaucer suggests that in the course of her marriages she has achieved the sort of immunity to the attractions of eros that Ovid outlines in the *Remedia amoris*, an elegiac poem written as a sequel to the *Ars amatoria* and often paired with the *Ars* in medieval manuscripts.[21] The *Remedia* offers a set of strategies designed to effectively end an affair; it playfully tutors the reader in the art of detachment as a means of gaining control of desire, and by extension, of the object of desire. But Chaucer's last words in the portrait of the Wife are the most telling: the reference to "the olde daunce" situates the Wife of Bath as a direct descendant of the Vieille and her Ovidian performance of female desire. The Middle English version of the *Roman de la Rose* employs identical vocabulary to translate the French phrase, "la vielle dance" (3908). At the moment the Vieille takes custody of Bel Acueil, the text describes her erotic skill:

> The whiche devel in hir enfaunce
> Hadde lerned of loves art,
> And of his pleyes tok hir part;
> She was expert in his servise.
> She knew ech wrench and every gise
> Of love, and every wile;
> It was [the] harder hir to gile.
> Of Bealacoil she tok ay hede,
> That evere he lyveth in woo and drede.
> He kepte hym koy and eke pryve,
> Lest in hym she hadde see

Ony foly countenaunce,
For she knew all the olde daunce.

(4288–300)

Although Chaucer tells us in the *Prologue to the Legend of Good Women* that he translated the *Roman de la Rose*, the surviving three fragments of a Middle English version of the *Rose* cannot be clearly attributed to him, and this passage from Fragment B is probably not Chaucer's version. It nonetheless demonstrates how closely the linguistic register of the *General Prologue* echoes the *Rose*. In the *Rose*, the phrase "la vielle daunce," or "the olde daunce" summarily concludes a survey of the Vieille's skill in the arts of love, and it situates the Vieille in a literary genealogy derived from the *Ars amatoria*.

The construction of the Vieille in the *Roman de la Rose* marks a particular moment in the vernacular reception of Ovid's *Ars amatoria*, and Chaucer's *Wife of Bath's Prologue* further develops the Ovidian discourse on the eroticization of violence. As we saw in chapter 4, the highly visual format of many manuscripts of the *Roman de la Rose* reifies the Ovidian thematics of the allegory, since the visual component often accentuates depictions of violent agency, particularly in the case of the Jaloux and the Vieille. In addition to the Ovidian discourse of the *Rose*, Chaucer also consulted the French version of the *Ars amatoria*, the *Art d'amours*, which, as we have seen, rendered the *Ars* as a crude handbook for sexual domination. The compelling figure of the Wife of Bath embodies the Ovidian discourse of the Vieille from the *Roman de la Rose*; in the process, the *Wife of Bath's Prologue* domesticates the erotic violence of the *Ars amatoria*.

The Vieille and the Widow

The *Wife of Bath* is, of course, not a wife but a widow; as sexually experienced women outside the regime of marriage and consequently beyond masculine control, widows explicitly troubled the normative categories of desire in medieval cultures.[22] As a widow who retrospectively describes her career as a married woman, the Wife of Bath appears to offer a record of embodied subjectivity: as she announces at the end of the *Man of Law's Tale*, "My joly body schal a tale telle" (1185). Like the Vieille's sermon in the *Roman de la Rose*, the *Wife of Bath's Prologue* is an extensive first-person narrative of sexual transgressions punctuated at the end by an anecdote of self-disclosure. In medieval culture the space that would elicit such narratives of transgression was the space of the confessional; not surprisingly, the discourse of the self that emerges in Chaucer's *Wife of Bath's Prologue*, like the *Pardoner's Prologue*, employs confessional rhetoric as the most readily available model of self-presentation.[23] Chaucer's text constructs his narrator through a series of sexual transgressions: in the first section of the *Prologue*, the Wife of Bath catalogues the ways in which she achieved dominance over her husbands in direct contradiction to the cultural norm that considered the husband to be the dominant partner in a marriage. The *Prologue* moves from her boastful recitation of her marital transgressions as a domineering wife to her admission that things got out of her control during her fifth marriage. Throughout the *Prologue* her character develops first as a wife who violates the principles of marriage, then as an experienced wife who violates her own principles. Chaucer's narrator appears to disclose more than she intends, and such confessional-seeming rhetoric contributes to her perceived authenticity. Foucault suggests that the veracity of a confession is a result of "the bond, the basic intimacy in discourse, between the one who speaks and what he is speaking about,"[24] so that the very act of speaking about the self in sexual terms creates an intimate bond that claims a truth-value for the confessional speech act.[25] Judith Butler extends Foucault's notion to emphasize the role of the body in confession, since the "speaker, in speaking, is presenting the body that did the deed."[26] The more compelling the confession, the more present the speaking body implicitly becomes. The intense transference that takes place between readers of Chaucer and the fictional Wife of Bath testifies to the efficacy of confessional rhetoric in constructing the body implied by the text. Dianne Chisholm argues that "bodies are not substituted by language nor is their corporeality reducible to textuality."[27] While Carolyn Dinshaw has illuminated the textual erotics of the Wife of Bath,[28] it is the Wife of Bath's "lingual performativity"[29] that seduces even the most sophisticated readers, as we have seen.

The exuberant verbal performance of the Wife of Bath, for all its perceived authenticity, is almost a transcription of the sermon of the Vieille from the *Roman de la Rose*; since the Vieille functions as a conduit for Ovidian discourse drawn from the *Ars amatoria*, the most compellingly "authentic" portions of the *Wife of Bath's Prologue* are the most Ovidian. Like the Vieille, the Wife of Bath is identified by her age, though at the age of forty, a serial widow such as the Wife would not be considered elderly as much as experienced.[30] The *Prologue* distinguishes between experience and authority by enacting the Wife of Bath's experience with authority. Authoritative discourse percolates to the surface throughout the *Prologue*, so that the rhetorical structure of the text pits the narrator against a range of authorities, and she emerges as a skeptical interlocutor arguing with a series of invisible authority figures.[31] She begins by interrogating a sermon on the marriage of Cana over the issue of multiple marriages;[32] she defends marital sexuality against the discourses that privileged virginity, and she proceeds to argue against a variety of misogynist and misogamous traditions. She repeatedly dismisses doctrinal precepts and proverbial wisdom, at one point stating "conseillyng is no comandement" (67). In the passages where she does not argue with authority, she narrates a life story. While these passages appear to offer personal anecdotes in order to disrupt or challenge authoritative discourse, many of them are translated directly from the Vieille's speech in the *Rose*, so that the Vieille and the Wife essentially speak the same language.[33] At her most personal or authentic, the Wife of Bath is most constructed.

The pedagogic discourse of the Vieille's sermon has ostensibly found an ideal disciple in the Wife of Bath: in describing her maneuvers, the Wife endorses the advice of the Vieille who urged Bel Acueil to cultivate rich men who are generous and thus vulnerable to being manipulated. The Vieille summarizes her strategy: "et soit tourjorz vers cues plus fiere / qui plus, por s'amor deservir, / se peneront de lui servir" (13244–46)[34] ["and always behave more cruelly towards those who will strive all the harder to serve her in order to win her love"]. She adds that that a woman who can take financial advantage of her lover will have the upper hand, and "car qui mieuz plumer le savra, / c'iert cele qui meilleur l'avra / et qui plus iert chiere tenue" (13669–71) ["The woman who can best fleece him will have the best of him, and will be held more dear because she was more dearly bought"]. The Vieille instructs Bel Acueil in the exchange value of desire when she tells him to sell his heart dearly, and always to the highest bidder (13008–9). The Wife of Bath expresses this doctrine in a pithy, mercantile aphorism: "Wynne whoso may, for al is for to selle" (414). In describing how she manipulated her first three husbands, she notes that her verbal cruelty elicited their attentive, even submissive, behavior; she measures their submission by the commodities that they purchased for her:

> I governed hem so wel, after my lawe,
> That ech of hem ful blisful was and fawe
> To brynge me gaye thynges fro the fayre.
> They were ful glad whan I spak to hem faire,
> For, God it woot, I chidde hem spitously.
>
> *(219–23)*

In keeping with the courtly register of the *Rose*, the Vieille recommends that Bel Acueil acquire gold and jewels; Chaucer by contrast depicts this exchange in terms of the urban, mercantile currency, the "gaye thynges" on offer at the fair, a phrase that echoes the *glose* to the *Art d'amours* at *Ars* 1.395–96, when the compiler details the sort of gifts that women extract from their lovers: "car es festes demandent et ont accoustumé les dames a demander cointises a leurs amis, et aussi es foires et aus marchiés demander joiaux et marchandises" (1362–63)[35] ["At festivals the ladies demand and are accustomed to ask for finery from their lovers. Furthermore, they ask for jewels and goods at fairs and markets"]. The Wife of Bath, however, raises the stakes when she threatens to trade sexual favors on the open market; in a close paraphrase of the Vieille's precepts, the Wife relates how she would taunt her old husbands: "For if I wolde selle my *bele chose* / I koude walke as fressh as is a rose" (447–48). This declaration depicts conjugal sexuality as part of the wider market economy. The Vieille suggests that a lady have her servant or mother put the same case to her lover: "S'el vousist fere, par saint Gile, / por tel a il en ceste vile, / conme reïne fust vestue / et chevauchast a grant sambue" (13699–702) ["By Saint Giles, if she were willing to yield to a certain man in this very town, she could dress like a queen and ride in great state"]. Both the Vieille and Alisoun provocatively claim the right to profit from their own sexuality; such assertions expose the economic dimensions of erotic desire that ideologies such as courtly love or the institutions of marriage work to obscure.[36]

The verbal performance of the *Wife of Bath's Prologue* illustrates the erotic value derived from the commodity fetishism that permeates the *Rose*. The Wife of Bath describes her husbands' rebukes in language reminiscent of the Jaloux's tirade and his obsession with his wife's public display of finery and the implied infidelity of that display. She exclaims: "Thou seyst also, that if we make us gay / With clothyng, and with precious array, / That it is peril of oure chastitee" (337–39). In her enthusiasm for attending church and undertaking pilgrimages, Alisoun follows the precepts of the Vieille who recommends that women who wish to acquire lovers negotiate the public sphere:

> *Et gart que trop ne sait enclose,*
> *quar, quant plus a l'ostel repose,*
> *mains est de toutes genz veüe*
> *et sa biauté mains conneüe,*
> *mains couvoitiee et mains requise.*
> *Sovant aille a la mestre iglise*
> *et face visitacions*
> *a noces, a processions,*
> *a geus, a festes, a queroles.*
>
> *(13487–95)*

[A woman must be careful not to lead too cloistered a life, for the more she stays at home, the less she is seen by everyone and the less her beauty is known, desired, and sought after. She ought often to go to the principal church and attend weddings, processions, games, festivals, and dances.]

The Vieille concludes this advice with instruction on using attire as a spectacle, advice that the well-accoutred Wife of Bath would seem to exemplify. This passage in the *Rose* closely resembles an assertion in the *glose* of the *Art d'amours* regarding well-dressed women in public; in commenting on *Ars* 1.49–50, the translator observes: "Au temps mesmes qui ores est vont elles aus festes et aus eglises, les plus cointes et les plus parees qu'elles pevent, et si faignent que ce soit en l'onneur de la feste" (285–88) ["Even in our day, ladies go to festivals and churches as elegantly and as well dressed as they can, and they pretend that this is in honor of the festival"]. The *Rose* specifies the sexual and erotic meanings that attach to a well-attired woman such as Alisoun of Bath who negotiates public and ceremonial spaces on her own.

As the Vieille advises, the Wife of Bath attends to the economic balance sheet and the market value for sexual favors. The Vieille instructs Bel Acueil to maintain a diversified set of investments, since "Mout a soriz povre secours / et fet en grant perill sa druige / qui n'a q'un pertuis a refuige" (13120–22) ["The mouse who has only one hole to retreat to has a very poor refuge and is in great danger when he goes foraging"]. The Wife, however, calculates her exchange value in terms of marriage when she describes how she had selected Jankyn as her fifth husband before her fourth husband had died: "I holde a mouses herte nat worth a leek / That hath but oon hole for to sterte to" (572–73). This moment in the *Prologue* also actualizes the advice that Ovid's *praeceptor* offers at *Ars* 3.431 that a new lover (*vir*) can be sought at the funeral of the previous one. In the final accounting, however, the Wife has received a much higher return on her investments than has the Vieille: by the time she has survived five husbands and makes the pilgrimage to Canterbury in order to assess the possibility of a sixth marriage, she has amassed considerable wealth which enhances her sexual agency.[37] The Vieille, by contrast, is destitute in her old age: "Les granz dons que cil me donaient / qui tuit a moi s'abandonoient / aus mieuz amez habandonaie" (14429–31) ["The great gifts I received from those who abandoned themselves wholly to me I relinquished to those I loved better"]. Despite the fact that the *Prologue* borrows heavily from the Vieille's speech in the *Roman de la Rose*, Chaucer's emphasis on the marital status of the Wife shifts the focus to her ability to reap financial returns on her investment in heterosexual desire.[38]

The Wife of Bath's Prologue evokes the legal concepts of marriage and its
·duties, particularly the notion of the conjugal debt and marital affection.
The *Prologue* attests to Chaucer's awareness of marital law—especially canon
law, the area of law most invested in regulating and disciplining sexuality.
The opening lines of the *Prologue* invoke marriage as a legal category when
the Wife of Bath declares: "sith I twelve yeer was of age, / Thonked be God
that is eterne on lyve, / Housbondes at chirche dore I have had fyve" (4–6).
Canon law set twelve as the minimum age at which a girl might marry; the
reference to the church door likewise refers to the requirement that marriage ceremonies take place in a public space with witnesses. The *Prologue* is
sprinkled throughout with language derived from the notion of the conjugal debt, a central tenet of canon law that presumes that each partner in a
marriage is legally obliged to comply when the other partner initiates sexual
intercourse.[39] The Wife repeatedly expresses a one-sided understanding of
the conjugal debt since she speaks of it as if it were the sole responsibility of
the husband: "Why sholde men elles in hir bookes sette / That man shal
yelde to his wyf hire dette" (129–30). She refers to the conjugal debt in
terms of the power it offers her: "Myn housbonde shal it have bothe eve and
morwe, / Whan that hym list come forth and paye his dette" (152–53). In
describing her first three, aged husbands, she uses the language of the conjugal debt to comment on their ability to perform sexually: "The thre were
goode men, and riche, and olde; / Unnethe myghte they the statut holde /
In which that they were bounden unto me" (197–200). A few lines earlier,
she has extended the language of the conjugal debt to make a general assertion about her understanding of her role in marriage:

> An housbonde I wol have—I wol not lette—
> Which shal be bothe my dettour and my thral,
> And have his tribulacion withal
> Upon his flessh, whil that I am his wyf.
>
> *(154–57)*

Although modern scholars consider the notion of the conjugal debt to be
the one area of medieval canon law where husband and wife are treated
with equality, the Wife of Bath does not appeal to the notion as a principle
of equality but as an authorization of her dominance, not only in bed, but in
the marriage as a whole.

As the Wife of Bath narrates how she alternated verbal abuse and kindness in managing her first three husbands, she volunteers that she is offering
this description for the benefit and enjoyment of the "wise wives" who are
listening to her *Prologue*, an oddly misplaced pedagogical goal, since the Wife

of Bath is the only nonreligious woman on the pilgrimage to Canterbury. In addressing this absent female audience, the Wife mimics the Vieille, who emphasizes the pedagogical applications of her sermon, not only in relation to Bel Acueil but to other, younger women who are not part of her immediate audience in the *Rose*. Alisoun's evocation of the absent "wise wyves" conjures up the spectral presence of the wives of the married pilgrims. Presumably, these wives are safely ensconced in their homes, away from the temptations and dangers of pilgrimage, and out of hearing of the *Prologue*. The interpellation of the absent wives signifies the threat embodied in an experienced widow who might transmit the knowledge gained in marriage to younger wives and women. As the Wife rehearses the speeches she used to chide her husbands, the *Prologue* becomes a transcript of her rhetorical performance. She argues directly with her dead husbands, repeatedly framing their side of the argument with the phrase "Thow seyst" and then dismissing their arguments:

> Thow seyst we wyves wol oure vices hide
> Til we be fast, and thanne we wol hem shewe—
> Wel may that be a proverbe of a shrewe!
>
> *(282–84)*

The content of these arguments against women, marriage, and especially wives that the Wife puts in the mouth of her dead husbands actually comes from Theophrastus' *Liber de nuptiis* as it was known and transmitted in Jerome's *Adversus Jovinianum*. In the larger sense, then, Chaucer pits the Wife, not against her elderly husbands, but against the textual tradition of misogamy and misogyny. In such a performance, her husbands play a role very similar to that of the Jaloux, who cites Theophrastus and "Valerius" as authorities, and whose verbal tirade borrows from the same sources as the arguments quoted by the Wife. The Wife energetically dismisses the entire set of arguments as an "olde barel-ful of lyes!" (302).

When the Wife of Bath speaks of her fourth husband, her display of rhetorical and sexual dominance starts to unravel. In the course of describing this marriage, she digresses on her own tendency to drink and carouse, and without transition, she veers into an exemplum from Valerius Maximus:

> Metellius, the foule cherl, the swyn,
> That with a staf birafte his wyf hir lyf,
> For she drank wyn, thogh I hadde been his wyf,
> He sholde nat han daunted me fro drynke!
>
> *(460–63)*

A gloss in the margins of the Ellesmere manuscript repeats this anecdote in Latin and thereby accords it a form of textual authority: "Valerius libro 6° capitulo 3° Metellius vxorem suam eo quod vinum bibisset fuste percussam interemit."[40] As we saw in Chapter 2, Valerius contrasts the severity of Metellius' punishment of his wife to the decadence of imperial Rome, where, as Ovid's *Ars amatoria* suggests, women were accustomed to drink wine. In the context of the *Wife of Bath's Prologue*, this graphic description of a wife being clubbed to death acquires an iconic quality. Clive Skidmore points out that Valerius regards "his historical examples as equal to a pictorial representation in their vividness and verisimilitude."[41] The vivid detail that Metellius killed his wife "with a staf" indirectly cites the illustrations from the *Rose* in which the Jaloux beats his wife with a staff (Figs. 19–23). Chaucer deploys the Metellius exemplum in a move that demonstrates the Wife's rhetorical skill at extending and transforming the implications of an exemplum she has heard: she does not cite the exemplum of Metellius to comment on uxoricide but rather to address the issue of women and wine-drinking.[42] When the Wife of Bath declares that she would not have let a homicidal husband such as Metellius keep her from her intoxicated revels, her assertion is hollow; had her fourth husband beaten her for drinking, she would have had little legal or social protection. Despite her boast, she does not seriously challenge the violence in the Metellius exemplum; instead, she concludes with the comment that "A likerous mouth moste han a likerous tayl. / In wommen vinolent is no defence— / This knowen lecchours by experience" (466–68). The notion that a drunken woman has no defense comes from the Vieille; however, the precept that drinking induces erotic desire also occurs in the *Ars*; indeed, the *Art d'amours* emphasizes Ovid's point in a *glose*: "Par maintes actorités trouvees en escript que le bon vin es-muet la luxure" (797–98) ["According to many authorities found in writings, good wine moves one to lasciviousness"]. Chaucer's Wife of Bath thus cites the premise that underlies Metellius' exemplum rather than its rhetorical purpose. Although Valerius invokes an extreme case of uxoricide for a wife who drank wine, the Wife of Bath claims the sexual citizenship that wine-drinking might authorize for women as proposed in the *Ars*; she simultaneously scoffs at the threat of violence.

While the Wife of Bath authoritatively uses the Metellius exemplum to dismiss the threat of violence in the description of her fourth marriage, her description of her fifth husband, Jankyn, acknowledges the erotic value of violence when she is the object, not the agent of violence. Despite her bravado in narrating her ability to dominate and even humiliate her first four husbands, it is the erotic violence of Jankyn that she ultimately celebrates:

Now of my fifthe housbonde wol I telle.
God lete his soule nevere come in helle!
And yet was he to me the mooste shrewe;
That feele I on my ribbes al by rewe,
And evere shal unto myn endyng day.
But in oure bed he was so fressh and gay,
And therwithal so wel koude he me glose,
Whan that he wolde han my *bele chose*;
That thogh he hadde me bete on every bon,
He koude wynne agayn my love anon.
I trowe I loved hym best, for that he
Was of his love daungerous to me.

                                        (503–14)

In this passage, the Wife of Bath ventriloquizes the end of the Vieille's speech when she describes her desire for the one lover who beat her. As we saw in chapter 4, the Vieille describes such violence as erotic, since her violent lover knows how to follow blows with sexual caresses: in this description, female desire is defined in terms of being the object of desire. As the Wife describes it, Jankyn's skill as a lover—his ability to "gloss"—is enhanced by his violence towards her. Both characters, despite their claims that they manipulate and dominate their lovers, express desire only for the one man who is violent. In both the Vieille's sermon and the Wife's *Prologue*, this "confessional" moment occurs after a long cynical disquisition on managing lovers or husbands; in both texts, this moment of self-disclosure contradicts the premises of the preceding speech and consequently appears to offer a more authentic-appearing version of female subjectivity and by extension, experience.

In her wistful memory of Jankyn, the Wife of Bath states that she can still feel the pain of his blows on her ribs, and will until her dying day; she says that she loved him best because he and his love were "daungerous." All three editions of the *Riverside Chaucer* gloss this term in this line as "standoffish, hard to get," a meaning that does not fully address the violence in this passage, although elsewhere in the *Prologue* "dangerous" denotes "haughty" or "withholding."[43] The Wife explains her response to Jankyn's erotic violence in terms that categorically connect gendered identity and desire:

We wommen han, if that I shal nat lye,
In this matere a queynte fantasye:
Wayte what thyng we may nat lightly have,
Therafter wol we crie al day and crave.
Forbede us thyng, and that desiren we;

Preesse on us faste, and thanne wol we fle.
With daunger oute we al our chaffare;
Greet prees at market maketh deere ware,
And to greet cheep is holde at litel prys:
This knoweth every womman that is wys.

(515–24)

In the comparable passage in the *Roman de la Rose*, the Vieille introduces the description of erotic violence with the assertion that her violent lover did not love her: "li ribauz, qui point ne m'amoit. / Fame a trop povre jugement, / et je fui fame droitement" (14458–60) ["scoundrel that he was, he never loved me. Women have very poor judgement, and I was a true woman"]. A similar precept is found in the *Art d'amours* which glosses *Ars* 1.717 with a similar concept: "Il en est maintes qui congnoissent celi qui se retrait et qui heent celi qui trop les enchauce" (2068–69) ["There are many women who desire the man who retreats and many women who hate the man who pursues them too much"]. If the Wife's "queynte fantasye" refers to the fact that Jankyn, like the lover in the *Rose*, does not love her despite his erotic skill and attention ("I trowe I loved hym best, for that he / Was of his love daungerous to me"), then "daungerous" would suggest that Jankyn plays emotionally "hard to get." But the *Middle English Dictionary* notes that as early as 1400 *daungerous* also denotes "fraught with danger; hazardous, risky, dangerous." The Old French noun *daunger* is derived from the Latin term *dominiarium*; the meaning of *daunger* is overdetermined, as George Braun demonstrated: " 'Dangier' does not occur in Old French before the middle of the twelfth century and emerges from the very beginning in two fundamental meanings in the dynamic, active sense of power and in the more static, passive sense of refusal."[44] In Old French, Anglo-Norman, and Middle English, *daunger* and its adjective *daungerous* may denote a range of meanings from explicit violence and the risk of physical harm to the more abstract violence of refusal.[45] Given the close relationship between the Wife of Bath's *Prologue* and the *Roman de la Rose*, the register of the term *daungerous* certainly includes the connotation of physical danger. The personification of "dangier" in the *Rose* figures the entire range of meanings of the term. Dangier represents the lady's refusal of Amant's advances, but he is also a figure who nonetheless threatens Amant with physical harm. *Rose* illustration invariably depicts Dangier as a man wielding a club (Figs. 24, 36), an instrument that rather crudely visualizes the connotations of physical danger and the risk of physical harm in the term *dangier*.[46] When the Wife comments that Jankyn's love was "daungerous," the term refers to the erotic value of his

FIGURE 36. Dangier threatens Amant. *Roman de la Rose*, BUV, MS 387, fol. 22v. By permission of the Biblioteca Històrica, Universitat de València.

violence towards her as well as his aloofness. When she claims that such responses to violence are constitutive of female heterosexual desire, she performs a version of feminine embodiment defined by physical vulnerability.

In the *ordinatio* of the Ellesmere manuscript, the *Wife of Bath's Prologue* is the most heavily glossed section of the *Canterbury Tales*. The presence of Latin glosses frames the vernacular performance of the Wife as an authoritative text; the manuscript also contains marginal comments in English that mark off the sections of the *Prologue* by reference to the wife's treatment of her husbands: "Of the fifth housbonde of this wyf and how she bar hir agens hym" appears in the margin at line 504.[47] Such *ordinatio* highlights the disputational quality of the *Prologue*. The struggle between Jankyn and Alisoun locates the physical violence of the *Prologue* within the traditions of rhetorical violence associated with disputation. As practiced in the schools, disputation was marked by aggressive language and a tendency towards physical violence. In disputation, words were considered blows, and little meaningful distinction would be made between verbal and physical violence, as Helen Solterer has shown.[48] Thus the clerkly husband Jankyn—shaped by the disputational structures of his education—attempts to claim mastery by preaching to his wife, reading to her, and reciting proverbs to her, actions that she considers violent. The Wife of Bath describes herself as a "verray jangleresse" (638), and she counters his magisterial performance of textual authority with the assertion: "Ne I wolde nat of hym corrected be. / I hate hym that my vices telleth me" (661–62). The Wife's refusal to be corrected constitutes a challenge to her readers as well as her husband, as the tradition of glosses in fifteenth-century manuscripts of the *Canterbury Tales* suggests. In Egerton 2864, for instance, a cluster of eight Latin glosses appears in the margin next to her assertion in line 661 that she will not be corrected. This dense set of glosses cites eight biblical proverbs that reiterate the value of *disciplina*—or correction: "correction is the high road to life," "he who loves correction loves knowledge," and so forth.[49] As Susan Schibanoff puts it, the Egerton glossator "attempts to shout the Wife down in a series of marginal remarks taken from Scripture."[50] The glossator's attempt to intervene in the rhetoric of this passage mimics the battle over the book of "wikked wyves."

Jankyn's Book of Wikked Wyves

The Wife's refusal to be corrected suggests that she claims the status of subject in her contest with Jankyn, yet the rhetoric of the *Prologue* shows that she becomes a subject by being an object of violence. The battle over the "Book of Wikked Wyves" illustrates her location in these two subject positions; since Jankyn's book includes the *Ars amatoria*, this battle exemplifies the centrality of Ovidian discourses on erotic violence to the textual subjectivities constructed in the *Wife of Bath's Prologue*. Every night Jankyn reads aloud to his wife from his book; she finds Jankyn's reading to be an intolerable experience, given the abusive language and the portrayal of women in his "cursed book" (789) as she calls it. She considers his clerical interpretation of texts to be textual violence, to which she reacts with physical violence. Since this abusive reading practice complements his sexual skill in "glossing," his reading is the first blow in an altercation in which the Wife is rhetorically and physically overmatched; his reading is simultaneously violent and erotic. As part of the explanation the Wife of Bath offers for her attack on Jankyn and his book, she provides an extensive catalogue of its contents:

He hadde a book that gladly, nyght and day,
For his desport he wolde rede alway;
He cleped it Valerie and Theofraste,
At which book he lough alwey ful faste.
And eek ther was somtyme a clerk at Rome,
A cardinal, that highte Seint Jerome,
That made a book agayn Jovinian;
In which book eek ther was Tertulan,
Crisippus, Trotula, and Helowys,
That was abbesse nat fer fro Parys,
And eek the Parables of Salomon,
Ovides Art, and bookes many on,
And alle thise were bounden in o volume.
And every nyght and day was his custume,
Whan he hadde leyser and vacacioun
From oother worldly occupacioun,
To reden on this book of wikked wyves.

(669–85)

The specificity of this table of contents has led scholars to attempt to locate an actual codex that might qualify as Jankyn's book.[51] Alisoun's sense of injury derives not from the texts themselves, but from the pleasure Jankyn takes in these texts which he "gladly" reads, night and day. Chaucer presents this fictional character as an illiterate consumer of texts, a woman who readily absorbs texts that are read or presented to her in any number of contexts, from the pulpit where she hears the sermons on the marriage of Cana to the texts Jankyn reads to her. The titles in Jankyn's book refer to Latin texts, and this highly dramatic and specific scene of reading in the *Prologue* represents Jankyn's construction as a clerical reader ("He som tyme was a clerk of Oxenford" [527]) who renders Latin authority as vernacular exempla. His subject position and his marital performance are shaped by the texts he reads in this book.

The label "wikked wyves" is not an accurate description of the entire contents of Jankyn's book. The clerical Latin tradition is represented by selections from "Valerius," Theophrastus, Jerome, Tertullian, and the book of Proverbs. This imaginary codex, however, also includes three texts— Heloise, Trotula, and Ovid—that do not fit the tradition of misogamy or misogyny suggested by the rubric "wikked wyves" and exemplified by the clerical tracts. All three of these texts were available both in their Latin originals and in vernacular translation—though a clerical reader such as Jankyn might be expected to read them in Latin. The inclusion of "Trotula" and Heloise adds two female authorities on sexual desire to Jankyn's book. As the gloss in the *Art d'amours* suggests, "Trotula" is a name associated with a textual tradition regarding women:

> *Selonc ce que Troculeus, qui enseigna la nature des femmes dist, ja soit ce que les femmes se facent simples et honteuses, si veullent elles bien c'om les prie et qu'on les esgart. . . . Et ne vont elles aus jeux ne mais pour ce que aussi voulentiers veoient elles les hommes comme les hommes elles. Et ce puet on veoir appertement, car aussi volentiers y vont les laides comme les belles.* (388–93)

[According to Troculeus, who taught about the nature of women, although women pretend to be unpretentious and bashful, they actually want men to court them and to look at them. . . . Women go to the games because they want to see men as much as men want to see them. This is quite obvious, because the ugly go there as willingly as the beautiful.]

Monica Green has demonstrated that the name "Trotula" was associated with a number of texts: while "Trotula" originally designated a text on gynecology written by a woman physician from Salerno known as "Trot," medieval textual traditions appropriated the name to represent a variety of texts on women, some of them profoundly misogynist, such as the *Secreta secretorum*.[52] The text designated in Jankyn's book might be the one described in the *Art d'amours*: a text that characterizes women by their desire to be courted by men. The text identified as "Heloise" refers to the collection of the letters of Abelard and Heloise. Chaucer may have known these letters in Jean de Meun's translation, or in their original Latin, or only as they are characterized in the *Roman de la Rose*—where Heloise's story is an exemplum in the tirade of the Jaloux, as we saw in chapter 4. In the context of this collection of Latin texts in Jankyn's book, Heloise's letters offer a performance of Ovidian desire that emphasizes the pleasures of female subjection, and the presence of Heloise's letters furthers the thematic emphasis on the female as object of desire suggested by the inclusion of Trotula. The final text in the list, "Ovides Art," the *Ars amatoria*, adds the weight of pre-Christian Latin learning to the more standard texts of clerical misogyny. Although the *Ars* in its original classical form might not lend itself easily to inclusion in an anthology on "wikked wyves," its medieval reception and vernacular adaptation demonstrate how the *Ars* could be decontextualized and its irony deactivated. Read in the clerical context of Jankyn's codex, the *Ars amatoria* becomes a treatise on the seduction of women. While Jankyn appears to resemble the Jaloux, his violence against his wife does not become the brutish, satirical violence of the Jaloux from the *Rose*. Jankyn's reading of "Ovides Art" enables him to go beyond the misogynous tirades of the Jaloux and develop an erotics of violence. The *General Prologue* notes the Wife of Bath's knowledge of Ovid's *Remedia amoris* as a way of characterizing her use of detachment as a method of manipulation. By contrast, Jankyn's reading of the *Ars amatoria* arms him with the methodologies necessary for his erotic encounter with Alisoun.

In the process of reading and thereby producing vernacular versions of the Latin texts in the codex, Jankyn performs a specific set of interpretations. As the Wife of Bath tells it, Jankyn mines these texts for their exempla of wicked women who betray, murder, or otherwise destroy their men: Eve, Delilah, Deianeira, Xanthippe, Pasiphaë, Clytemnestra, and so forth. Such exempla are interspersed with biblical proverbs (from the "Parables of Salomon," (679) and verses (651–52) that set forth generalizations on the character or danger of women, or standards of female conduct. The Wife of Bath's description of Jankyn's reading anatomizes the interpretive violence he does to the texts in his book, as well as the relentless verbal tirade against women that his reading generates. It is not simply Jankyn's reading, but his reading for a specific exemplarity that Alisoun finds so painful; as she exclaims in response to these exempla: "Who wolde wene, or who wolde suppose, / The wo that in myn herte was, and pyne?" (786–87). Exempla, however, are seldom delimited by the rhetorical framework in which they appear. This series of biographies of women such as Clytemnestra or Pasiphaë offers remarkable portraits of female agency and even sexual autonomy; these brief accounts of wicked wives actually authorize the agency the Wife of Bath herself exhibits when she becomes violent towards Jankyn's book and Jankyn himself. Although the Wife does not interrogate these exempla, her rehearsal of the stories of wicked wives leads directly into her account of her own transgressive behavior towards Jankyn.

The battle over Jankyn's book moves from rhetorical to physical violence: when the Wife of Bath perceives that he will never stop reading from it, she tears three leaves out of it and gives him a blow with her fist to his cheek. He falls over into the fire but immediately jumps up and delivers a blow to her head that causes her to pass out: "That in the floor I lay as I were deed. / And whan he saugh how stille that I lay, / He was agast and wolde han fled his way, / Til atte laste out of my swogh I breyde" (796–99). Jankyn's fear that he might have killed his wife illustrates his awareness of the limitations on violence against women in marriage: had he killed her with this blow, he would have gone beyond the level of the violence allowed to a husband who wished to chastise or correct his wife. When the Wife of Bath revives, she accuses him of trying to murder her, and he apologizes. She re-

ports that she struck him repeatedly in a vengeful complaint about his violence, and eventually "We fille acorded by us selven two" (812). Given the
earlier description of Jankyn as a lover who knows how to move from physical violence to sexual caress, the term "accorded" suggests that he resorts to
his seductive or erotic skill at "glossing," thereby explicitly eroticizing this
battle. He has learned the same lessons that Amant has learned at the end of
the *Rose* regarding the erotics of violence. The *Prologue* concludes with a vision of marital concord: Jankyn apologizes for striking his wife ("As help me
God, I shal thee nevere smyte!" [805]), and after having Jankyn burn the
book of wicked wives and after renegotiating the terms of their marriage,
the Wife of Bath states:

> After that day we hadden never debaat.
> God helpe me so, I was to hym as kynde
> As any wyf from Denmark unto Ynde,
> And also trewe, and so was he to me.
>
> *(822–25)*

This concluding statement that she was the kindest wife in the world from
Denmark to India contrasts sharply with the image of international dominance that emerges from the portrait of the Wife of Bath in the *General Prologue*. Her subjection at the end of her *Prologue* is contextualized within the
same vast, global landscape that formed the backdrop for the earlier image of
the Wife of Bath as a well-traveled pilgrim whose economic stature added
to her erotic power. This vision of marital harmony stands in direct contrast
to the iterative force of her introductory statement about Jankyn, that of her
five husbands he was the "most shrewe" and that she can still feel his blows
on her ribs, and will until the end of her life. The combination of violence
and affection in the Wife's fifth marriage is consistent with the portrait of
marriage that emerges from canon law: while a husband had the right to
"correct" or physically punish his wife, he had a simultaneous duty to treat
her with "marital affection." As John Noonan has shown, "marital affection"
is best considered a "dynamic disposition" that predisposes spouses to a "loving state of mind."[53]

In a reiteration of the Ovidian script of the Vieille from the *Rose*, the
Wife of Bath performs a femininity in which the female subject gains
recognition by imagining herself to be the object of violence.[54] Teresa de-
Lauretis, in a revision of René Girard, articulates the difference between
subject-subject violence and subject-object violence.[55] Subject-subject violence presumes a contractual relation between its participants, who engage
with one another as equals who agree to disagree. The Wife of Bath is not an

equal match for Jankyn, whose clerical training gives him a distinct advantage in deploying texts and interpretations, and whose physical strength appears to give him an edge in trading blows for blows. She can knock him down; he can—and does—knock her out. At the end of her *Prologue*, the Wife may have the bridle in her hand, but the violence of the struggle has left her "somdel deaf" (446). Though she asserts that she will not be corrected, she expresses an unceasing desire for the physically violent eroticism of her fifth husband. While the Wife might appear momentarily on top—like Phyllis on top of Aristotle—her discourse nonetheless cites and thereby enacts the Ovidian tradition of erotic violence so precisely scripted in the *Roman de la Rose* and so pointedly identified as an ethical problem by Christine de Pizan, as we shall see in chapter 6. Perhaps more than any other text in the Chaucerian corpus, the *Wife of Bath's Prologue* earned Chaucer the praise lavished on him by Deschamps, who identifies Chaucer not only as a translator of the *Roman de la Rose* but also as an Ovidian poet: "Ovides grans en ta poëterie" ["A great Ovid in your poetry"].[56]

Coda: The Wife of Bath's Tale

Textual evidence suggests that Chaucer originally intended the Wife of Bath to tell what is now the *Shipman's Tale*. The *Shipman's Tale* is a narrative of marital negotiations within a mercantile ethos that privileges wifely appearances even as it laments the cost of keeping up these appearances, not to mention the risks of failing to do so:

> The sely housbonde, algate he moot paye,
> He moot us clothe, and he moot us arraye,
> Al for his owene worshipe richely,
> In which array we daunce jolily.
> And if that he noght may, par aventure,
> Or ellis list no swich dispence endure,
> But thynketh it is wasted and ylost,
> Thanne moot another payen for oure cost,
> Or lene us gold, and that is perilous.
>
> *(11–19)*

Not only is the linguistic register of the *Shipman's Tale* consistent with the *Wife of Bath's Prologue*, but the tale offers a view of bourgeois marriage in which the wife unabashedly trades in sexual favors: the wife in the *Shipman's Tale* practices the motto that the Wife of Bath preaches, that "al is for to selle." If the Wife of Bath were to tell this tale of a merchant and his sly, sexy wife, it would offer rhetorical support for the economic discourse in the *Wife of Bath's Prologue*, and it would reinforce the Wife's self-presentation as a shrewd player on the marriage market. But the textual evidence as it now stands assigns to the Wife of Bath an Arthurian romance in a courtly rather than mercantile register that turns on an act of sexual violence rather than the economic exchange of the *Shipman's Tale*. As such, the *Wife of Bath's Tale* glances back towards the erotic violence of the *Wife of Bath's Prologue*. In privileging the aspect of the *Prologue* that grounds female heteroerotics in violence, the *Wife of Bath's Tale* contributes to the construction of Alisoun's recognizable, "authentic" subjectivity.

The *Wife of Bath's Tale* suggests that violence remains part of the psychic residue of chivalric identity. Set in the Arthurian otherworld, the *Tale* nostalgically evokes a distant past when fairies, elves—and rapist-knights—roamed the land. Chaucer's version of this romance is the only one of the analogues to depict the knight's transgressions as rape:[57] "He saugh a mayde walkynge hym biforn, / Of which mayde anon, maugree hir heed, / By verray force, he rafte hire maydenhed" (886–88). Unlike other depictions of sexual assault in the *Canterbury Tales*, the representation of this scene specifies that the volition of the knight went against the will of the maiden. Yet despite the violence of this transgression, the queen offers the rapist-knight an opportunity to redeem himself by discovering what women desire most. In the course of narrating the knight's recuperation, the Wife has recourse to an exemplum from Ovid's *Metamorphoses* that she adjusts to illustrate the premise that women cannot keep secrets.[58] This exemplum concerns the mythical figure of Midas who has ass's ears; in Ovid's version, only Midas' barber knows this secret, but Chaucer changes the details in the exemplum so that it is Midas' wife who knows his secret. Since the erotic volubility of a wife's body means that she cannot physically keep a secret, she goes to a marsh and whispers it to the reeds. A similar discourse on wives and secrets circulates in the *Roman de la Rose*, where Genius expounds at length on the fact that women cannot keep secrets and that a man who trusts his wife with a secret puts himself in her power:

> *A son avis morte seroit*
> *s'il ne li saillet de la bouche,*
> *s'il i a perill ou reprouche.*
> *Et cil qui dit le li avra,*
> *s'il est tex, puis qu'el le savra,*
> *qu'il l'ose anprés ferir ne batre,*
> *une foiz, non pas .iii. ne .iiii.,*

ja plus tost ne la touchera
conme el le li reprouchera ;
mes ce sera tout en apert.
                (16336–45)

[She imagines she would die if it did not burst from her lips, even if danger and blame are involved. And now that she knows it, if the man who revealed it to her dares to strike or beat her just once, not three or four times, the moment he touches her, she will reproach him with it, and she will do it in public.]

Though he intends to illustrate the physical incapability of women to keep secrets, Genius inadvertently observes that a husband cannot beat a wife who knows his secret. In the *Wife of Bath's Tale*, the description of a wife who cannot keep a secret echoes Genius' assertions: "But nathelees, hir thoughte that she dyde / That she so longe sholde a conseil hyde" (965–66). Chaucer's text does not include the notion that a woman who knows her husband's secrets has thereby acquired an immunity from his violence. Indeed, Chaucer's narrator, the Wife of Bath, specifically grounds the premise that wives cannot keep secrets in the authority of Ovid, whom she cites even though she misrepresents the exemplum she ascribes to him: "we kan no conseil hyde. / The remenant of the tale if ye wol heere, / Redeth Ovyde, and ther ye may it leere" (980–82). But it is the *Roman de la Rose*, not Ovid, that elucidates the libidinal economy suggested by the exemplum: the exuberant verbal eroticism of a wife should not be met with violence.

✒ CHAPTER 6

The *Querelle de la Rose*
Erotic Violence and the Ethics of Reading

> By looking beyond the immediacy of our historical
> "now," it becomes conceivable to think of feminisms,
> including theoretical feminisms, as engaged in an on-
> going process of debate, contestation, and critical re-
> vision. Theoretical feminisms then appear as positions
> "with attitude," certainly not with a brazen, brash at-
> titude, but with a critical, even ethical (never a moral-
> izing) one, in line with the original meaning of that
> time-honored word *ethos*.
>
> —Beatrice Hanssen

As a conduit for Ovidian discourse on sexual-
ity, the *Roman de la Rose* offered readers an ambiguous perspective on erotic
violence, as we saw in chapter 4. The *Rose* proved to be the most widely read
and most influential poem of its era, and *Rose* manuscripts continue to be
produced for three centuries after Jean de Meun completed Guillaume de
Lorris' allegory. Both Geoffrey Chaucer and Christine de Pizan were
equally shaped by Ovidian discourse and poetically schooled by the *Rose*,
though at times their responses to Jean de Meun's portion of the allegory di-
verge greatly. Neither Chaucer nor Christine could have known the other's
work: Christine's literary career begins in the 1390s just as Chaucer's approaches its end. Given her intense dislike of the English and her reverence
for continental texts, especially of Italian origin, Christine would not have
read English texts.[1] Her critique of the Ovidian discourse of the *Roman de
la Rose* nonetheless elucidates the salient features of Chaucer's appropriation
of the *Rose* in the *Wife of Bath's Prologue*.

Chaucer's translation of the *Roman de la Rose* constituted a textual ap-
prenticeship for a poet composing in a fledgling literary language; the language of the *Rose* subsequently haunts his poetry just as the Vieille haunts
the Wife of Bath. Chaucer, however, acknowledges that the ethos of the *Rose*
might pose interpretive difficulties for some readers. In the *Prologue to the
Legend of Good Women*, he offers a playful critique of his own poetic practice

when he depicts the God of Love accusing him of heresy for the transparency of his translation of the *Rose*:

> Thow mayst it nat denye,
> For in pleyn text, it nedeth nat to glose,
> Thow hast translated the Romauns of the Rose,
> That is an heresye ageyns my lawe,
> And makest wise folk fro me withdrawe . . .
>
> *(G. 253–57)*[2]

In staging this challenge, Chaucer suggests that the "pleyn text" of the *Rose* could be read as a narrative that discourages lovers and disparages love. The God of Love proceeds to castigate Chaucer for depicting the "wikednesse" (269) of women, and he diagnoses Chaucer's failing as a form of feeble-mindedness that comes with age: "Wel wot I therby thow begynnyst dote, / As olde foles whan here spiryt fayleth; / Thanne blame they folk, and wite nat what hem ayleth" (G. 261–63). The God of Love's comment echoes the sharply worded observation of the Wife of Bath regarding clerks and misogyny:

> The clerk, whan he is oold, and may noght do
> Of Venus werkes worth his olde sho,
> Thanne sit he doun, and writ in his dotage
> That wommen kan nat kepe hir mariage!
>
> *(707–10)*

Both comments derive from the biography of Ovid in Jean le Fèvre's *Livre de Leesce*, where Jean ascribes Ovid's misogyny to the fact that he had supposedly been castrated at the time of his exile and consequently became bitter towards women.[3] In the course of the *Prologue*, Chaucer agrees to do penance by producing the *Legend of Good Women*, a collection of classical stories drawn largely from Ovid's *Heroides*.[4] The notion that composing texts based on the *Heroides* might compensate for translating the *Rose* suggests that the "heresye" of the *Rose* derives from its status as a medieval version of the *Ars amatoria*. Despite the playfulness of the judgments pronounced in this literary court, the *Prologue* identifies the ethical problems posed by the Ovidian discourse of the *Rose*. In her *Epistre au dieu d'amours*, Christine de Pizan stages a similar hearing on the interpretive issues inherent in treating the *Rose* as a poetic authority.

Epistolary Rhetoric

In her *Epistre au dieu d'amours* (1399), Christine de Pizan attempts to recuperate the God of Love from his mythical origins in Ovid's *Ars amatoria* and his allegorical role in the *Roman de la Rose*. Christine's God of Love, Cupido, dictates a letter to loyal lovers on behalf of women who feel aggrieved by the prevalence of misogynist discourse. Deriving authority from his epistolary performance (Fig. 37), Christine's God of Love distances himself from his namesake in the *Ars* and the *Rose* by satirically subjecting these two texts to a critique of their amatory politics. To this end, the God of Love declares that Ovid's *Ars amatoria* does not offer advice on the conduct of love but instead tutors its readers in the deception of women: "Et pour ce est li livres mal nommez, / Car c'est livre d'Art de grant decevance!" (376–77)[5] ["And this book is poorly named, because it is a book on the art of great deception"]. He characterizes Jean de Meun's portion of the *Roman de la Rose* in precisely the same terms, since the lengthy discourse of the *Rose* is ultimately aimed at the deception of a single maiden: "Quel long procès. / quel difficile chose!" (390) ["What a long process! What a difficult task!"]. In response to the misogynist arguments that form the basis of the grievance brought before him, the God of Love categorically dismisses this textual tradition because it is authored by men: "Je leur respons que les livres ne firent / Pas les femmes, ne les choses n'i mirent / Que l'en y list contre elles et leurs meurs" (409–11) ["I answer that women did not write the books, nor did they put into them the things one reads there against women and their behavior"]. Despite its whimsical tone, the *Epistre au dieu d'amours* exemplifies Christine's authorial approach to textual traditions,[6] and its satiric register did not keep Christine from citing it later during the *Querelle de la Rose* and from repeating some of its assertions almost verbatim. As one of the earliest of her long works, the *Epistre* allowed Christine to articulate a vehement correction to the textual tradition of misogyny.[7]

A model for producing a purposeful argument against misogyny was available to Christine in the *Livre de Leesce* (1380–87), the poem Jean le Fèvre composed in refutation of Matheolus' *Lamentations*, which Le Fèvre himself had translated. As we saw in chapter 5, Chaucer had likewise employed Jean Le Fèvre's text in his construction of the Wife of Bath. Christine later names Matheolus as an arch-misogynist in the *Livre de la cité des dames* (1405); as in the *Cité des dames*, poetic agency in the *Epistre* emerges from the rhetorical critique of other texts, and the *Epistre* singles out both Ovid's *Ars amatoria* and the *Roman de la Rose* for analysis. In the process, the *Epistre* articulates an approach to the *Rose* that would gain significant currency a few

FIGURE 37.   Cupid dictates his letter. *Epistre au Dieu d'amours*, BnF, fr. 835, fol. 45r. By permission of the Bibliothèque nationale de France.

years later in the *Querelle de la Rose*, an epistolary debate in prose that addresses the ethical implications of reading Jean de Meun's portion of the *Roman de la Rose*. In the three letters Christine contributed to the *Querelle* in 1401–2, she develops a critique of the narrative and allegory of the *Rose*; as part of this critique, she identifies the issue of erotic violence as a critical category that could be recognized and analyzed as such. Christine's three letters, even taken together, do not provide a coherent reading of the *Rose*; rather, they are epistolary interventions whose critical discourse is structured within the medieval tradition of the *ars dictaminis*. The *Querelle* offers a case study in the medieval practices of an ethics of reading, and Christine's contributions to the *Querelle* articulate some of the interpretive problems the Ovidian discourse in the *Roman de la Rose* posed for the medieval reader. And it is precisely this set of interpretive problems that Chaucer had already negotiated in the composition of the *Wife of Bath's Prologue*.

Christine's interlocutors in the *Querelle* were all members of the royal chancellery, and as such, their profession involved the composition of letters.[8] Christine, herself the widow of a royal secretary, challenges the most authoritative practitioners of epistolography of her day. As a collection of letters, the *Querelle de la Rose* enacts all the interpretive difficulties that epistolary rhetoric might pose: although these letters appear to have arrived at their destinations, they are animated throughout by rhetorical refusals; they are read by interloping readers and redirected to readers other than their addressees. Christine enters the *Querelle* in the summer of 1401 when she composes a letter to Jean de Montreuil, provost of Lille, in which she criticizes a treatise he had authored in praise of the *Rose* against its critics.[9] Christine comments that this treatise, though forwarded to her by Montreuil, was neither addressed to her nor did it require a response: ("combien que a moy ne soit adreçant ne response ne requiert" [12]).[10] Nonetheless, she sends Montreuil a letter in which she develops a sustained critique of his position on the *Rose*. In this letter, she takes issue, not with the *Rose* as such, but with Montreuil's praise of the *Rose* as a model for good social conduct; he had described it as a "mirouer de bien vivre, exemple de tous estas de soy politiquement gouverner et vivre religieusement et saigement" (21) ["A mirror of living well, an example for all classes of politic self-governing and of living religiously and wisely"]. Although Montreuil never responds directly to Christine's letter, he directs several other letters to various other people regarding the *Rose*. A few months later, however, Gontier Col—a notary and royal secretary—responds negatively to Christine's critique of Montreuil in two separate letters addressed directly to Christine. In his first letter, Gontier Col requests a copy of her "invective" on the *Rose*, and he expresses his dismay that she dared to challenge the authority of Jean de Meun. Indeed, Gontier Col demands that Christine retract her argument, even before he has read her letter. A few days later, having read her letter, he puts his case even more forcefully, employing language appropriate to a *disputatio* when he asserts his disagreement with her critique: t'ay . . . exortee, avisee et priee de toy corrigier et admender de l'erreur manifeste, folie ou demence a toy venue par presompcion ou oultrecuidance et comme femme passionnee en ceste matiere" (23) ["I have . . . exhorted, advised and prayed you to correct and amend your obvious error, the madness or lunacy that has come over you, from self-conceit or overweening pride, and like a woman impassioned in this matter"]. In response, Christine wrote her second letter to Gontier Col.

As a professional author, Christine was in a position to "publish" the epistles in the *Querelle* and exert authorial control over their circulation. Early in 1402, she collected the two letters each that she and Gontier Col had written in a dossier she called the "epistres du debat sus *le Romant de la Rose*." She composed two cover letters for this dossier, one addressed to Queen Isabeau and one to the Provost of Paris, Guillaume de Tignonville. The *Querelle*, however, was not to be neatly closed with the completion of this initial dossier. In May 1402, Jean Gerson—chancellor of the University of Paris—authored a treatise against the *Rose*, and several months later Pierre Col, brother of Gontier and also a royal secretary, wrote to Christine to assert yet again that her reading of the *Rose* was erroneous. In response, Christine composed a long and detailed reply in which she painstakingly reiterated and developed the views she had already expressed in her earlier two letters. As this schematic outline of the *Querelle* shows, Christine addressed one letter to Montreuil, one to Gontier Col, and one to Pierre Col and each letter expands on her previous letter. The original dossier on the *Querelle* was included in the first edition of her collected works in June 1402. She later expanded the dossier to incorporate her letter to Pierre Col, and this expanded dossier appears in both deluxe manuscripts of her collected works, one presented to the duke of Berry, the other to Queen Isabeau.[11] With the "publication" of these letters, the *Querelle* took its place among Christine's literary works, and it consequently became a literary text in its own right. In the course of the *Querelle*, Jean Gerson aligned himself with Christine; besides his treatise on the *Rose*, he preached a series of sermons against Jean de Meun and his supporters.[12]

Like the letters of Abelard and Heloise, and like most medieval letter collections, the epistles in the *Querelle* are simultaneously personal and public, so that the texture of each letter works against its arrival at a single destination.[13] While the letters exchanged between Abelard and Heloise rhetorically shape and circulate desire, the letters in the *Querelle* stage a *disputatio* regarding the status and interpretive impact of the categories of desire in Jean de Meun's portion of the *Roman de la Rose*. Medieval rhetorical treatises recognize the potential of letters to articulate opposing sides of an argument; indeed, Brunetto Latini's thirteenth-century *Livres dou tresor* follows Cicero in identifying controversy as a constitutive component of epistolary rhetoric. According to Latini, the letter writer, by definition, takes an argumentative stance: "Et celes letres apertienent a recthorique, autresi comme la chançons dont il uns amans parole a l'autre autresi com s'il fust devant lui a la contençon" ["And these letters belong to rhetoric just like the chansons in which one lover speaks to the other, just as if there was a quarrel between them"].[14] The structure and texture of the *Querelle* are entirely consistent with Latini's synthetic description of the disputational potential of epistolary rhetoric: the uncompromising positions adopted by all the interlocutors in the *Querelle* reflect this rhetorical formula for the argumentative shape of letters. In addition, Latini's comparison of letters to *chansons d'amor* suggests that the circulation of desire in letters such as those exchanged between Abelard and Heloise is rhetorically analogous to the oppositional discourse generated in more public letters, such as those in the *Querelle de la Rose*.

The rhetorical contours of the letters between Abelard and Heloise were known in early fifteenth-century Paris; Jean de Meun's translation of these letters survives in a manuscript in Gontier Col's hand, which points to these letters' currency in the royal chancery. Christine knew the letters of Abelard and Heloise well enough to refer specifically to Heloise's use of the Latin term *meretrix*; she tells Pierre Col: "Tu ressembles Helouye du Paraclit qui dist que mieux ameroit estre *meretrix* appellee de maistre Pierre Abalart que estre royne couronnee; si appert bien que les voulantés qui mieux plaisent ne sont pas toutes raisonnables" (146) ["You resemble Heloise of the Paraclete who said that she would prefer to be called the *meretrix* of Master Pierre Abelard than to be crowned queen; it appears that the wishes that are most pleasing are not the most reasonable"]. While Christine elsewhere refers to Jean de Meun's translations, which included this collection of letters,[15] her reference to the Latin term *meretrix*, rather than to Jean de Meun's translation of *meretrix* as *putain*, points to her knowledge of the letters in Latin. In suggesting a rhetorical equivalence between Heloise and Pierre Col, Christine identifies Pierre Col's position with the feminine abjection claimed by Heloise, a position she designates as unreasonable. In this paradigm, she emerges as the master of the argument.

The *Querelle* demonstrates the reach of the Latin rhetorical tradition into vernacular practice since vernacular letters generally followed the rhetorical conventions of letter composition as codified in the *ars dictaminis*.[16] As we saw in chapter 3, epistolary discourse—whether Latin or vernacular—enacted social hierarchy in its *salutatio*: according to the *ars dictaminis*, the *salutatio* acknowledges the social significance of the office—or lack of office—held by both sender and addressee.[17] For a woman such as Christine—excluded by her gender from occupying any bureaucratic office—epistolary rhetoric required her to acknowledge both her own lack of position as well as the authority of her male interlocutors whose status as royal secretaries authorized their social and intellectual agency as the authors of the letters in the *Querelle*.

This social—and thus rhetorical—inequity accounts for the tone of self-deprecation in Christine's initial letter addressed to Montreuil: "de par moy Cristine de Pizan, femme ignorant d'entendement et de sentement legier—pour lesquelles choses vostre sagesce aucunement n'ait en despris la petitesse de mes raisons, ains vueille supploier par la consideracion de ma femmenine foiblece" (12) ["from me, Christine de Pizan, a woman untutored in judgment, and of frivolous sense, on account of which factors may your wisdom not in the least despise the smallness of my arguments, but rather take into consideration my feminine weakness"]. Such *salutatio* is rhetorically prescribed and entirely appropriate to Christine's position; nonetheless, such expression of *humilitas* could be disabling for a woman composing a letter to intervene in a *disputatio* with a royal secretary.

When she collected the epistles that had circulated in the first stage of the *Querelle* and dedicated them to Queen Isabeau, Christine published all of them, including Gontier Col's, under her signature. In addressing the queen, Christine articulates an empowering "destination" for her critique of the *Rose*, an addressee who did not require that she perform a debilitating *salutatio* to a clerk: this dedicatory letter to Isabeau revises the social structure of the *Querelle* since Christine addresses another woman, the only woman in the realm who outranked her interlocutors. In her letter to the queen, moreover, Christine characterizes her subject position as a woman writing in defense of women. This rhetorical framework allowed her to refuse the anger of Gontier Col and deflect the "destination" of his critical letters. Having authorized her agency as a letter writer in addressing the Queen, Christine expresses no self-abasing discourse in her subsequent letter to Gontier Col, which she composed several months after the cover letter to Isabeau. Instead, in keeping with the disputational potential of epistolary rhetoric, her letter to Col challenges him by identifying the rhetorical violence of his two letters to her: "O clerc subtil d'entendement philosophique, stilé es sciences, prompt en polie rethorique et subtile poetique, ne vueilles par erreur voluntaire repprendre et reprimer ma veritable oppinion justement meue pour tant se elle n'est a ta plaisance" (24) ["O clerk discerning in philosophical judgment, well versed in learning, quick with polished rhetoric and subtle poetics; do not try by a capricious distortion to criticize and put down my legitimate opinion, justly conceived, simply because it does not please you"]. She describes his letter as abusive (injurieuses [25]), although she declares that she does not feel any sting from his criticism: "saiches de vray que ce ne tiens je a villenie ou aucun repprouche" (25) ["You should know truly that I have not taken it as an insult nor any sort of reproach"]. She stands her ground with the statement: "Si ne cuides aucune-

ment moy estre meue ne desmeue par legiereté, par quoy soye tost des-
ditte—ja soit ce que en moy disant vilenie me menaces de tes subtilles
raisons" (26) ["Don't think me to be in any way moved or deterred through
fickleness, so that I could be soon overruled, although while saying offensive
things to me, you threaten me with your clever discourse"]. In his demand
that Christine correct (*corrigier*) her position, Col simultaneously deploys the
pedagogical language of *disputatio* and invokes the power relations implicit
in epistolary rhetoric as codified in the *ars dictaminis*.[18] But since Christine
writes to Gontier Col and the queen simultaneously as part of her dossier
on the *Rose*, she articulates a destination for her letter that allows her to reject the subject position he identifies for her.

Christine also sent the dossier to Guillaume de Tignonville, the Provost
of Paris, with a cover letter asking him to judge the debate and rule in her
favor: "proprement eslire le bon droit de mon oppinion" (7) ["to appropriately recognize the justice of my opinion"]. Guillaume de Tignonville was
one of the twenty-four ministers in the *cour amoureuse* from its inception in
1400; his role in this literary and poetic court dedicated to defending the
honor of women made him—like the God of Love in the *Epistre au dieu
d'amours*—an appropriate adjudicator of the *Querelle*.[19] Yet although the letter to the queen characterizes Christine's intention in the debate as the defense of women[20]—the ostensible purpose of the *cour amoureuse*—the letter
to the provost appeals instead to his wisdom and sense of justice. Guillaume
de Tignonville had translated a text of ethical proverbs, the *Dicta philosopho-
rum*. In appealing to Guillaume in this way, Christine explicitly frames the
issue in the *Querelle* as a question of the ethical implications of Jean de
Meun's *Roman de la Rose*.

The Ethics of Reading the *Rose*

The epistles in the *Querelle* participate in a tradition of textual responses to
the *Rose* that dates to the beginning of the fourteenth century; nonetheless,
the rhetorical skirmishes in the *Querelle* tend to obscure the interpretive
performances of these letters as readerly engagements with Jean de Meun's
text.[21] Although Christine, Montreuil, and the Col brothers disagree about
the value of the *Rose*, they all share the same assumptions regarding the purposes of literary texts. A. J. Minnis has demonstrated that both sides of the
Querelle assume that the *Rose* should be read for its *utilitas*: "its usefulness in
behavioral and pedagogic terms," an assumption that emerges from their
shared premise that "poetry showed its audience both what to do and what
to avoid."[22] In her letter to Gontier Col, Christine summarizes her anxiety

about the ethical implications of the *Rose* when she designates it a "perverse exortacion en tres abhominables meurs confortant vie dissolue" (26) ["a wicked exhortation to abominable conduct, endorsing the dissolute life"]. In addition, as we have seen, texts were thought to acquire their ethical urgency through their memorability.[23] The visuality of the *Rose* made it particularly memorable; the more memorable a text, the more it would need to be evaluated for its potential impact on the behavior of readers. The illustrations of the "Jaloux qui bat sa fame," given their stark iconic quality, exemplify how the visual programs in the *Rose* manuscripts must be carefully negotiated, as we have seen: the image of a husband beating his wife works to thematize the category of erotic violence as a component of the allegorical narrative.[24] In her letter to Montreuil, Christine comments on the memorability of the *Rose*: "Neantmoins demoura en ma memoire aucunes choses traictees en lui que mon jugement condempna moult" (13) ["Nevertheless there remained in my memory some things treated there that my judgment condemned greatly"]. Christine later specifies the issue of violence in marriage as a critical issue for readers of the *Rose*.

Although Christine's letters in the *Querelle* suggest that her critical assumptions regarding texts and their readers were conventional, her reading of the *Rose* as it emerges from her letters is directly opposed to that expounded by Montreuil and the Col brothers. Christine's critical difference from her interlocutors results from cultural differences in their textual repertoires as readers and in their pedagogical preparation for literary activity. Most specifically, Christine's different approach to Jean de Meun is to some degree a consequence of the difference in her access to and experience of Ovid's texts, particularly the *Ars amatoria*. At various moments in the *Querelle*, the status of Ovid as an important precursor to Jean de Meun becomes a contested issue, since several participants in the *Querelle* evoke the intertextual quality of the *Rose* as an Ovidian text.[25] Gerson, for instance, singles out Ovid when he expresses outrage at Jean de Meun's selection of pre-texts:

> *Et que tele oeuvre soit pieur que celle d'Ovide, certes je le maintieng; car* L'Art d'amour, *laquelle escript Ovide, n'est pas seulement toute enclose ou dit livre, mais sont translatés, assemblés et tirés come a violance et sans propos autres livres plusseurs . . . qui ne sont point moins deshonnestes et perilleux (ainssy que sont les dis de Heloys et de Pierre Abelart et de Juvenal et des fables faintes . . .) Ovide par exprés protesta qu'il ne vouloit parler des bonnes matronnes et dames mariees, ne de celles qui ne seroient loisyblement a amer. (76–77)*

[And this work is worse than that of Ovid, I certainly maintain. Because the *Art of Love*, which Ovid wrote, is not only completely enclosed in this book, but there are many other books translated, compiled, and forcefully and improperly drawn in . . . which are not any less dishonorable or dangerous (thus there are the writings of Heloise and of Pierre Abelard, and of Juvenal and many fables . . .) Ovid certainly declared that he did not wish to speak of good matrons and married ladies, nor of those whom it would not be lawful to love.]

Gerson's disapproval of Ovid is noticeably extended to include the letters of Abelard and Heloise; as we saw in chapter 3, this collection develops the implications of the Ovidian discourse of desire as scripted in the *Ars amatoria*.

With the exception of his mention of Juvenal, Gerson's catalogue of offending texts is completely within an Ovidian tradition. For Gerson, a major issue in a consideration of the *Ars* concerns the identity of its implied audience. In opposition to Gerson, Pierre Col later disputes Gerson's claims regarding the audience of Ovid's text: "quant il escript *L'Art d'amours*, il escript en latin, lequel n'entendent fammes: et ne le bailla qu'aux assaillans pour aprandre a asaillir le chastel" (105) ["When he wrote the *Art of Love*, he wrote it in Latin, which women do not understand; and he gave it only to the assailants to learn how to attack the castle"]. Pierre Col's defense of Ovid—like Gerson's attack—presumes that a reader's understanding of Ovid's *Ars amatoria* will determine that reader's approach to the *Roman de la Rose*. Both Gerson and Pierre Col allude to the *Ars* as the cause of Ovid's exile, and both claim that Ovid wrote the *Remedia amoris* in hopes of being recalled from exile. Comments such as these reflect the influence of the *accessus ad auctores* which shaped the clerical understanding of Ovid's *Ars*. In her *Epistre au dieu d'amours*, Christine refers to the clerical uses of Ovid's *remedia amoris*:

> Si ont les clers apris trés leur enfance
> Cellui livret en premiere science
> De gramaire, et aux autres l'aprenent
> A celle fin qu'a femme amer n'emprenent.
> *(291–94)*

[Clerks are taught this book from their earliest youth, in their beginning grammar classes, and they teach it to others, so that none will undertake to love a woman.]

Christine's gender denied her the formal education available to a clerk; as an autodidact, she consequently developed a less institutional and more idiosyncratic appreciation of the *Ars amatoria* than her interlocutors. In response to Pierre Col's characterization of the *Ars*, she repeats in her own voice the God of Love's sarcastic dismissal of the *Ars* from the *Epistre au dieu d'amours*: "Ha! livre mal nommé *L'Art d'amours*! Car d'amours n'est il mie! mais art de faulse malicieuse industrie de decepvoir fanmes puet il bien estre appellés" (138–39) ["Ha! *The Art of Love*: a book badly named! Because there is hardly anything of love in it. It could be better called the art of the false, malicious skill of deceiving women"].

Removed from the satire of the *Epistre*, this response to Ovid's text becomes a considered literary judgment. Christine's lack of formal education makes it likely that she read the *Ars amatoria* in the thirteenth-century French prose translation, the *Art d'amours*, rather than in the original Latin, though Christine was certainly proficient in Latin, as her citation of the Latin text of the letters of Heloise demonstrates.[26] As we have seen, the *Art d'amours* renders the poetic and rhetorical brilliance of Ovid's Latin couplets in an unambiguous French prose, accompanied by extensive glosses. The glosses explain in detail the mechanics of the various approaches to seduction that the *praeceptor* playfully suggests in Ovid's Latin text. The *Art d'amours* thus transforms Ovid's text into a rather crude manual for sexual manipulation and seduction; in the process, it thematizes deception as the most effective means for acquiring and retaining a lover, which accounts for Christine's view that the art taught in the *Ars amatoria* is the art of deception. Having read the *Ars amatoria* in French prose translation would situate Christine to read Ovid, and by extension, Jean de Meun, in an entirely different register from her clerical interlocutors.

Christine's understanding of Ovid conditions her to develop a similarly critical approach to the *Roman de la Rose;* indeed, she links the two texts together in her *Enseignemens* when she warns her son to avoid reading both Ovid and the *Rose*.[27] Christine's critique of the *Rose* emphasizes that Jean de Meun defames the female sex by portraying women as deceitful and wanton. In this respect, Christine considers the *Rose* to be an instance of injurious language, as Helen Solterer has shown.[28] But beyond the verbal violence of the text, Christine also evaluates the *Rose* specifically for its potential impact on the lives of married women. In her letter to Montreuil, she criticizes Jean de Meun for suggesting that wives deceive their husbands, and she asks: "a quelle bonne fin pot ce estre, ne quel bien ensuivre? N'y sçay entendre fors empeschement de bien et de paix, et rendre les maris qui tant oyent de babuises et fatras, se foy y adjoustent, souspeçonneux et pou amant leurs femmes" (18) ["What good purpose could it have, and what good could come of it? All I expect from it is the obstruction of happiness and peace, and it makes husbands who hear such babbling and rubbish, if they give it any credence, suspicious and less loving to their wives"]. Not only might the *Rose* lead to marital discord by encouraging husbands to mistreat their wives, but many women already endure difficult marriages: "est et sera moult de plus vaillans femmes, plus honnestes . . . et pluseurs qui ont esté cause du reconciliement de leurs maris, et porté leurs affaires et leurs secréz et leurs passions doulcement et secretement, non obstant leur feussent leurs maris rudes et mal amoureux (19) ["And [there are] many [women] who have been instrumental in obtaining absolution for their husbands and who put up with their affairs and their secrets and their passions quietly and discreetly, even if their husbands were brutal and unloving to them"]. Such comments illustrate the ethical premises of reading that Christine articulates and develops in her three letters in the *Querelle*: Christine evaluates the *Rose* as though it were a set of exempla that could authorize or justify particular conduct on the part of married male readers. Jean de Montreuil and Gontier Col were both familiar with cases of marital discord; Montreuil at one point penned a diatribe he attributes to Gontier Col's unhappy wife, who complains about her husband's dissolute ways and his disregard for her. According to Montreuil, she describes the lot of married women: "Nous ne sommes pas des épouses et des compagnes, mais des captives faites sur l'ennemi ou des esclaves achetées"[29] ["We are not spouses and companions, but captives taken by the enemy or purchased slaves"]. The existence of this complaint composed by Montreuil in the voice of Gontier Col's wife suggests that the humanist circles of early fifteenth-century Paris were well attuned to issues of marital ethics. In her reading of the *Rose*, Christine attempts to specifically address the issue of marital unhappiness from the perspective of wives.

Throughout the *Querelle*, Christine appeals to the notion of the "common good" ("bien commun" [133]), a category for the evaluation of social utility derived from Aristotle's *Ethics*. This text had tremendous presence in the literary cultures of early fifteenth-century Paris, since Charles V had commissioned a French translation from Nicole Oresme. This version first appeared in 1370 and survives in two luxury manuscripts from the late fourteenth century that were part of Charles V's library.[30] Oresme's *Livre de éthiques* is a vernacular rendition of Robert Grosseteste's thirteenth-century Latin version of Aristotle's text, and Oresme includes extensive glosses to Aristotle's philosophical text. As a treatise on the cultivation and development of virtue through *habitus* or reiteration, the *Livre de éthiques* emphasizes moderation, temperance, and self-control. While Aristotle's text develops a discourse on political justice suitable to the social organization of the ancient world, Oresme's text and glosses develop a political theory responsive to a medieval Christian ethos. Thus the *Ethiques* recuperates the marital relationship of husband and wife to integrate the conjugal couple into the political discourses of virtue, community, justice and friendship; a synthetic statement from book 8 illustrates this point: "L'amistié qui est entre le mari et sa femme semble estre amistié selon nature. Car les gens sont plus ordenéz par nature a communiquer ensemble en mariage que en policie ou communité civile" (443)[31] ["The friendship which is between a husband and his wife seems to be friendship according to nature, because people are more inclined by nature to unite together in marriage than in a polity or a civil community"]. Nonetheless, while disagreement and dissent might belong to friendship, a marriage marked by accusation and complaints would degenerate into jealousy and foolishness.[32] The *Livre de éthiques* promotes a notion of a just and reasonable marriage in the aid of virtue and the good; in her letters in the *Querelle*, Christine appeals to an ethos of marriage derived from Oresme's *Ethiques*.

Christine's critique of the *Rose* treats it as a set of exempla measured against a marital ideal derived from Oresme's version of the *Ethics*. Christine states that she is critical only of certain parts of the *Rose* ("trop traicte deshonnestment en aucunes pars" [13]), and she specifically identifies the speeches of Reason, Genius, the Vieille, and the Jaloux as problematic portions of the text. Christine, however, returns several times to the figures of the Vieille and the Jaloux—the two most Ovidian figures in the *Rose*—both of whom she assesses for their exemplarity, their effect on the conduct and ethics of specific readers:

> quel horribleté! quel deshonnesteté! Et divers reprouvéz enseignemens recorde ou chapitre de la Vieille! Mais pour Dieu! qui y pourra noter fors ennortemens sophistez tous plains de laidure et toute vilaine memoire? . . . Et a quel utilité ne a quoy prouffite aux oyans tant oïr de laidures? Puis ou chapitre de Jalousie, pour Dieu! quelx grans biens y peuent estre notéz, n'a quel besoing recorder les deshonnestetés et laides paroles qui asséz sont communes en la bouche des maleureux passionnéz d'icelle maladie? Quel bon exemple ne introducion puet estre ce? (15)

[What atrocity! What dishonor! And the malicious, despicable teachings recorded in the Chapter of the Vieille! By God! What can one observe there except sophistical advice too full of abuse and utterly repulsive recollection? . . . And for what *utilitas* or for what profit do listeners hear such abuse? Then in the chapter on Jealousy, by God! What great good can be discovered there, what need is there to record the dishonorable and abusive words that are very common in the mouths of those unhappy ones afflicted with this malady? What good model or example could this be?]

In pairing the Vieille and the Jaloux in this passage, Christine questions the *utilitas* of the desire they perform in relation to one another in the allegorical reiterations of the *Rose*. Unlike Genius and Reason who personify abstract values, the Vieille and the Jaloux represent contemporary stereotypes of the Old Woman and the Jealous Husband, stereotypes drawn on the ambient culture as much as on textual tradition; indeed, Pierre Col asserts that each of these characters speaks according to his or her nature: "dy que maistre Jehan de Meung en son livre introduisy personnaiges, et fait chascun personnaige parler selonc qui luy appartient: c'est assavoir le Jaloux comme jaloux, la Vielle come la Vielle" (100) ["I say that Master Jean de Meun in his book introduced characters and makes each character speak appropriately: so that the Jaloux is understood as a jealous husband and the Vieille as an old woman"]. Such stereotypical values could make the Vieille and the Jaloux appear especially persuasive to some readers. In her critique of the Jaloux, Christine acknowledges that his is not the normative voice in the text. As she says in her letter to Montreuil:

> *Et la laidure qui la est recordee des femmes, dient pluseurs en lui excusant que c'est le Jaloux qui parle, et voirement fait ainsi comme Dieu parla par la bouche Jeremie. Mais sans faille, quelxque addicions mençongeuses qu'il ait adjoustees, ne peuent—Dieu mercy!—en riens amenrir ne rendre empirees les conditions des femmes. (15)*

[And as for the vile nature that is there accorded to women, many say in excusing him [Jean de Meun] that it is the Jaloux who speaks, and indeed that [Jean de Meun] does exactly what God does in speaking through the mouth of Jeremiah. But without fail whatever deceitful additions he has added, thank God, they cannot make worse the condition of women.]

Nonetheless, Christine's awareness of the rhetorical irony of the Jaloux's tirade does not appear to mitigate her anxiety about the content of his speech.

Christine's approach to the Jaloux as an exemplum is evident throughout the *Querelle*, but it takes vivid shape in her final letter, addressed to Pierre Col. This letter, however, is especially haunted by the possibility that it might not arrive: its tone of exasperation and its repetition of earlier statements all suggest that Christine was aware that her earlier letters had not truly reached their destinations. In this letter Christine takes pains to develop more thoroughly the issues that she had treated in the earlier two letters, so that the letter to Pierre Col can almost be read as a gloss to her earlier two letters. She clarifies how a reader might read the *Rose*, and the conduct that such reading might authorize. Christine specifically challenges Pierre Col's assumptions regarding marital behavior. In his letter, Pierre Col judges the Jaloux's behavior as an extreme, but predictable response to his wife's behavior: "c'est a mon avis que regulierement ung chascun homme marié, avant qu'il soit jaloux, cuide avoir la milleur fame, ou au moins auxi bone comme il en soit point. Et vient ceste cuidance, come je tieng, partie pour l'amour qu'il a a elle . . . supposé qu'en son absence elle se tiengne a baudement" (100–101) ["It is my opinion that each married man usually, before he becomes jealous, thinks that he has the best wife, or at least as good as any that might be. And this belief comes, as I think, out of the love that he has for her . . . Suppose that in his absence that she behaves bawdily"]. In these comments, Pierre Col accepts without question the Jaloux's complaint that his wife has been unfaithful, and this acceptance implicitly provides a legitimate basis for his verbal abuse, despite the fact that in the *Rose* the Jaloux's accusations are without foundation. In this way, Pierre Col apologizes for the violent jealousy of the husband as an understandable, even excusable, response to a wife who behaves "baudement."

Pierre Col assumes that Jean de Meun, having been a foolish lover himself, wrote the *Rose* to teach his readers how to overcome foolish love; he offers an anecdote to support this assumption: "En verité je cognois home fol amoureux, lequel pour soy oster de fole amour a emprunté de moy *Le Ronmant de la Rose*, et luy ay oÿ jurer par sa foy que c'est la chose qui plus li a aidié a s'en oster" (106) ["In truth I know a man, a foolish lover, who in order to recover from foolish love borrowed the *Roman de la Rose* from me, and I have heard him swear by his faith that this is the thing that most helped him recover from it"]. Christine shares Pierre Col's assumption that the *Rose* will have an impact on the behavior and attitudes of its readers. To counter Pierre Col's anecdote, she describes the conduct of a more violent reader:

> *Et je te diray ung aultre exemple sans mentir, puis que nous sommes es miracles du* Romant de la Rose: *je oÿ dire, n'a pas moult, a ·i· de ces compaingnons de l'office dont tu es et que tu bien congnois, et homme d'auctorité, que il congnoit ung home marié, lequel ajouste foy au* Ronmant de la Rose *comme a l'Euvangile; celluy est souverainnement jaloux, et quant sa passion le tient plus aigrement il va querre son livre et list devant sa fame, et puis fiert et*

frappe sus et dist: "Orde, telle come quelle il dist, voir que tu me fais tel tour.
Ce bon sage homme maistre Jehan de Meung savoit bien que femmes savoient
fere!" Et a chascun mot qu'il treuve a son propos il fiert ung coup ou deux du
pié ou de la paume; si m'est advis que quiconques s'en loe, telle povre famme
le compere chier. (139–40)

[And I will tell you another true example, since we are on [the subject of] the miracles of the *Roman de la Rose.* I heard not long ago from one of the members of the profession to which you belong, with whom you are well acquainted, a man of authority, that he knew a married man who put as much faith in the *Roman de la Rose* as in the gospel. This man is often jealous, and when his passion takes hold of him most intensely, he goes to find his book and reads it in front of his wife, and then he strikes and hits her and says, "Filthy thing [you are] just like what he says; it is true that you play such tricks on me. This good wise man, Master Jean de Meun, knew full well what women could do." And at each word that he finds to his purpose, he strikes her once or twice with his foot or with his hand. So it seems to me that no matter who may praise [this book], unfortunate women such as this one pay dearly for it.]

This anecdote is the only time during the *Querelle* when Christine describes a scene of reading. In her description, she pointedly assigns this story to an authoritative source when she attributes it to one of Pierre Col's bureaucratic colleagues, a "man of authority." Christine considers how the *Rose* might be read within a bourgeois marriage; in direct opposition to Pierre Col's reader who focused thematically on the "foolish lover," Christine narrates a scene that closely mirrors the behavior of the Jaloux. Given the vivid quality of the Jaloux's violence—especially in an illustrated manuscript of the *Rose*—the Jaloux would offer a more compelling exemplum than the "foolish lover" evoked by Pierre Col. As such, the *Rose* does not encourage the temperance and moderation extolled in the *Livre de éthiques.*

In the course of this long letter addressed to Pierre Col, Christine returns repeatedly to the figure of the Vieille whose sermon represented, along with the tirade of the Jaloux, one of the most problematic sections in the *Rose.* She questions how the evil teaching ("vil enseignment") of the Vieille could contribute to the common good:

Puis que celuy livre de la Rose est tant necessaire et expedient pour doc-
trine de bien vivre tant prouffitablement, je te pry que tu me dies a quel
proffit du bien commun puet venir tant avoir assemblé de disolucions que

dist le personnage de la Vielle. Car se tu vuelz dire que c'est affin que on se
garde, je cuide qu'il ait la plus grant partie des gens qui onques n'orent que
faire de telles dyableries come elle recorde, et ne sevent que ce puet estre.
(133)

[Since this book of the *Rose* is so necessary and expedient for the doctrine of good, beneficial living, I ask you to tell me what profit for the
common good can come from having compiled the debauched sayings which the character of the Vieille spoke. For if you wish to say
that it is so that one might be on guard, I believe that most people will
have never heard of such devilry as she narrates, nor do they know
that it can exist.]

While Pierre Col claims that the Vieille represents the essential qualities to
be found in an old woman, Christine, for her part, objects that the Vieille is
not culturally normative, nor do her teachings qualify as conventional wisdom. Christine criticizes the cynicism of the Vieille's instructions to Bel
Acueil and states that Bel Acueil would not need the manipulative skills
taught by the Vieille in order to avoid being deceived. As we saw in chapter
4, since the Vieille concludes her speech by celebrating the memory of a violent lover, she becomes an exemplum of female conduct and experience
that ultimately eroticizes the sort of violence performed by the Jaloux.
Christine does not refer to this confessional moment in the speech of the
Vieille, but she does repeatedly denounce the Vieille's performance as a
whole: "ce malicieuse maniere de decepvoir" (140) ["This malicious manner
of deception"]. While the Jaloux models violence against women, the Vieille
unapologetically promotes feminine deceit: as such, Jean de Meun constructs a highly distasteful character in the Vieille.

Scattered among Christine's critical comments on the *Rose* are her repeated objections to the end of the poem, which she claims noblewomen
would cover their faces and blush to hear (135), so that the ending renders
the *Rose* a text that cannot be honorably read in the presence of ladies
("honnestement ne puet estre leue en leur presence" [136]). Such comments
reflect her judgment regarding the appropriate register for poetic discourse;
in addition, she questions the thematic closure offered by the final inflated
scene of heroic conquest in the *Roman de la Rose*. In her letter to Pierre Col,
she asserts that a conclusion retrospectively emphasizes the purposes and
threads of an argument: "et car tu sés se ung dicteur veult user d'ordre de
rethorique, il fait ses premisses de ce que il veult traictier, et puis entre de
propos en propos et parle de plusseurs choses s'il luy plaist, puis revient a sa

conclusion de ce pour quoy il a faite sa narracion" (135) ["And as you know, if a poet wishes to employ rhetorical order, he states his premises regarding that which he wishes to treat, and then from proposition to proposition he speaks of as many things as he pleases, then he returns in his conclusion to the reason why he had made his narrative"]. In her assessment of the *Rose*, Christine identifies "les orribletés qui sont en la fin tant abhominables" (136) ["the horrible things that are in so abominable an ending"]. For Christine, the violent conquest of the rose that concludes the poem should be read as a thematic summary of its central premises. Read in this manner, the ending of the *Rose* reinforces the discourse of the Jaloux and the Vieille, since the narrator/lover's acquisition of the rose demonstrates the extent to which he has learned the lessons of Ami and the Vieille, as we have seen. In focusing on the conclusion, Christine identifies the thematic emphasis on erotic violence in the development of the *Rose*.

Critical Approaches to Marital Violence

The argumentative edge in Christine's approach to the *Rose* and its representation of violence and desire becomes evident by contrast to Gerson's more normative reactions to the *Rose*. Early in 1403, partially as a response to Pierre Col's praise of the *Rose* in his second letter, Gerson composed a series of sermons on the seven deadly sins.[33] These sermons—preached in the vernacular—were designed to reach a popular audience and to address issues of everyday conduct for Parisian Christians. As Eric Hicks says, "Les sermons de la série *Poenitemini* témoignent de l'intérêt soutenu du public comme de l'actualité des problèmes."[34] Gerson's sermon on marital chastity, delivered on January 7, 1403, explicitly identifies violence as part of the conduct of marriage. Gerson suggests that violence is inherent in marriage when he pragmatically encourages women to steer clear of angry husbands. He asserts that the husband must use physical and psychological violence responsibly: "S'elles sont juenes, le mary les peut chastoier, premierement de paroles doulcement, puis de verges"[35] ["If the wife is young, the husband may chastise her, first gently with words, then with rods"]. To Gerson, violence is a standard component of marriage, and the ethical issues it raises involve the appropriate levels of force in a given context.

Christine's scattered references to violence in marriage demonstrate her awareness that many married women lived with the threat or fact of violence. In the third section of her conduct book for women, the *Livre des trois vertus*, she speaks of the "love and faith" ("amor et foy" [172]) that wives owe their husbands; she asserts that wives must be governed by their husbands, whether their husbands are "peaceful or quarrelsome" ("paisibles ou rio-teux" [172]).[36] Christine points out that many wives who had endured the mistreatment of their husbands reaped their rewards as widows because their abusive husbands repented of their wrongs on their deathbeds and left all their worldly goods to their long-suffering wives. Such advice in the *Trois vertus* is striking in its utterly pragmatic approach to marital violence; this advice echoes very similar comments from the end of the *Livre de la cité des dames*. Christine's acceptance of marital violence in the *Cité* and the *Trois vertus* stands in stark contrast to her critique of the violent husband in the epistle she wrote to Pierre Col. Marital violence was part of the quotidian reality negotiated by married women in late medieval Paris; for instance, James Brundage comments on its ubiquity in the years for which legal records survive.[37] But since husbands had a legal right—and in Gerson's terms, a moral responsibility—to "discipline" their wives within limits, Christine could not address the problem of physical violence in marriage as a moral issue, nor even as an issue of appropriate marital conduct. Unlike a sermon or a conduct book—both of which reinforce the status quo—the rhetorical strategies of an epistle offer an opportunity to develop a critical discourse. In the course of the *Querelle*, Christine develops a critique of mar-ital violence as an issue in the ethics of reading; such an ethical framework makes it possible for her to articulate a connection between marital violence and reading practices by questioning the purpose to which a reader might put sections of the *Rose*—specifically the sections that eroticize violence. In-deed, the persistence with which she interrogates the *Rose* in relation to erotic violence suggests that she sees violence against women as one of the critical issues of an ethics of reading any given text.

In gathering her letters together into a dossier and including it in her col-lected works, Christine dramatizes her subject position as a critical reader; the dossier, however, adopts an antagonistic tone towards the *Rose* and specifically Jean de Meun. Although modern scholars have often been put off by Christine's irreverent attitude towards Jean de Meun,[38] her antagonis-tic stance, however, ought to be recognized as a strategic engagement with the authoritative status of the *Rose*; indeed, the *ars dictaminis* expressly as-sumes that a letter writer would adopt an antagonistic tone. Doris Sommer sees antagonism as a constitutive feature of an ethical reading: "Antagonism, to put it simply, is built into the asymmetries between texts and readers. . . . The operative esthetic for antagonistic, or politely offputting, postures in-cludes a set of conventions for reminding powerful interlocutors of the in-equalities they would rather forget. And the name for these literary and locutionary conventions is what we popularly call 'attitude.' "[39] The argumentative structure of epistolary rhetoric allowed Christine to develop a critical approach towards Jean de Meun's section of the *Roman de la Rose*, and that attitude in turn allowed her to consider the ethical implications of reading practices. Despite her criticism of the *Rose*, much recent scholarship suggests that many texts in the Christine corpus address issues first raised in the *Querelle de la Rose* and demonstrates her close and careful reading and rewriting of the *Rose*.[40] In addition, Christine continued to employ an epistolary format in several later texts, which suggests that she found epistolary rhetoric to be an efficacious format for developing a critical perspective.[41]

Epistolary rhetoric allowed Heloise to develop a discourse of desire that situated her as a submissive lover; two centuries later, Christine's location in the bureaucratic cultures of late medieval Paris enabled her to deploy epistolary rhetoric in the development of a critical discourse in order to reject the category of female experience as it is developed in the *Roman de la Rose*. In her initial letter to Montreuil, Christine appeals to experience in support of her position on the *Rose:*

> *Et ne croiéz, chier sire . . . que je die ou mette en ordre ces dictes deffenses par excusacion favourable pour ce que femme suis: car veritablement mon motif n'est simplement fors soustenir pure verité . . . et de tant comme voirement suis femme, plus puis tesmoingnier en ceste partie que cellui qui n'en a l'experience, ains parle par devinailles et d'aventure. (19)*

> [And do not believe, dear sir . . . that I speak or arrange these critical sayings for the simple reason that I am a woman: because truly my purpose is only to uphold the pure truth . . . and since I am obviously a woman, I can better testify on this topic than one who does not have experience of it and thus speaks by supposition and by chance.]

She invokes experience again at the start and at the conclusion of her letter to Pierre Col (116, 148).[42] Christine's rhetorical appeal to her own version of lived experience as a form of truth allows her to reject the Ovidian version of female identity and desire articulated by the Vieille in the *Roman de la Rose*. Unlike Chaucer's reiteration of Ovidian erotics in the *Wife of Bath's Prologue*, Christine develops a critical discourse and even a critical subjectivity. The argumentative and adversarial rhetoric of the *ars dictaminis*—its rhetorical violence—offered her a subject position from which she could develop a language of female embodiment as a form of authority.

Afterword

> Sexual difference entails the existence of a sexual
> ethics, an ethics of the ongoing negotiations between
> beings whose differences, whose alterities, are left in-
> tact but with whom some kind of exchange is
> nonetheless possible.
>
> —Elizabeth Grosz

Ironically presented as a handbook for eroti-
cizing sexual difference, Ovid's *Ars amatoria* is structured around the lessons
of a *praeceptor amoris* to would-be lovers, both male and female. The reception of the *Ars* in medieval textual cultures emphasized its didactic rhetoric
at the expense of its irony, and the presence of the *Ars* in the schools guar-
anteed its status as authoritative instruction on desire. The *Roman de la Rose*
is likewise an inflated and contradictory tutorial on *amor*, extensively ampli-
fied by the various interlocutors who speak to Amant. The instruction of
Ami and the lessons of the Vieille owe their shape to the *Ars amatoria*, and
Ovid's Art is one of the texts bound in Jankyn's book of "wikked wyves" in
Chaucer's *Wife of Bath's Prologue*. The *Prologue* takes its cue from the pedagogical authority of the *Ars* and the *Rose* so that the violent eros of pedagogy and the eroticizing of violence converge in Chaucer's text. Indeed, the
Wife's assertion that she is of "fyve husbondes scoleiyng" (44f) suggests the
intensive pedagogy required to reproduce the sort of "heterosexual" experience she performs en route to Canterbury. Nonetheless, as we have seen, the
Wife of Bath's Prologue often appears uncannily familiar to modern readers.
Of all these texts, only the *Wife of Bath's Prologue* remains a "school" text: its
presence in the *Norton Anthology* assures that this text continues to perform
a pedagogical function, often in the comparatively dehistoricized context of
survey courses on English literature in North American universities. In this

pedagogical space, the constructed quality of the Wife's "experience" might not always be evident.

In interviews in the early 1980's, Foucault more than once compared medieval erotic practices to contemporary S/M.[1] In one instance he specified the nature of the comparison: "S/M is the *use* of a strategic relationship as a source of pleasure (physical pleasure). It is not the first time that people have used strategic relations as a source of pleasure. For instance, in the Middle Ages there was the institution of 'courtly love,' the troubadour, the institutions of the love relationships between the lady and the lover, and so on"[2] The "strategic relations" Foucault identifies as the source of pleasure in medieval erotic institutions are especially evident in Ovidian discourses of desire. The highly codified gestures encouraged by the *praeceptor* provide the theatricality that enabled the rhetorical excesses evident in Heloise's discourse of submission or the confessional performances of the Vieille and the Wife of Bath. As we have seen, it is the scripted quality of such rhetorical violence that allowed Christine de Pizan to develop a critical discourse: her intervention in the Ovidian tradition manifest in the *Roman de la Rose* proposes an ethical engagement with the categories of erotic violence.

When traced through to its discursive formations, the *Wife of Bath's Prologue* allows us to see the ways in which heteroerotics has historically been constructed so that it has the potential to eroticize violence. The erotics of sexual difference that emerge from the textual traditions of Ovid's *Ars amatoria* achieves legibility through violence, so that the power erotics Ovid ironically proposes in the context of Roman colonial culture become domesticated as a feature of medieval marriage and desire. Both the *Roman de la Rose* and Chaucer's depiction of the Wife of Bath reiterate the erotic potentials of clothing and accessories, a legacy of the imperial possibilities of heteroerotics as proposed by the *praeceptor* in the third book of the *Ars amatoria*. Likewise, the erotic potential of intimate violence in the Latin love elegy, particularly from Ovid's *Amores* 1.7, depends on the precise meanings attributed to violence within the hierarchies of a colonial, slave-owning culture. The emergence of erotic violence in medieval constructions of subjectivity and erotic agency shows traces of these Roman discourses on coloniality and desire. The *Roman de la Rose* and the *Wife of Bath's Prologue* suggest that the erotic and amatory structures of the medieval West were haunted by the Roman imperial structures of eros and *amor*. And the extent that modern readers recognize the Wife of Bath as a familiar figure suggests that the categories of erotic violence that emerge in Ovid's *Ars amatoria* and circulate in medieval textual cultures continue to shape the "strategic relations" of erotic cultures in the contemporary West.

✒ ABBREVIATIONS

The following source abbreviations are used in the notes and illustration captions.

BnF	Bibliothèque nationale de France
BUV	Universitat de València, Biblioteca Històrica
CR	*Chaucer Review*
MS	*Mediaeval Studies*
PMLA	*Publications of the Modern Language Association*
SAC	*Studies in the Age of Chaucer*

✒ NOTES

Introduction

1. Dallas Beal, et al., "Review into Women's Studies Conference at SUNY New Paltz, November, 1997," unpublished report, SUNY New Paltz, 1997.

2. Carole Vance, ed., *Pleasure and Danger: Exploring Female Sexuality*, New York, 1990.

3. 4. For a survey of the "sex wars" see Ruby B. Rich, "Feminism and Sexuality in the 1980's," *Feminist Studies* 12 (1986), 525–61; see also Carla Freccero, "Notes of a Post-Sex Wars Theorizer," in *Conflicts in Feminism*, ed. Marianne Hirsch and Evelyn Fox Keller, London, 1990, 305–25; Lisa Duggan and Nan D. Hunter, *Sex Wars: Sexual Dissent and Political Culture.* New York, 1995.

4. 5. For a separate example of sadomasochism as a sex-panic, see David M. Halperin, *Saint Foucault: Towards a Gay Hagiography*, Oxford, 1995, 81–104.

5. Thomas S. Weinberg and Martha S. Magill, "Sadomasochistic Themes in Mainstream Culture," in *S&M: Studies in Dominance and Submission*, ed. Thomas S. Weinberg, Amherst, N.Y., 1995, 223–30.

6. Kaja Silverman, *Male Subjectivity at the Margins*, London, 1992; Eve Kosofsky Sedgewick, "A Poem is Being Written," in *Tendencies*, Durham, N.C., 1993, 177–214; Mandy Merck, *Perversions: Deviant Readings*, New York, 1993; Anne McClintock, "Maid to Order: Commercial S/M and Gender Power," in *Dirty Looks: Women, Pornography, Power*, ed. Pamela Church Gibson and Roma Gibson, London, 1993, 207–31; McClintock, "The Return of Female Fetishism and the Fiction of the Phallus," *Perversity* 19 (1993), 1–22; and McClintock, "Confessions of a Psycho-Mistress: An Interview with Mistress Vena," in *Social Text* 37 (1993), 65–72; Lynda Hart, *Between the Body and the Flesh: Performing Sadomasochism*, New York, 1998; Dorothy Allison, "Public Silence, Private Terror," in *Pleasure and Danger*, 101–99; and Pat Califia and Robin Sweeny, eds., *The Second Coming: A Leatherdyke Reader*, Los Angeles, 1996; Sue Golding, "Sexual Manners," *Public* 8 (1993), 61–68; Pat Califia, "The Limits of the S/M Relationship," *Outlook* 15 (1992), 16–21; "Feminism and Sadomasochism," *Heresies* 12 (1981), 30–34.

7. Parveen Adams, "Of Female Bondage," in *Between Feminism and Psychoanalysis*, ed. Teresa Brennan, London, 1989, 264.

8. Tania Modleski, *Feminism Without Women: Culture and Criticism in a "Postfeminist" Age*, New York, 1991; see also, Leo Bersani, *Homos*, Cambridge, Mass., 1995 83–97.

9. Pat Califia, *SM: Sensuous Magic: A Guide for Adventurous Couples*, New York, Masquerade, 1998, 14. See also Bill Thompson, *Sadomasochism: Painful Perversion or Pleasurable Play*, London, 1994, 124; Thomas S. Weinberg, "Sadism and Masochism:

Sociological Perspectives," in S&M: *Studies in Dominance*, 119–37; Liz Highleyman, aka Mistress Veronika Frost, "Professional Dominance," in *Whores and Other Feminists*, ed. Jill Nagle, New York, 1997, 145–55. As Thomas Weinberg and G. W. Levi Kamul comment: "Much S&M involves very little pain . . . it is the illusion of violence, rather than violence itself, that is frequently arousing to both sadists and masochists." ("S&M: An Introduction to the Study of Sadomasochism," in *S&M: Studies in Dominance*, 19.)

10. "Violence against women" refers to violence in intimate or domestic contexts, usually within the home; see Elizabeth Stanko, "Models of Understanding Violence against Women," in *Violence Against Women,* ed. Susan Bewley, John Friend, and Gillian Mezey, London, 1997, 13. Given its intimate nature, violence against women usually includes a sexual and erotic dimension; see Siobhan Lloyd, "Defining Violence against Women," in *Violence Against Women*, 7. Current sociological research suggests that violence against women is pervasive; see Isabel Marcus, "Reframing 'Domestic Violence': Terrorism in the Home," in *The Public Nature of Private Violence: The Discovery of Domestic Violence*, ed. Martha Albertson Fineman and Roxane Mykitiuk, London, 1994, 11–35; Judith Lewis Herman, *Trauma and Recovery: From Domestic Abuse to Political Terror*, London, 1992. See also Daniel G. Saunders, "Wife Abuse, Husband Abuse, or Mutual Combat: A Feminist Perspective on the Empirical Findings," in *Feminist Perspectives on Wife Abuse*, ed. Kersti Yllö and Michele Bograd, London, 1988.

11. See R. Emerson Dobash and Russell Dobash, "The Response of the British and American Women's Movements to Violence Against Women," in *Women, Violence and Social Control*, ed. Jalna Hanmer and Mary Maynard, Atlantic Highlands, N. J., 1987, 169–79; Anne Edwards, "Male Violence in Feminist Theory: An Analysis of the Changing Conceptions of Sex/Gender Violence and Male Dominance," in ibid., 13–29. See also Linda Gordon, *Heroes of Their Own Lives: The Politics and History of Family Violence*, London, 1989.

12. Domestic violence is so widespread in the contemporary West that some researchers see it as a normative component of marriage; as Michelle Bograd puts it: "the widespread prevalence of wife abuse suggests that it may be more a function of the normal psychological and behavioral patterns of men than the aberrant actions of a very few husbands." Michelle Bograd, "Feminist Perspectives on Wife Abuse," in *Feminist Perspectives on Wife Abuse*, 17. Various theories, such as "traumatic bonding," or the "Stockholm Syndrome" have been proposed as explanations for the erotic intensity of desire and identification on the part of women who experience abuse. Several decades ago, Leonore Walker identified what has come to be known as the "cycle theory of violence," which has three parts: tension building, acute battering incident, and loving contrition. Leonore E. Walker, *The Battered Woman Syndrome*, New York, 1984, 95. Jeff Hearn summarizes the erotic nature of violence against women: "violence has often taken on sexual meanings for men. Dominance, including violence, has become eroticized for most men and some women." Jeff Hearn, "Men's Violence to Known Women: Historical, Everyday and Theoretical Constructions by Men," in Hannah Bradby, *Defining Violence*, Avebury, 1996, 32. Domestic violence often results from sexual jealousy on the part of the male perpetrator, so that the violence itself intersects with sexual coercion and sexual possessiveness. Case studies also suggest that men who batter see their violence "as a response to women's

verbal aggressiveness," as James Ptacek has found: "these men seem to regard verbal aggressiveness as equivalent to physical aggressiveness, as if a woman's verbal behavior somehow excuses them of responsibility for their violence." James Ptacek, "Why Do Men Batter Their Wives?" in *Feminist Perspectives on Wife Abuse*, 145.

13. See Arthur Kleinman, "The Violences of Everyday Life: The Multiple Forms and Dynamics of Social Violences," in *Violence and Subjectivity*, ed. Veena Das, Arthur Kleinman, Mamphela Ramphele, and Paula Reynolds, Berkeley, Calif., 2000, 227; Gail Mason, *The Spectacle of Violence: Homophobia, Gender, and Knowledge*, London, 2002. For a theoretical discussion of violence, see David Riches, "The Phenomenon of Violence," in *The Anthropology of Violence*, Oxford, 1987, 2–27; Lauro Martines, "Introduction: The Historical Approach to Violence," in *Violence and Civil Disorder in Italian Cities 1200–1500*, Berkeley, Calif., 1972.

14. The most notorious case of S/M policing is the Spanner case in the UK, in which gay men who practiced consensual S/M were prosecuted for assault. See www.commex.org/whatever/spanner/spanner.html

15. Michel Foucault, "Sexual Choice/Sexual Act," in *Michel Foucault: Essential Works of Foucault: 1954–1984*, ed. Paul Rabinow. vol. 1: *Ethics*, New York, 1997, 151.

16. John K. Noyes, *The Mastery of Submission: Inventions of Masochism*, Ithaca, N.Y., 1997, 4–5. See also Thompson, who comments: "what was really intriguing about sadomasochism was that it appeared prevalent in its organizing form only in literate societies full of symbolic meanings," 118.

17. Maria Marcus, A Taste for Pain: On Masochism and Female Sexuality, London, 1981, 17.

18. Slavoj Žižek, *The Metastases of Enjoyment: Six Essays on Woman and Causality*, London, 1994, 89.

19. Anna Freud, "Beating Fantasies and Daydreams," in *Essential Papers on Masochism*. ed. Margaret Ann Fitzpatrick Hanly, New York, 1995, 290–91.

20. See Jeffrey J. Cohen, *Medieval Identity Machines*, Minneapolis, 2003. Cohen uses a Deleuzian paradigm to examine what he calls a "masochistic assemblage" (78) in medieval cultures; see especially 78–115.

21. On the representation of rape in medieval texts, see Kathryn Gravdal, *Ravishing Maidens: Writing Rape in Medieval French Literature and Law*, Philadelphia, 1991; Christine M. Rose and Elizabeth Ann Robertson, *Representing Rape in Medieval and Early Modern Literature*, New York, 2001.

22. See for instance, Roger M. Walker, "A Possible Source for the 'Afrenta de Corpes' Episode in the 'Poema de Mio Cid,'" *Modern Language Review* 72 (1977), 335–47.

23. *Pornography and Sexual Violence: Evidence of the Links. The Complete Record of Public Hearings for Experts, Witnesses and Victims of Sexual Assault Involving Pornography*, London, 1988, 46–47.

24. William Burgwinkle, *Sodomy, Masculinity, and Law in Medieval Literature: France and England, 1050–1230*, Cambridge, 2004, 5. Under the influence of Foucault, it has become fashionable for medievalists to consider the Middle Ages as a time "before heterosexuality" and the ancient world as a time "before sexuality." See James A. Schultz, "Bodies That Don't Matter: Heterosexuality before Heterosexuality in Gottfried's *Tristan*," in *Constructing Medieval Sexuality*, ed. Karma Lochrie, Peggy McCracken, and James A. Schultz, Minneapolis, 1997, 91–110; David M.

Halperin, John J. Winkler, Froma I. Zeitlin, *Before Sexuality: The Construction of Erotic Experience in the Ancient World,* Princeton, 1990. However, James Brundage argues that the sexual regimes of the modern West were formed to a large degree by medieval legal discourse designed to regulate sexuality and desire; see James A. Brundage, *Law, Sex, and Christian Society in Medieval Europe,* Chicago, 1987, 1–9.

25. Ivan Illich, *In the Vineyard of the Text: A Commentary to Hugh's Didascalicon,* Chicago, 1993.

26. Stephanie Jed, *Chaste Thinking: The Rape of Lucretia and the Birth of Humanism,* Bloomington, 1989.

Chapter 1. Sexual Difference and the Ethics of Erotic Violence

1. Emmanuel Lévinas, *Totality and Infinity: An Essay on Exteriority,* trans. Alphonso Lingis, Pittsburgh, 1969.

2. Luce Irigaray, "The Fecundity of the Caress: A Reading of Levinas, *Totality and Infinity,* Section IV, B. 'The Phenomenology of Eros,' " in *Face to Face with Lévinas,* ed. Richard A. Cohen, Albany, N.Y., 1986, 235.

3. Michel Foucault, "What Is Enlightenment?" in *Michel Foucault: Essential Works of Foucault 1954–1984,* ed. Paul Rabinow. vol. 1: *Ethics,* New York, 1997, 319. See Beatrice Hanssen, *Critique of Violence: Between Poststructuralism and Critical Theory,* New York, 2000, 30–96.

4. Philippe Delhaye, "L'Enseignement de la philosophie morale au XIIe Siècle," *MS* 11 (1949), 77–99; Delhaye, "Grammatica" et "Ethica" au XIIe siècle," *Recherches de Théologie Ancienne et Médiévale* 25 (1958), 59–110.

5. Alastair J. Minnis, *Medieval Theory of Authorship: Scholastic Literary Attitudes in the Later Middle Ages,* Oxford, 1984; Judson Boyce Allen, *The Ethical Poetic of the Later Middle Ages: A Decorum of Convenient Distinction,* Toronto, 1982, 9–10. Paule Demats, *Fabula: Trois Études de mythographie antique et médiévale,* Geneva, 1973, 116–17.

6. John Dagenais suggests that an examination of the ethics of reading in a manuscript culture should attend to "what people do as they read and with what they read," as well as "what scribes, glossators, readers, and commentators did." *The Ethics of Reading in a Manuscript Culture: Glossing the Libro de Buen Amor.* Princeton, 1994, 29.

7. See Mary Carruthers, "Memory and the Ethics of Reading," in *The Book of Memory: A Study of Memory in Medieval Culture,* Cambridge, 1990, 156–88. See also Dagenais, 8–29.

8. Brian Stock, *After Augustine: The Meditative Reader and the Text,* Philadelphia, 2001, 24–37; Stock, "Reading, Ethics and the Literary Imagination," *New Literary History* 34 (2003), 1–17.

9. Derek Attridge describes the ethical possibilities of an innovative reading as "one that brings about unexpected reshapings of the familiar." "Innovation, Literature, Ethics: Relating to the Other," *PMLA: Ethics and Literary Study* 114 (1999), 25.

10. Michel Foucault, *Madness and Civilization: A History of Insanity in the Age of Reason,* trans. Richard Howard, New York, 1965, 210.

11. For a survey of the "mounted Aristotle," see Susan L. Smith, *The Power of Women: A Topos in Medieval Art and Literature,* Philadelphia, 1995, 66–136; Smith suggests that the visual tradition of the "Mounted Aristotle" is an illustration of the textual tradition. Other surveys include: Pietro Marsilli, "Réception et diffu-

sion iconographique du conte de 'Aristote et Phillis' en Europe depuis le Moyen Age," in *Amour, mariage et transgressions au Moyen Age*, ed. Danielle Buschinger and André Crépin, Göppingen, 1984, 239–69; Cornelia Herrmann, *Der "Gerittene Aristoteles": Das Bildmotiv des "Gerittenen Aristoteles" und seine Bedeutung für die Aufrechterhaltung der gesellschaftlichen Ordnung vom Beginn des 13. Jahrhundert bis um 1500*, Pfaffenweiler, 1991; Raffaele de Cesare, "Di nuovo sulla leggenda di Aristotele cavalcato," *Miscellanea del Centro di Studi Medievali*, n.s. 57 (1956), 181–238; de Cesare, "Due recenti studi sulla leggenda di Aristotle cavalcato," *Aevum* 31 (1957), 85–101. In the early modern period, the best-known examples are the woodcuts by the Housebook Master and Hans Baldung Grien. See Jane Campbell Hutchison, "The Housebook Master and the Folly of the Wise Man," *Art Bulletin* 48(1966), 73–78.

12. On the status of marginal illustration, see Lillian M. C. Randall, *Images in the Margins of Gothic Manuscripts*, Berkeley, Calif., 1966.

13. For the entire manuscript tradition of this illustration to the *Trionfi d'Amore*, see de Cesare, "Di nuovo," 239–43.

14. I am grateful to Karen Winstead for bringing this image to my attention. Another image in the iconographic tradition of the "mounted Aristotle" has recently come to light in the newly discovered *Macclesfield Psalter*, fol 110v. See *The Cambridge Illuminations: Ten Centuries of Book Production in the Medieval West*. ed. Paul Binski and Stella Panayotova, London, 2005, fig. 2.

15. Natalie Zemon Davis, "Woman on Top," in *Society and Culture in Early Modern France*, Stanford, Calif., 1975, 124–51.

16. Helen Solterer, *The Master and Minerva: Disputing Women in French Medieval Culture*, Berkeley, Calif., 1995, 23–26.

17. Smith, 103–36. On the correct positions for heterosexual intercourse, see Pierre J. Payer, *The Bridling of Desire: Views of Sex in the Later Middle Ages*, Toronto, 1993, 76.

18. For a text of Vitry's exempla, see Joseph Greven, *Die exempla aus den Sermones feriales et communes des Jakob von Vitry*, Heidelberg, 1914, 15.

19. Smith, 66–102.

20. For a text of the *Lai d'Aristote*, see *Les Dits d'Henri d'Andeli*, ed. Alain Corbellari, Paris, 2003.

21. *Li Livres dou Tresor de Brunetto Latini*, ed. Francis J. Carmody, Berkeley, Calif., 1948, II, 106.2; see also de Cesare, "Di nuovo," 184–85.

22. *Les Lamentations de Matheolus et le Livre de leesce de Jehan Le Fèvre, de Ressons*, vol. 1 ed. A.-G. Hamel, Bibliothèque de l'école des hautes études 95, Paris, 1892.

23. Guillaume de Machaut alludes to the "mounted Aristotle" in a list of ancient figures overcome by love, see *Livre de la fonteinne amoureuse* 1817–19; Froissart likewise includes Aristotle in a similar list, see *Le Joli Buisson de Jonece*, 3369–71; see also, Eustache Deschamps, the *Miroir de mariage*, 1385. For more citations, see de Cesare, "Di Nuovo."

24. G. C. Macaulay, ed., *The English Works of John Gower*, London, 1957.

25. On the status of Aristotle in the *Confessio Amantis*, see James Simpson, *Sciences and the Self in Medieval Poetry: Alan of Lille's* Anticlaudianus *and John Gower's* Confessio Amantis, Cambridge, 1995, 198–229.

26. For a magisterial survey of equestrian metaphors in medieval texts, see Beryl

Rowland, "The Horse and Rider Figure in Chaucer's Works," *University of Toronto Quarterly* 35 (1966), 246–59.

27. James Joyce, *Ulysses*, New York, 1961, 467.

28. Thaïs E. Morgan, " 'A Whip of One's Own' ": Dominatrix Pornography and the Construction of a Post-Modern (Female) Subjectivity," *The American Journal of Semiotics* 6 (1980), 130. Riding crops are especially valued by S/M practitioners. In her how-to handbook on S/M practices, Pat Califia notes that the riding crop is a highly versatile implement; Pat Califia, *SM: Sensuous Magic: A Guide for Adventurous Couples,* New York, 1998, 125. Edward Anthony, in his celebration of "ecstatic flagellation," extols the riding crop since it is "capable of great returns of severity for the expenditure of minimal effort. . . . it is an elegant weapon." Edward Anthony, *Thy Rod and Staff,* London, 1995, 225.

29. Amy Richlin, *The Garden of Priapus: Sexuality and Aggression in Roman Humor,* rev. ed., Oxford, 1992, 219; see also Otto Kiefer, *Sexual Life in Ancient Rome,* trans. Gilbert and Helen Highet, London, 1934, 23. Eva C. Keuls comments on ancient Greece: "that men regularly resorted to physical violence *against* their wives in Classical Athens is not indicated, but then, who would have recorded it if it did take place?" *The Reign of the Phallus: Sexual Politics in Ancient Athens,* Berkeley, Calif., 1993, 108. On the status of the wife in Roman marriage, see Percy Ellwood Corbett, *The Roman Law of Marriage*, Oxford, 1930, 107–21; Suzanne Dixon, *The Roman Family,* Baltimore, 1992, 71–83.

30. M. I. Finley, *Ancient Slavery and Modern Ideology,* London, 1980, 93. See also K. R. Bradley, *Slaves and Masters in the Roman Empire: A Study in Social Control*, Brussels, 1984, 113–37; Richard Saller, "Symbols of Gender and Status Hierarchies in the Roman Household," in *Women and Slaves in Greco-Roman Culture,* ed. Sandra R. Joshel and Sheila Murnaghan, London, 1998, 85–91; Peter Garnsey, *Social Status and Legal Privilege in the Roman Empire,* Oxford, 1970. On violence and citizenship in ancient Greece, see John. J. Winkler, *The Constraints of Desire: The Anthropology of Sex and Gender in Ancient Greece,* Routledge, 1990, 48.

31. On the status of women in the Latin love elegy, see Jasper Griffin, *Latin Poets and Roman Life*, London 1985, 55, 112–41; R. O. A. M. Lyne, *The Latin Love Poets: From Catullus to Horace*, Oxford, 1980, 8–13.

32. Paul Veyne, "La famille et l'amour sans le Haut-Empire romain," *Annales ESC* 3 (1978), 35–63.

33. On violence in the late antique household, see Brent D. Shaw, "The Family in Late Antiquity: The Experience of Augustine," *Past & Present* 115 (1987), 4–51. Peter Brown, *Power and Persuasion in Late Antiquity: Towards a Christian Empire,* Madison, Wis., 1992, 50–52.

34. *Patrologia Latina* 32.772. On Augustine's mother, see Beverly Mayne Kienzle and Nancy Nienhuis, "Battered Women and the Construction of Sanctity," *Journal of Feminist Studies in Religion* 17 (2001), 33–61. See also Richard Saller, "*Patria potestas* and the Stereotype of the Roman Family," *Continuity and Change* 1 (1986), 7–22.

35. *Patrologia Latina* 41.644–45. On the *patria potestas*, see Saller.

36. *Corpus Christianorum, Series Latina* 40.2077; on this passage, see Shaw, 29.

37. Shaw, 48.

38. See Jean Verdon, "La femme et la violence en Poitou pendant la Guerre de

Cent Ans d'après les lettres de rémission," *Annales du Midi* 102 (1990), 367–74; David Nicholas, *The Domestic Life of a Medieval City: Women, Children, and the Family in Fourteenth-Century Ghent*, Lincoln, Neb., 1985, 17–52; J. R. Hale, "Violence in the Late Middle Ages: A Background," in *Violence and Civil Disorder in Italian Cities 1200–1500*, ed. Lauro Martines, Berkeley, 1972, 19–37; Stanley Chojnacki, "Crime, Punishment, and the Trecento Venetian State," in *Violence and Civil Disorder*, 212; Guido Ruggiero, *The Boundaries of Eros: Sex Crime and Sexuality in Renaissance Venice*, New York, 1985, 101–2. For the early modern period, see Anthony Fletcher, *Gender, Sex, and Subordination in England 1500–1800*, New Haven, Conn., 1995, 192–203; Susan Dwyer Amussen, "The Gendering of Popular Culture in Early Modern England," in *Popular Culture in England, c. 1500–1850*, ed. Tim Harris, New York, 1995, 48–68; J. A. Sharpe, "Domestic Homicide in Early Modern England," *Historical Journal* 24 (1981), 29–48.

39. Thomas Wright, ed., *The Book of the Knight of La Tour-Landry*, Early English Text Society, original series, vol. 33 London, 1906, 25.

40. Georgine E. Brereton and Janet M. Ferrier, eds., *Le Menagier de Paris*, Oxford, 1981.

41. For a discussion of these three conduct books, see Roberta L. Krueger, " 'Nouvelles choses': Social Instability and the Problem of Fashion in the *Livre du Chevalier de la Tour Landry*, the *Ménagier du Paris*, and Christine de Pizan's *Livre des Trois Vertus*," in *Medieval Conduct*, ed. Kathleen Ashley and Robert L. A. Clark, Minneapolis, 2001, 49–85.

42. James A. Brundage, "Domestic Violence in Classical Canon Law," in *Violence in Medieval Society*, ed. Richard W. Kaeuper, Cambridge, 2000, 183–96. See also Pierre Cuzacq, *La naissance, le mariage et le décès*, Paris, 1902, 114–15; Guido Rossi, "Statut juridique de la femme dans l'histoire du droit italien," *Recueils de la Société Jean Bodin* 12 (1962), 115–34; John Gilissen, "Le Statut de la femme dans l'ancien droit belge," ibid., 255–321.

43. See R. H. Helmholz, *Marriage Litigation in Medieval England*, Cambridge, 1974; see also John M. Biggs, *The Concept of Matrimonial Cruelty*, London, 1962, 10–27.

44. Helmholz, 101–2.

45. On the concept of "maritalis affectio," see John. T. Noonan Jr., "Marital Affection in the Canonists," *Studia Gratiana* 12 (1967), 479–509. See also Margaret Aston, *Thomas Arundel: A Study of Church Life in the Reign of Richard II*, Oxford, 1967, 41–42.

46. Sir Frederick Pollock and Frederic William Maitland, *The History of English Law Before the Time of Edward I*. 2nd ed. Vol. 2, Cambridge, 1952, 436; see also, Philippa Maddern, "Interpreting Silence: Domestic Violence in the King's Courts in East Anglia, 1422–1442," in *Domestic Violence in Medieval Texts*, ed. Eve Salisbury, Georgiana Donavin, and Merrall Llewelyn Price, Gainesville, Fla., 2002, 31–56; Philippa C. Maddern, *Violence and Social Order: East Anglia 1422–1442,* Oxford, 1992, 99–105 and 232–34.

47. Margaret Kerr, "Husband and Wife in Criminal Proceedings in Medieval England," in *Women, Marriage, and Family in Medieval Christendom: Essays in Memory of Michael M. Sheehan, C. S. B.*, ed. Constance M. Rousseau and Joel T. Rosenthal, Kalamazoo, Mich., 1998, 214–15. See also L. R. Poos, "The Heavy-Handed Marriage Counselor: Regulating Marriage in Some Later-Medieval English Local

Ecclesiastical-Court Jurisdictions," *American Journal of Legal History* 39 (1995), 291–309; Charles I. Hammer, Jr., "Patterns of Homicide in a Medieval University Town: Fourteenth-Century Oxford," *Past & Present* 78 (1978), 3–23.

48. Robert Palmer, "Contexts of Marriage in Medieval England: Evidence from the King's Court circa 1300," *Speculum* 59 (1984), 42–67.

49. See Maddern, "Interpreting Silence," 48.

50. Jean-Louis Flandrin, *Families in Former Times: Kinship, Household, and Sexuality in Early Modern France*, Cambridge, 1979, 123–29.

51. F. R.P. Akehurst, *The Coutumes de Beauvaisis of Philippe de Beaumanoir*, Philadelphia, 1992, 595.

52. See James Buchanan Given, *Society and Homicide in Thirteenth-Century England*, Stanford, Calif., 1977, 205; Barbara A. Hanawalt, *Crime and Conflict in English Communities 1300–1348,* Cambridge, Mass., 1979, 165–65; A. J. Finch, "The Nature of Violence in the Middle Ages: An Alternative Perspective," *Historical Research* 70 (1997), 261–64.

53. So Emmanuel Le Roy Ladurie notes when he introduces his chapter on marriage in his study of the village of Montaillou: "Every married woman could expect a fair amount of beating sometime or other." see *Montaillou: The Promised Land of Error*, New York, 1978, 192.

54. See Emma Hawkes, "The 'Reasonable' Laws of Domestic Violence in Late Medieval England," in *Domestic Violence in Medieval Texts*, 57–70. See also Sara M. Butler, "Spousal Abuse in Fourteenth-Century Yorkshire: What Can We Learn from the Coroner's Rolls?" *Florilegium* 18 (2001), 61–78; Alison McRae-Spencer, "Putting Women in Their Place: Social and Legal Attitudes towards Violence in Marriage in Late-Medieval England," *The Ricardian: Journal of the Richard III Society* 10 (1995), 185–93; Andrew Finch, "Women and Violence in the Later Middle Ages: The Evidence of the Officialty of Cerisy," *Continuity and Change* 7 (1992), 23–45. On the relationship between law and lived experience, see Emma Hawkes, " 'She will . . . protect and defend her rights boldly by law and reason . . . ': Women's Knowledge of Common Law and Equity Courts in Late-Medieval England," in *Medieval Women and the Law*, ed. Noël James Meunge, Suffolk, 2000, 145–61. See also Anthony Musson, *Medieval Law in Context: The Growth of Legal Consciousness from Magna Carta to the Peasants' Revolt*, Manchester, 2001, 84.

55. Sarah Kay, *Courtly Contradictions: The Emergence of the Literary Object in the Twelfth Century*, Palo Alto, Calif., 2001, 216–58. Julie B. Miller, "Eroticized Violence in Medieval Women's Mystical Literature: A Call for a Feminist Critique," *Journal of Feminist Studies in Religion* 15 (1999), 25–49; Martha Easton, "Saint Agatha and the Sanctification of Sexual Violence," *Studies in Iconography* 16 (1994), 83–118. The seminal work on the sacral functions of violence is René Girard, *Violence and the Sacred*, trans. Patrick Gregory, Baltimore, 1977; for a critique of Girard, see Teresa de Lauretis, "The Violence of Rhetoric: Considerations on Representation and Gender," in *The Violence of Representation: Literature and the History of Violence*, ed. Nancy Armstrong and Leonard Tennenhouse, London, 1989, 239–58; Nancy Jay, *Throughout Your Generations Forever: Sacrifice, Religion, and Paternity*, Chicago, 1992.

56. See Kienzle and Nienhuis; Ulrike Wiethaus, "Naming and Un-naming Violence against Women: German Historiography and the Cult of St. Elisabeth of

Thuringia," *Studies in Medievalism* 7 (1999), 187–208; André Vauchez, *Sainthood in the Later Middle Ages*, trans. Jean Birrell, Cambridge, 1997, 148–49.

Chapter 2. Ovid's Art and the Wounds of Love

1 For a study of the *Ars*, see Molly Myerowitz, *Ovid's Games of Love*, Detroit, 1985; see also Peter Toohey, "Eros and Eloquence, Modes of Amatory Persuasion in Ovid's *Ars amatoria*," in *Roman Eloquence: Rhetoric in Society and Literature*, ed. William J. Dominik, New York, 1997, 198–211. For a general discussion of Ovid and issues of gender and sexuality, see Alison Sharrock, "Gender and Sexuality," in *The Cambridge Companion to Ovid*, ed. Philip R. Hardie, Cambridge, 2002, 95–107; and Warren Ginsberg, "Ovid and the Problem of Gender," in *Ovid in Medieval Culture*, ed. Marilynn Desmond, special issue, *Mediaevalia* 13 (1989), 11–28. For a discussion of the discourse of the hunt and *Ars* 1, see C. M. C. Green, "Terms of Venery: *Ars Amatoria* I," *Transactions of the American Philological Association* 126 (1996), 221–63.

2. Pál Csillag, *The Augustan Laws on Family Relations*, trans. József Decsényi, Budapest, 1976; Eva Cantarella, *Pandora's Daughters: The Role and Status of Women in Greek and Roman Antiquity*, Baltimore, 1987, 112–14; Jane F. Gardner, *Women in Roman Law and Society*, London, 1986, 77–82, 127–30; Susan Treggiari, *Roman Marriage: Iusti Coniuges from the Time of Cicero to the Time of Ulpian*, Oxford, 1991, 277–98; Suzanne Dixon, *The Roman Family*, Baltimore, 1992, 79–82; Alison R. Sharrock, "Ovid and the Politics of Reading," *Materiali e discussioni per l'analisi dei testi classici* 33 (1994), 97–122; Ellen O'Gorman, "Love and the Family: Augustus and Ovidian Elegy," *Arethusa* 30 (1997), 103–24; Philip Hardie, "Ovid and Early Imperial Literature," in *Cambridge Companion*, 34–45.

3. See P. A. Brunt, *Italian Manpower: 225 BC–AD 14*, Oxford, 1971.

4. On Ovid's exile, see John C. Thibault, *The Mystery of Ovid's Exile*, Berkeley, Calif., 1964; Ronald Syme, *History in Ovid*, Oxford, 1978, 215–29; A. S. Hollis, "The *Ars amatoria* and *Remedia amoris*," in *Ovid*, ed. J. W. Binns, London, 1973, 84–115. See also R. J. Dickinson, "The *Tristia*: Poetry in Exile," ibid., 154–72; J. C. McKeown, "*Fabula Proposito Nulla Tegenda Meo*: Ovid's *Fasti* and Augustan Politics," in *Poetry and Politics in the Age of Augustus*, ed. Tony Woodman and David West, Cambridge, 1984, 169–87. On Ovid and Augustus, see P. J. Davis, "*Praeceptor Amoris*: Ovid's *Ars amatoria* and the Augustan Idea of Rome," *Ramus* 24 (1995), 181–95.

5. On performance and desire, see Judith Butler, *Gender Trouble: Feminism and the Subversion of Identity*, New York, 1990; Butler, *Undoing Gender*, New York, 2004, 207–19.

6. C. S. Lewis, *The Allegory of Love: A Study in Medieval Tradition*, London, 1936, 7.

7. Texts from P. Ovidi Nasonis, *Amores, Medicamina, Faciei Femineae, Ars Amatoria, Remedia Amoris*, ed. E. J. Kenney, Oxford, 1961, rpt. 1995.

8. Claude Nicolet, *The World of the Citizen in Republican Rome*, trans. P. S. Falla, London, 1980, 90; on the poetic implications of military discourse, see Leslie Cahoon, "The Bed as Battlefield: Erotic Conquest and Military Metaphor in Ovid's *Amores*," *Transactions of the American Philological Association* 118 (1988), 293–307.

9. Amy Richlin, *The Garden of Priapus: Sexuality and Aggression in Roman Humor*, Oxford, 1992, 225; see also Timothy Wiseman, *Catullus and His World: A Reappraisal*, Cambridge, 1985, 12.

10. See Werner A. Krenkel, "Fellatio and Irrumatio," *Wissenschaftliche Zeitschrift der Wilhelm–Pieck–Universität Rostock* 29 (1980), 77–88.

11. On this passage, see Thomas Habinek, "The Invention of Sexuality in the World-City of Rome," in *The Roman Cultural Revolution*, ed. Thomas Habinek and Alessandro Schiesaro, Cambridge, 1997, 30–31; for a theoretical discussion of colonialism and erotic violence, see Ali Behdad, "Eroticism, Colonialism and Violence," in *Violence, Identity, and Self-Determination*, ed. Hent de Vries and Samuel Weber, Stanford, 1997, 201–7.

12. John T. Davis, *Fictus Adulter: Poet as Actor in the Amores*, Amsterdam, 1989, 46–47.

13. Saara Lilja, *The Roman Elegists' Attitude to Women*, Helsinki, 1965, 35–41.

14. Lilja, 36; in *Tristia* 11.303, Ovid states that the *Ars* was addressed to *meretrices;* see Ronald Syme, *History in Ovid*, 18. See also, Treggiari, 307–9; Jasper Griffin, *Latin Poets and Roman Life*, Chapel Hill, 1986, 55; 112–41; R. O. A. M. Lyne. *The Latin Love Poets: From Catullus to Horace*, Oxford, 1980, 8–13.

15. Alison Sharrock, *Seduction and Repetition in Ars amatoria 2*, Oxford, 1994, 288.

16. See A. S. Hollis, ed., *Ars amatoria, Book I*, Oxford, 1977, 96–97; Paul Veyne, *Roman Erotic Elegy: Love, Poetry, and the West*, trans. David Pellauer, Chicago, 1988, 71–86.

17. See Roland Auguet, *Cruelty and Civilization: The Roman Games*, London, 1972; Keith Hopkins, *Conquerors and Slaves*, Cambridge, 1978; William V. Harris, *War and Imperialism in Republican Rome 327–70 BC*, Oxford, 1979; Claude Nicolet, *Space, Geography, and Politics in the Early Roman Empire*, Ann Arbor, Mich., 1991; H. S. Versnel, *Triumphus: An Inquiry into the Origin, Development and Meaning of the Roman Triumph*, Leiden, 1970; Thomas Habinek, "Ovid and Empire," in *Cambridge Companion*, 46–61.

18. Nicolet, *World of the Citizen*, 343–81.

19. Csillag, 174.

20. Nicolet, *Space*, 44.

21. Keith Hopkins, *Death and Renewal*, Cambridge, 1983, 22. On the gladiator, see Carlin A. Barton, *The Sorrows of the Ancient Romans: The Gladiator and the Monster*, Princeton, N.J., 1992; 11–84; Michael Grant, *Gladiators*, London, 1967.

22. See Myerowitz, 64–65; Amy Richlin, "Reading Ovid's Rapes," in *Pornography and Representation in Greece and Rome*, ed. Amy Richlin, Oxford University Press, 1992, 158–79; A. E. Wardman, "The Rape of the Sabines," *Classical Quarterly* 15 (1965), 101–3; J. S. C. Eidinow, "A Note on Ovid's *Ars amatoria 1.117–19*," *American Journal of Philology* 114 (1993), 413–17.

23. For a discussion of the violence in this passage in relation to erotic elegy as a whole, see Duncan F. Kennedy, *The Arts of Love: Five Studies in the Discourse of Roman Love Elegy*, Cambridge, 1993, 55–56; E. W. Leach, "Georgic Imagery in the *Ars amatoria*," *Transactions of the American Philological Association* 95 (1964), 142–54; Marjorie Curry Woods, "Rape and the Pedagogical Rhetoric of Sexual Violence," in *Criticism and Dissent in the Middle Ages*, ed. Rita Copeland, Cambridge, 1996, 56–86.

24. On violence in *Amores 1.7*, see Ellen Greene, *The Erotics of Domination: Male Desire and the Mistress in Latin Love Poetry*, Baltimore, 1998, 84–92; David Frederick, "Reading Broken Skin: Violence in Roman Elegy," in *Roman Sexualities*, ed. Judith P.

Hallet and Marilyn Skinner, Princeton, N.J., 1998, 172–93; Alison Sharrock, "Ovid and the Discourses of Love: the Amatory Works," in *Cambridge Companion*, 150–62. For a general discussion of *Amores* 1.7, see J. V. Morrison, "Literary Reference and Generic Transgression in Ovid, *Amores* 1.7: Lover, Poet, and *Furor*," *Latomus* 51 (1992), 571–89. Tibullus also represents violence as erotic; see *Carmina* 1.6 and 1.10.

25. On this passage, see Nicolet, *Space*, 44–45.

26. Judith Hallett, "The Role of Women in Roman Elegy: Counter-Cultural Feminism," *Women in the Ancient World: The Arethusa Papers*, ed. John Peradotto and J. P. Sullivan, Albany, N.Y., 1984, 250. See also Lilja, 76–89; Kathleen McCarthy, "*Servitium amoris: Amor Servitii*," in *Women and Slaves in Greco-Roman Culture: Differential Equations*, ed. Sandra R. Joshel and Sheila Murnaghan, London, 1998, 174–92.

27. See Maria Wyke, "Woman in the Mirror: The Rhetoric of Adornment in the Roman World," in *Women in Ancient Societies: An Illusion of the Night*, ed. Léonie J. Archer, Susan Fischler, and Maria Wyke, New York, 1994, 134–51.

28. Holt N. Parker, "Love's Body Anatomized: The Ancient Erotic Handbooks and the Rhetoric of Sexuality," in *Pornography and Representation*, 104. See also Simon Goldhill, *Foucault's Virginity: Ancient Erotic Fiction and the History of Sexuality*, Cambridge, 1995. 74.

29. Otto Kiefer notes that the Roman matron was forbidden to drink wine; see *Sexual Life in Ancient Rome*, trans. Gilbert Highet and Helen Highet, London, 1934, 22; for a discussion of the prohibition on wine drinking in the early republic, see Cantarella, 118–19; Treggiari, 430–31; Geoffrey MacCormack, "Wine Drinking and the Romulan Law of Divorce," *Irish Jurist* 10 (1975), 170–74.

30. Valerius Maximus compiled his ethical anecdotes a few decades after the composition of the *Ars amatoria*; however, they record a set of values that had been part of Roman culture for centuries. See W. Martin Bloomer, *Valerius Maximus and the Rhetoric of the New Nobility*, Chapel Hill, N.C., 1992; Clive Skidmore, *Practical Ethics for Roman Gentlemen: The Work of Valerius Maximus*, Exeter, 1996; see also Fergus Millar, "Ovid and the *Domus Augusta*: Rome Seen from Tomoi," *Journal of Roman Studies* 83 (1993), 1–17. ·

31. John Briscoe, ed., *Valeri Maximi, Facta et Dicta Memorabilia*, 2 vols. Leipzig, 1998.

32. See *Tristia* 11.8; Alessandro Barchiesi, *The Poet and the Prince: Ovid and Augustan Discourse*, Berkeley, 1997, 28–34.

33. See Ralph J. Hexter, *Ovid and Medieval Schooling: Studies in Medieval School Commentaries on Ovid's* Ars amatoria, Epistulae ex Ponto, *and* Epistulae Heroidum, Munich, 1986, 7; James H. McGregor, "Ovid at School: From the Ninth to the Fifteenth Century," *Classical Folia* 32 (1978), 29–51; E. J. Kenney, "The Manuscript Tradition of Ovid's *Amores, Ars amatoria* and *Remedia amoris*," *Classical Quarterly* 12 (1962), 1–31; for an overview of Ovid in the Middle Ages, see Jeremy Dimmick, "Ovid in the Middle Ages: Authority and Poetry," in *Cambridge Companion*, 264–87. For general studies of Ovid in medieval culture, see *Mediaevalia*; 13 (1989) E. K. Rand, *Ovid and His Influence*, Boston, 1925; L. P. Wilkinson, *Ovid Recalled*, Cambridge, 1955; Salvatore Battaglia, "La tradizione di Ovidio nel medioevo," *Filologia Romanza* 6 (1959), 185–224; Franco Munari, *Ovid im Mittelalter*, Zurich, 1960.

34. On Ovid in the medieval schools, see Hexter, 23–25; R. J. Tarrant, "Ovid," in

Texts and Transmission: A Survey of Latin Classics, ed. L. D. Reynolds, Oxford, 1983, 261–84; Peter L. Allen, *The Art of Love: Amatory Fiction from Ovid to the Romance of the Rose*, Philadelphia, 1992, 46–52; John W. Baldwin, "*L'Ars amatoria* au XIIe siècle en France: Ovide, Abélard, André le Chapelain et Pierre le Chantre," in *Histoire et Société: Mélanges offerts à Georges Duby*, vol. 1, Aix-en-Provence, 1992, 19–29; Gerald A. Bond, *The Loving Subject: Desire, Eloquence, and Power in Romanesque France*, Philadelphia, 1995, 56–69.

35. D. E. H. Alton, "Ovid in the Mediaeval Schoolroom," *Hermathena* 95(1961), 73; R. B. C. Huygens, ed., *Accessus ad auctores, Bernard d'Utrecht, Conrad d'Hirsau*, Leiden, 1970, 33; see also E. A. Quain, "The Medieval Accessus ad Auctores," *Traditio* 3 (1945) 215–64; Paule Demats, *Fabula: Trois Études de mythographie antique et médiévale*, Geneva, 1973. Judson Boyce Allen, *The Ethical Poetic of the Later Middle Ages: A Decorum of Convenient Distinction*, Toronto, 1982, 4–66. A. J. Minnis, *Medieval Theory of Authorship: Scholastic Literary Attitudes in the Later Middle Ages*, 2nd ed., Philadelphia, 1988, 22, 57–58; Warren Ginsburg, "'*Ovidius Ethicus?*' Ovid and the Medieval Commentary Tradition," in *Desiring Discourse: the Literature of Love*, ed. James J. Paxson and Cynthia A. Gravlee, Selinsgrove, P.A., 1998, 62–71.

36. Fausto Ghisalberti, "Mediaeval Biographies of Ovid," *Journal of the Warburg and Courtauld Institute* 9 (1946), 45.

37. Hexter, 72; See also Woods.

38. J. P. Migne, ed., *Patrologia Latina*, Paris, 1854, 184.379. Translations are from Thomas X. Davis, *William of St. Thierry: The Nature and Dignity of Love*, Kalamazoo, Mich., 1981, 47.

39. *Patrologia Latina* 184.381; Davis, 49.

40. Marie de France's *Guigemar* offers a brief comment on Ovid's status in twelfth-century literary cultures: in *Guigemar*, the Jealous Husband has imprisoned his wife in a chamber decorated with wall paintings depicting Venus endorsing the "nature" and "obligations" of love; as part of this tableau, Venus tosses an Ovidian text into the fire; the text is described as "Le livre Ovide, ou il enseigne / Comment chascun s'amur estreine"(239–40) ["The book of Ovid where he teaches how one controls love"]. Marie de France, *Lais*, ed. Jeanne Lods, Paris, 1959. While the text in question is often taken to be the *Remedia amoris*, the description could just as readily denote the *Ars amatoria* and its cynical advice on the manipulation of lovers outside of marriage. A jealous husband would not wish to endorse the pedagogical objectives of the *Ars*.

41. For a discussion of the presence of the *Ars amatoria* in the romances of Chrétien de Troyes, see Lewis, 24–32.

42. The *Ars amatoria* was not translated into English until the early sixteenth century; see M. L. Stapleton, *Thomas Heywood's Art of Love: the First Complete English Translation of Ovid's Ars amatoria*, Ann Arbor, Mich., 2000. For French printed versions of the *Ars amatoria*, see W. L. Wiley, ed., *Pierre Le Loyer's Version of the Ars amatoria*, University of North Carolina Studies in the Romance Languages and Literature 3, Chapel Hill, 1941.

43. See Judith L. Kellogg, "Transforming Ovid: The Metamorphosis of Female Authority," in *Christine de Pizan and the Categories of Difference*, ed. Marilynn Desmond, Minneapolis, 1998, 181–94.

Chapter 3. Dominus/Ancilla

1. The text for the *Historia calamitatum* is taken from *Historia calamitatum*, ed. Jacques Monfrin, Paris, 1962; for the letters, J. T. Muckle, "The Personal Letters between Abelard and Heloise," *MS* 15 (1953), 47–94; "The Letter of Heloise on the Religious Life and Abelard's First Reply," ibid., 17 (1955), 240–81.

2. There exists an anonymous collection of Latin letters, most of which are in prose, that may be identified as the letters exchanged between Abelard and Heloise early in their relationship. See Constant J. Mews, *The Lost Love Letters of Heloise and Abelard*, New York, 1999; see also Constant J. Mews, "Philosophical Themes in the *Epistolae duorum amantium:* The First Letters of Heloise and Abelard"; John W. Ward and Neville Chiavaroli, "The Young Heloise and Latin Rhetoric: Some Preliminary Comments on the 'Lost' Love Letters and Their Significance," in *Listening to Heloise: The Voice of a Twelfth-Century Woman*, ed. Bonnie Wheeler, New York, 2000, 35–52, 53–119. The letters show similar sensitivity to the prescriptions of the *ars dictaminis*, and the letter writers, especially the woman, are well versed in Ovid. For the purposes of this study, I have focused on the later letters that are signed by Heloise and that were collected by her at the Paraclete, what Mary Martin McLaughlin calls the "Paraclete Letters"; see Mary Martin McLaughlin, "Heloise the Abbess: The Expansion of the Paraclete," in *Listening to Heloise*, 1–18.

3. Robert L. Benson, "Protohumanism and Narrative Technique in Early Thirteenth-century Italian "Ars Dictaminis," in *Boccaccio: Secoli di vita: Atti del Congresso Internazionale: Boccaccio 1975. Università di California, Los Angeles 17–19 Ottobre, 1975*, eds. Marga Cottino-Jones and Edward F. Tuttle, Ravenna, 1977, 31–50; Ronald Witt, "Medieval 'Ars Dictaminis' and the Beginnings of Humanism: a New Construction of the Problem," *Renaissance Quarterly* 35 (1982), 1–35; Martin Camargo, "Where's the Brief?: The *Ars dictaminis* and Reading/Writing between the Lines," *Disputatio* 1 (1996), 1–17; "Toward a Comprehensive Art of Written Discourse: Geoffrey of Vinsauf and the *Ars Dictaminis*," *Rhetorica* 6 (1988), 167–94; Carol Dana Lanham, "Freshman Composition in the Early Middle Ages: Epistolography and Rhetoric before the *Ars dictaminis*," *Viator* 23 (1992), 115–34; William D. Patt, "The Early 'Ars dictaminis' as Response to a Changing Society," ibid., 9 (1979), 133–55; Jean Leclerq, "Le genre epistolaire au Moyen Age," *Revue des deux mondes* 2 (1946), 63–70.

4. James J. Murphy, *Rhetoric in the Middle Ages: A History of Rhetorical Theory from Saint Augustine to the Renaissance*, Berkeley, Calif., 1974, 194–268.

5. Giles Constable, "The Structure of Medieval Society according to the *Dictatores* of the Twelfth Century," in *Law, Church and Society: Essays in Honor of Stephan Kuttner*, eds. Kenneth Pennington and Robert Sommerville, Philadelphia, 1977, 253–67.

6. For a study of the *Heroides* and medieval epistolary collections, see Gerald A. Bond, *The Loving Subject: Desire, Eloquence, and Power in Romanesque France*, Philadelphia, 1995, 42–69. On *Heroides* 7, see my *Reading Dido: Gender, Textuality, and the Medieval Aeneid*, Minneapolis, 1994, 33–45.

7. As Barbara Newman puts it: "It is likely that Heloise had read both Ovid and Jerome, as well as Seneca, Lucan, Cicero, and a variety of ecclesiastical authors, before she ever laid eyes on Abelard." "Authority, Authenticity and the Repression of Heloise," in *From Virile Woman to WomanChrist: Studies in Medieval Religion and Liter-*

ature, Philadelphia, 1995, 69. On the education of Heloise, see Joan M. Ferrante, "The Education of Women in the Middle Ages in Theory, Fact, and Fantasy," in *Beyond Their Sex: Learned Women of the European Past*, ed. Patricia H. Labalme, New York, 1980, 9–42; on Heloise's citations of classical material, see Helen C. R. Laurie, *The Making of Romance: Three Studies*, Geneva, 1991, 96–118. On the significance of Heloise's reading of Seneca, see Martin Irvine, "Heloise and the Gendering of the Literate Subject," in *Criticism and Dissent in the Middle Ages*, ed. Rita Copeland, Cambridge, 1996, 87–114. On Heloise and Augustine, see Nancy A. Jones, "By Woman's Tears Redeemed: Female Lament in St. Augustine's *Confessions* and the Correspondence of Abelard and Heloise," in *Sex and Gender in Medieval and Renaissance Texts: The Latin Tradition* ed. Barbara K. Gold, Paul Allen Miller, and Charles Platter, Albany, N.Y., 1997, 15–39. For a romanticized view of Heloise's reading of Ovid, see Michael Calabrese, "Ovid and the Female Voice in the *De amore* and the Letters of Abelard and Heloise," *Modern Philology* 95 (1997), 1–26. On Heloise and the discourse of monasticism, see Linda Georgianna, "Any Corner of Heaven: Heloise's Critique of Monasticism," *MS* 49 (1987), 221–53. See also, Michael T. Clanchy, *Abelard: A Medieval Life,* Oxford, 1997.

8. On the importance of the *Ars amatoria* in the medieval classroom, see Ralph Hexter, *Ovid and Medieval Schooling: Studies in Medieval School Commentaries on Ovid's* Ars amatoria, Epistulae ex Ponto, *and* Epistulae Heroidum, Munich, 1986, 23–25; see also John Baldwin, *The Language of Sex: Five Voices from Northern France Around 1200*, Chicago, 1994, 20–23.

9. Peter Dronke, *Women Writers of the Middle Ages*, Cambridge, 1984, 112. For a thorough study of Heloise's use of the *Heroides*, see Phyllis R. Brown and John C. Pfeiffer II, "Heloise, Dialectic, and the *Heroides*," in *Listening to Heloise*, 143–60.

10. Dronke, *Women Writers*, 107–39.

11. Leonard Barkan, *Transuming Passion: Ganymede and the Erotics of Humanism*, Stanford, 1991, 48–49. On violence in the medieval classroom, see Jody Enders, *Medieval Theater of Cruelty: Rhetoric, Memory, Violence*, Ithaca, N.Y., 1999, 63–67, 129–52; Enders discusses this passage in "Rhetoric, Coercion and the Memory of Violence," in *Criticism and Dissent*, 24–55.

12. On corporal punishment in the classical era, see Stanley F. Bonner, *Education in Ancient Rome: From the Elder Cato to the Younger Pliny*, Berkeley, Calif., 1977, 143–45; for the medieval era, see Pierre Riché, *Les écoles et l'enseignement dans l'Occident chrétien de la fin du Ve siècle au milieu du XIe siècle*, Paris, 1979, 208–9; James J. Murphy, "The Teaching of Latin as a Second Language in the 12th Century," *Historiographia linguistica* 7 (1980), 159–75; Cora E. Lutz, *Schoolmasters of the Tenth Century*, Hamden, Conn., 1977, 75–86.

13. On the intensity of the relationship between *magister* and *discipulus* in the medieval classroom, see Stephen C. Jaeger, *Envy of Angels: Cathedral Schools and Social Ideals in Medieval Europe, 950–1200*, Philadelphia, 1994, 104–6.

14. Catherine Brown comments specifically on this scene: "Such violence resists interpretation as a powerful man's abuse of a helpless woman. Abelard's introduction of the erotic scene leads one to expect this, but the *Historia* delivers something more disturbing because less easily explained: a passionate relation mutually constructed through mutual violence to pleasurable ends." *"Muliebriter:* Doing Gender in the

Letters of Heloise," in *Gender and the Text in the Later Middle Ages*, ed. Jane Chance, Gainesville, Fla., 1996, 30.

15. For a general discussion of public and private in the letters of Heloise, see Glenda McLeod, " 'Wholly Guilty, Wholly Innocent': Self-Definition in Heloise's Letters to Abelard," in *Dear Sister: Medieval Women and the Epistolary Genre*, ed. Karen Cherewatuk and Ulrike Wiethaus, Philadelphia, 1993, 64–86.

16. See Peggy Kamuf, *Fictions of Feminine Desire: Disclosures of Heloise*, Lincoln, Neb. 1982, 43. For a psychoanalytic discussion of castration in relation to Abelard, see Jean-Charles Huchet, "La Voix d'Héloïse," *Romance Notes* 25 (1985), 271–87.

17. On Abelard's castration, see Bonnie Wheeler, "Origenary Fantasies: Abelard's Castration and Confession," in *Becoming Male in the Middle Ages*, ed. Jeffrey Jerome Cohen and Bonnie Wheeler, New York, 1997, 107–28; Yves Ferroul, "Abelard's Blissful Castration," ibid., 129–49; and Martin Irvine, "Abelard and (Re)Writing the Male Body: Castration, Identity, and Remasculinization," ibid., 87–106.

18. Jacques Derrida, *The Post Card: From Socrates to Freud and Beyond*, trans. Alan Bass, Chicago, 1987, 477. For Lacan's seminar, see *The Purloined Poe: Lacan, Derrida, and Psychoanalytic Reading*, ed. John P. Muller and William J. Richardson, Baltimore, 1988.

19. See Newman, Irvine. For a discussion of sublimation as an explanation of Heloise's dedication to learning, see Nancy Partner, "No Sex, No Gender," *Speculum* 68 (1993), 419–43.

20. Kaja Silverman, *Male Subjectivity at the Margins*, London, 1992, 47.

21. For a discussion of the *salutatio* as the unit of the *ars dictaminis* that expresses social hierarchy, see Martin Camargo, *Ars dictaminis, ars dictandi*, Turnhout, 1991, 22. For the history of salutation formulas, see Carol D. Lanham, *Salutatio Formulas in Latin Letters to 1200: Syntax, Style, and Theory*, Münchener Beiträge zur Mediävistik und Renaissance-Forschung 22, Munich, 1975.

22. See Pat Califia, "The Limits of the S/M Relationship," *Outlook* 15 (1992), 16–21; Califia, "Feminism and Sadomasochism," *Heresies* 12 (1981), 30–34; and Susan Farr, "The Art of Discipline: Creating Erotic Dramas of Play and Power," in *Coming to Power: Writings and Graphics on Lesbian S/M*, 3d ed., Boston, 1987, 183–91.

23. Jessica Benjamin, *The Bonds of Love: Psychoanalysis, Feminism, and the Problem of Domination*, New York, 1988, 52.

24. "non mihi, sacrilegas meretricum ut persequar artes, / cum totidem linguis sint satis ora decem" (*Ars* 1.435–36) ["Not ten mouths, nor as many tongues would be enough for me to tell the profane arts of the meretrix"]. Ovid employs *meretrix* to denote the female lover in the following poems: *Amores* 1.10.21, 1.15.18, 3.14.0; *Ep. Sappho* 63.

25. Claire Nouvet, "The Discourse of the 'Whore': An Economy of Sacrifice," *Modern Language Notes* 105 (1990), 761.

26. Helen Solterer asserts the significance of the medieval investment in an "analogy between words and physical blows. In a preprint society such as the medieval world, this link was acutely felt, and with it the fundamental connection between words and action." *The Master and Minerva: Disputing Women in French Medieval Culture*, Berkeley, Calif., 1995, 11.

27. Text and translation from *Peter Abelard's Ethics*, ed. and trans. D. E. Luscombe,

Oxford, 1971, 13–15. For a discussion of the "ethic of intention" as a philosophical category elaborated by both Abelard and Heloise in the exchange of letters, see Mary McLaughlin, "Abelard as Autobiographer," *Speculum* 42 (1967), 485; John Marenbon, "Abelard's Ethical Theory: Two Definitions from the *Collationes*," in *From Athens to Chartres: Neoplationism and Medieval Thought*, ed. Haijo Jan Westra, Leiden, 1992, 301–14; William E. Mann, "Ethics," in *The Cambridge Companion to Abelard*, ed. Jeffrey E. Brower and Kevin Guilfoy, Cambridge, 2004, 279–304; Maurice de Gandillac, "Intention et loi dans l'éthique d'Abélard," in *Pierre Abélard—Pierre le Vénérable*, Paris, 1975, 585–610; D. E. Luscombe, "The *Ethics* of Abelard: Some Further Considerations," in *Peter Abelard: Proceedings of the International Conference, Louvain May 10–12, 1971*, ed. E. M. Buytaert, Louvain, 1974, 65–84. As Chris D. Ferguson notes, "Abelard completed the *Ethica* (c. 1135–39) not long after the *Historia calamitatum* (c. 1132), and likely was working on the *Ethica* while also composing the *Historia calamitatum*"; see "Autobiography as Therapy: Guibert de Nogent, Peter Abelard, and the Making of Medieval Autobiography," *Journal of Medieval and Renaissance Studies* 13 (1983), 204. Although Abelard is historically credited with the concept of the "ethic of intention," it is significant that both Abelard and Heloise seem to share a philosophical command of the concept, and it emerges in both the letters and his treatise at roughly the same time. As Peter Dronke notes in another context, "the parallels between Heloise's third letter and contributions to the *Problemata*, and works of Abelard's such as the *Sic et Non* and the *Ethica*, may be better explicable in terms of Abelard's and Heloise's shared pursuit of certain problems than in terms of her slavishly repeating things he had already set down in written form" (*Women Writers*, 112).

28. Martin Irvine generally characterizes the desire in the Abelard/Heloise correspondence as repressed, and he sees this passage as emblematic of Heloise's "unfulfilled desire" (105).

29. See Monfrin, 60; On the various issues surrounding the authenticity of Heloise's letters, see Newman. Newman comments that the letters "could have been preserved only at the Paraclete, where it was Heloise and not Abelard who had leisure to put them in publishable form" (55).

30. On references to the letter collection in the medieval period, see Peter Dronke, *Intellectuals and Poets in Medieval Europe*, Rome, 1992, 247–94.

31. Peter Abelard, *La Vie et les epistres: Pierres Abaelart et Heloys sa fame: Traduction du XIIIe siècle attribuée à Jean de Meun*, ed. Eric Hicks, Paris, 1991.

32. See Carla Bozzolo, "L'humaniste Gontier Col et la traduction française des lettres d'Abélard et Héloïse," *Romania* 95 (1974), 199–215.

33. See Hicks, xx.

34. See Leslie C. Brook, "The Translator and His Reader: Jean de Meun and the Abelard-Heloise Correspondence," in *The Medieval Translator*, vol. 2, ed. Roger Ellis, London, 1991, 99–122; Brook, "Reiterated Quotations and Statements in Jean de Meun's Translation of the Abelard-Heloise Correspondence," *Zeitschrift für romanische Philologie* 105 (1989), 81–91. See also Dronke, *Intellectuals*, 275.

35. See Leslie C. Brook, ed., *Two Late Medieval Love Treatises: Heloise's Art d'Amour and a Collection of Demandes d'Amour*, Medium Aevum Monographs, Exeter, 1993.

Chapter 4. *Tote Enclose*

1. Text of the *Roman de la Rose* from Félix Lecoy, *Le Roman de la Rose*, 3 vols., Paris, 1970. Translations from Frances Horgan, *The Romance of the Rose*, Oxford, 1994.

2. On clothing and sexuality in medieval sexualities, see E. Jane Burns, "Refashioning Courtly Love: Lancelot as Ladies' Man or Lady/Man?" in *Constructing Medieval Sexuality*, ed. Karma Lochrie, Peggy McCracken, and James A. Schultz, Minneapolis, 1997, 111–34.

3. On this passage in relation to the text as a whole, see Sarah Kay, "Sexual Knowledge: The Once and Future Texts of the *Romance of the Rose*," in *Textuality and Sexuality: Reading Theories and Practices*, ed. Judith Still and Michael Worton, Manchester, 1993, 69–86. For discussions of sexuality and the *Rose*, see Sarah Kay, "The Birth of Venus in the *Roman de la Rose*," *Exemplaria* 9 (1997), 7–37; Sylvia Huot, "Bodily Peril: Sexuality and the Subversion of Order in Jean de Meun's *Roman de la Rose*," *Modern Language Review* 95 (2000), 41–61.

4. On Jean de Meun's use of Alain de Lille, see Susan Schibanoff, "Sodomy's Mark: Alan of Lille, Jean de Meun, and the Medieval Theory of Authorship," in *Queering the Middle Ages*, ed. Glenn Burger and Steven F. Kruger, Minneapolis, 2001, 28–56; Winthrop Wetherbee, "The Literal and the Allegorical: Jean de Meun and the *De Planctu Naturae*" *MS* 33 (1971), 264–91.

5. The editor of Jacques d'Amiens' *Art d'amours* suggests that this translation could be dated in the late fourteenth century; Jakes d'Amiens, *L'Art d'amours (XIIe eeuw)*, ed. Deeuwes Talsma, Utrecht, 1925, xlv.

6. Ernest Langlois identified Jean de Meun as a poet-translator; see *Origines et Sources du Roman de la Rose*, Paris, 1890, 173–74. See also Peter F. Dembowski, "Learned Latin Treatises in French: Inspiration, Plagiarism, and Translation," *Viator* 17 (1986), 255–69; on the relationship between the *Ars amatoria* and Guillaume's section of the *Rose*, see H. Marshall Leicester Jr., "Ovid Enclosed: The God of Love as *Magister Amoris* in the *Roman de la Rose* of Guillaume de Lorris," *Res Publica Litterarum: Studies in the Classical Tradition* 7 (1984), 107–29. For a general discussion of Ovid and the *Roman de la Rose*, see E. K. Rand, "The Metamorphosis of Ovid in 'Le Roman de la Rose,'" *Studies in the History of Culture*, ed. Percy W. Long, Menasha, Wis., 1942, 103–21; Edmond Faral, "*Le Roman de la Rose* et la pensée Française au XIIIe siècle," in *Revue des Deux Mondes* 35 (1926), 430–52. On the Ovidian discourse in the *Rose*, see Peter L. Allen, *The Art of Love: Amatory Fiction from Ovid to the Romance of the Rose*, Philadelphia, 1992.

7. For a text of the *Art d'amours*, see Bruno Roy, *L'Art d'amours: Traduction et commentaire de la "Ars amatoria" d'Ovide. Edition critique*, Leiden, 1974; translations from Lawrence B. Blonquist, trans., *L'art d'amours*, New York, 1987. See also Nico H. J. Van den Boogaard, "*L'Art d'aimer* en prose," in *Études de civilisation médiévale (IXe–XIIe siècles): Mélanges offerts à Edmond-René Labande*, Poitiers, 1974, 687–98. On the medieval translations of the *Ars amatoria*, see Gaston Paris, "Chrétien Legouais et autres traducteurs ou imitateurs d'Ovide," *Histoire Littéraire de la France* 29 (1885), 455–525; Robert H. Lucas, "Mediaeval French Translations of the Latin Classics to 1500," *Speculum* 45 (1970), 241–42. On the *Art d'amours*, see Alastair J. Minnis, *Magister amoris: The Roman de la Rose and Vernacular Hermeneutics*, Oxford, 2001, 44–62. Paul

Demats places the *Roman de la Rose* in the tradition of the medieval translations of the *Ars amatoria*. See "Poésie et doctrine courtoise au XIIIe siècle: *Le Roman de la Rose*," *Histoire de la literature française*, ed. Jacques Roger and Jean-Charles Payen, Vol. 1, Paris, 1969, 70–81. See also Pierre-Yves Badel, *Le Roman de la Rose au XIVe siècle: Étude de la réception de l'oeuvre*, Geneva, 1980, 144–60.

8. See Blonquist, xxvii–xxvix.

9. For text, see *La Clef d'amors: Texte critique*, ed. Auguste Doutrepont, Halle, 1890.

10. On the relationship between the *Clef d'amors* and Guillaume de Lorris' section of the *Roman de la Rose*, see Langlois, 160–65.

11. For text, see Louis Karl, ed. "L'Art d'Amors par Guiart," *Zeitschrift für Romanische Philologie* 44 (1924), 66–80, 181–87; On the *Clef d'amors*, see Reginald Hyatte, "Ovidius, Doctor Amoris: The Changing Attitudes towards Ovid's Eroticism in the Middle Ages as Seen in the Three Old French Adaptations of the *Remedia amoris*," *Florilegium* 4 (1982), 123–36.

12. Text of Maistre Elie from H. Kühne, ed., *Maître Elie's Überarbeitung der ältesten französischen Übertragung von Ovid's Ars amatoria,* Marburg, 1886.

13. For the text of Jacques d'Amiens, see above, note 5.

14. On the allegorical form of Guillaume's portion of the *Rose*, see Hans Robert Jauss, "La transformation de la forme allégorique entre 1180 et 1240: D'Alain de Lille à Guillaume de Lorris," in *L'Humanisme médiéval dans les littératures romanes du XIIe au XIVe siècle*, ed. Anthime Fourrier, Paris, 1964, 107–46; on Jean de Meun and allegory, see Marc-René Jung, "Jean de Meun et l'Allégorie," *Cahiers de l'Association Internationale des Etudes Françaises* 28 (1976), 21–36.

15. Huot notes that citations from the *Ars amatoria* frequently show up in marginal glosses in *Rose* manuscripts; see specifically her discussion of Arsenal Ms. 3337 and BnF fr. 24390. *The Romance of the Rose and Its Medieval Readers: Interpretation, Reception, Manuscript Transmission*, Cambridge, 1993, 48, 55, 65.

16. See Pierre-Yves Badel, *Le Roman de la Rose au XIVe siècle*, 142–43; Francesco Novati, *Attraverso il medio evo*, Bari, 1905.

17. Huot, *The Romance of the Rose and Its Medieval Readers*, 59.

18. For a discussion of the use of Ovidian myths from the *Metamorphoses* as a "thematic system" that integrates the two sections of the *Rose*, see Sylvia Huot, "The Medusa Interpolation in the *Roman de la Rose:* Mythographic Program and Ovidian Intertext," *Speculum* 62 (1987), 865–77. See also Huot, "From *Roman de la Rose* to *Roman de la Poire*: The Ovidian Tradition and the Poetics of Courtly Literature," *Medievalia et Humanistica*, n.s. 13 (1985), 95–111.

19. See John V. Fleming, "Jean de Meun and the Ancient Poets," in Kevin Brownlee and Huot, *Rethinking the Romance of the Rose*, Philadelphia, 1992, 81–100; on Jean de Meun and the *Amores*, see Leslie Cahoon, "Raping the Rose: Jean de Meun's Reading of Ovid's *Amores*," *Classical and Modern Literature* 6 (1986), 261–85.

20. Langlois demonstrated that adaptations from Ovid's *Ars amatoria* account for about thirteen hundred lines of Jean de Meun's *Rose*; more than half of these citations are drawn from *Ars amatoria* 3, the book in which Ovid's *praeceptor* addresses female readers, 119–21.

21. Thérèse Bouché, "Ovide et Jean de Meun," *Le Moyen Age* 83 (1977), 71–87.

22. Huot notes that from Michel Alès, the clerical scribe of BnF fr. 25525, "Ami's recommendation . . . that the Lover use force to pluck the Rose, drew two

"Nota bene" signs, placed at vv. 7661–62 and 7666–70, and the comment 'Dum locus affuerit te precor esses virum' [when the opportunity presents itself, I pray you, be a man (fol. 158r), var. of *Pamphilus.*, v. 546]." *The Romance of the Rose and Its Medieval Readers,* 44.

23. For a discussion of the Jaloux's point of view as separate from that of Jean de Meun and Ami, see Lionel J. Friedman, "Jean de Meung, 'Antifeminism,' and 'Bourgeois Realism,' " *Modern Philology* 57 (1959–60), 13–23; for a discussion of the Jaloux in relation to the *fabliaux* see Richard Spencer, "The Treatment of Women in the *Roman de la Rose,* the *Fabliaux* and the *Quinze Joyes de Mariage,*" *Marche romane* 28 (1978), 207–14. For a general discussion of the ambiguity of speaking voices in the *Roman de la Rose,* see David F. Hult, "Closed Quotations: the Speaking Voice in the *Roman de la Rose,*" *Yale French Studies* 67 (1984), 248–69; on the status of the narrator, see Claire Nouvet, "A Reversing Mirror: Guillaume de Lorris' *Romance of the Rose,*" in *Faux Titre: Études de langue et littérature françaises* 179 (2000), 189–205; Eva Martin, "Away from Self-Authorship: Multiplying the 'Author' in Jean de Meun's *Roman de la Rose,*" *Modern Philology* 96 (1998), 1–15.

24. On the myth of the Golden Age, see Paul B. Milan, "The Golden Age and the Political Theory of Jean de Meun: A Myth in *Rose* Scholarship," *Symposium* 23 (1969), 137–49; F. W. A. George, "Jean de Meung and the Myth of the Golden Age," in *The Classical Tradition in French Literature: Essays Presented to R. C. Knight by Colleagues, Pupils and Friends,* ed. H. T. Barnwell, London, 1977, 31–39; Marc-René Jung, "Jean de Meun et son lecteur," *Romanistische Zeitschrift für Literaturgeschichte* 2 (1978), 241–45.

25. Huot notes that BnF fr. 25524 has cut the Jaloux from the discourse of the Ami, *The Romance of the Rose and Its Medieval Readers,* 140. The speech of the Jaloux has not always troubled twentieth-century scholars; for instance, see the comment on the Jaloux in Charles Muscatine, *Chaucer and the French Tradition,* Berkeley, Calif., 1957, 88–90.

26. See Peter Dronke, "Abelard and Heloise in Medieval Testimonies," in *Intellectuals and Poets in Medieval Europe,* Rome, 1992, 247–94.

27. For a discussion of Heloise in the *Roman de la Rose,* see Emmanuèle Baumgartner, "De Lucrèce a Héloise, Remarques sur deux *exemples* du *Roman de la Rose* de Jean de Meun," *Romania* 95 (1974), 433–42.

28. On the castration of Abelard in relation to the text as a whole, see David F. Hult, "Language and Dismemberment: Abelard, Origen, and the *Roman de la Rose,*" in Brownlee and Huot, 101–30.

29. On the visuality of the *Rose,* see Claire Nouvet, "On the Way toward Love," *American Imago* 50 (1993), 325–51; Patricia J. Eberle, "The Lovers' Glass: Nature's Discourse on Optics and the Optical Design of the *Roman de la Rose,*" *University of Toronto Quarterly* 46 (1976–77), 241–62. On the topic of optics in the *Rose,* see Claire Nouvet, "An Allegorical Mirror: The Pool of Narcissus in Guillaume de Lorris' *Romance of the Rose,*" *Romanic Review* 91 (2000), 353–65.

30. For discussions of *Rose* illustration, see Marilynn Desmond and Pamela Sheingorn, *Myth, Montage, and Visuality in Late Medieval Manuscript Culture: Christine de Pizan's Othea,* Ann Arbor, Mich., 2003, 47–83; Deborah McGrady, "Reinventing the *Roman de la Rose* for a Woman Reader: The Case of Ms. Douce 195," *Journal of the Early Book Society for the Study of Manuscripts and Printing History* 4 (2001), 202–

27; Simon Gaunt, "Bel Acueil and the Improper Allegory of the *Romance of the Rose*," *New Medieval Literatures* 2 (1998), 65–93l Suzanne Lewis, "Images of Opening, Penetration and Closure in the *Roman de la Rose*," *Word and Image* 8 (1992), 215–42; Meradith T. McMunn, "Representations of the Erotic in Some Illustrated Manuscripts of the *Roman de la Rose*," *Romance Languages Annual* 4 (1992), 125–30; Lori Walters, "A Parisian Manuscript of the *Romance of the Rose*," *Princeton University Library Chronicle* 51 (1989), 31–55; John V. Fleming, *The Roman de la Rose: A Study in Allegory and Iconography*, Princeton, N.J., 1970. Rosemund Tuve, *Allegorical Imagery: Some Mediaeval Books and Their Posterity*, Princeton, 1966, 246–80. Several manuscripts are available in complete digitized form on the *Romance of the Rose* site: http: // rose.mse.jhu.edu

31. See Philippe Ménard, "Les Représentations des vices sur les murs du verger du *Roman de la Rose*: Le texte et les enluminures," *Texte et Image: Actes du colloque international de Chantilly (3 au 15 octobre 1982)*, Paris, 1984, 177–90.

32. Huot, *The Romance of the Rose*.

33. Patrick de Winter dates this manuscript to 1403–4; he suggests that the artist of this manuscript is the same who illustrated two manuscripts of Christine's *Chemin de long estude*. This date makes this manuscript too late to have shaped either Chaucer's understanding of the *Roman de la Rose* or Christine's characterizations of the *Rose* during the *Querelle de la Rose*. See Patrick de Winter, *La Bibliothèque de Philippe le Hardi, duc de Bourgogne (1364–1404): Étude sur les manuscrits à peintures d'une collection princière à l'époque du "style gothique international,"* Paris, 1985, 298–99.

34. For a discussion of the violent tenor of the Valencia manuscript, see Desmond and Sheingorn, 50–53.

35. On the embrace, see Pamela Sheingorn, "The Bodily Embrace or Embracing the Body: Gesture and Gender in Late Medieval Culture," in *The Stage as Mirror: Civic Theatre in Late Medieval Europe*, ed. Alan E. Knight, Cambridge, 1997, 51–89.

36. Jody Enders, *Medieval Theater of Cruelty: Rhetoric, Memory, Violence*, Ithaca, N.Y., 1999, 66–78.

37. On the cultural connections between prostitution and sexuality, see Ruth Mazo Karras, *Common Women: Prostitution and Sexuality in Medieval England*, New York, 1996.

38. Heather Arden briefly discusses the Vieille in relation to the Jaloux, see "Women as Readers, Women as Text in the *Roman de la Rose*," in *Women, the Book and the Worldly: Selected Proceedings of the St. Hilda's Conference, 1993*, vol. 2, ed. Lesley Smith and Jane H. M. Taylor, Cambridge, 1995, 111–17.

39. Gaunt; see also: Jo Ann Moran, "Literature and the Medieval Historian," *Medieval Perspectives* 10 (1995), 49–66; Marta Powell Harley, "Narcissus, Hermaphroditus, and Attis: Ovidian Lovers at the Fontaine d'Amors in Guillaume de Lorris's *Roman de la rose*," *PMLA* 101 (1986), 324–37.

40. On the category of experience in the *Rose*, see Nancy Freeman Regalado, " 'Des Contraires Choses': La Fonction poétique de la citation et des *exempla* dans le *Roman de la Rose* de Jean de Meun," *Littérature* 41 (1981), 62–81; Kevin Brownlee, "Reflections in the *Miroër aus Amoreus*: The Inscribed Reader in Jean de Meun's *Roman de la Rose*," in *Mimesis: From Mirror to Method*, ed. John D. Lyons and Stephen G. Nichols Jr., Hanover, N.H., 1982, 60–70, 257–58.

41. Sarah Kay notes that the speech of the Vieille functions as a university lec-

ture, see "Women's Body of Knowledge: Epistemology and Misogyny in the *Romance of the Rose*," in *Framing Medieval Bodies*, ed. Miri Rubin and Sarah Kay, Manchester, 1994, 211–35.

42. Langlois, 122–23. On *Amores* 1.8, see Nicolas Gross, "Ovid, *Amores* 1.8: Whose Amatory Rhetoric?" *Classical World* 89 (1996), 197–206.

43. See Melinda Marsh Heywood, "The Withered Rose: Seduction and the Poetics of Old Age in the *Roman de la Rose* of Guillaume de Lorris," *French Forum* 25 (2000), 5–22. On the *de Vetula*, see, Dorothy Robathan, *The Pseudo-Ovidian de Vetula: Text, Introduction and Notes*, Amsterdam, 1968; Michèle Gally, "'La Vieille' ou Ovide réinventé," in *Lectures d'Ovide, Publiées à la mémoire de Jean-Pierre Néraudau*, Paris, 2003, 165–74

44. BnF fr. 800, fol. 70v.

45. For a discussion of the text and image of Dido's death in the *Roman de la Rose*, see Marilynn Desmond, *Reading Dido: Gender, Textuality, and the Medieval Aeneid*, Minneapolis, 1994, 50–54.

46. BnF fr. 25524 omits the speech of the Vieille altogether, see Huot, *The Romance of the Rose and Its Medieval Readers*, 141; Rennes, Bib. Mun. 15963 cuts it down, see ibid., 192, no. 25. Most notably, the Rennes manuscript cuts lines 14470–76 from the end of the Vieille's speech where she recounts the beating she received from the one man she says she loved. See also Huot, *The Romance of the Rose and Its Medieval Readers*, 35–36.

47. Indeed, scholars have often noted that *Ars amatoria* 3 seems to be more closely evoked in the speech of the Vieille than are *Ars amatoria* 1 and 2 in the speech of Ami; see Bouché, 77–85.

48. For a discussion of these images, see Desmond and Sheingorn, 51–53.

49. See Joan Cadden, *Meanings of Sex Difference in the Middle Ages: Medicine, Science, and Culture*, Cambridge, 1993, 142–43, 158–59.

50. Kathryn Gravdal, *Ravishing Maidens: Writing Rape in Medieval French Literature and Law*, Philadelphia, 1991, 68.

Chapter 5. The *Vieille Daunce*

1. All quotations from Chaucer's texts from *The Riverside Chaucer*, ed. Larry D. Benson, 3d ed., Boston, 1987.

2. Arlyn Diamond, "Chaucer's Women and Women's Chaucer," in *The Authority of Experience: Essays in Feminist Criticism*, ed. Arlyn Diamond and Lee R. Edwards, Amherst, Mass., 1977, 68.

3. For example, see S. H. Rigby, "The Wife of Bath, Christine de Pizan, and the Medieval Case for Women," *CR* 35 (2000), 133–65; Catherine S. Cox, "Holy Erotica and the Virgin Word: Promiscuous Glossing in the Wife of Bath's Prologue," *Exemplaria* 5 (1993), 207–37; Charles A. Owen, Jr., "Fictions Living Fictions: The Poetics of Voice and Genre in Fragment D of the *Canterbury Tales*," in *Poetics: Theory and Practice in Medieval English Literature* eds. Piero Boitani and Anna Torti, Suffolk, 1991, 37–55; Susan Schibanoff, "Taking the Gold out of Egypt: The Art of Reading as a Woman," in *Gender and Reading*, ed. Elizabeth A. Flynn and Patrocinio Schweickart, Baltimore, 1986, 83–106; Katharina M. Wilson, "*Figmenta vs. Veritas*: Dame Alice and the Medieval Literary Depiction of Women by Women," *Tulsa Studies in Women's*

Literature 4 (1985), 17–32; Marjorie M. Malvern, " 'Who peyntede the leon, tel me who?': Rhetorical and Didactic Roles Played by an Aesopic Fable in the *Wife of Bath's Prologue*," *Studies in Philology* 80 (1983), 238–52. For a discussion of this tendency in Chaucerian criticism, see Elaine Tuttle Hansen, *Chaucer and the Fictions of Gender*, Berkeley, Calif., 1992, 26–57.

4. Frederick J. Furnivall, ed., *Hoccleve's Works*, vol. 1, Early English Text Society, extra series 61, Oxford, 1970.

5. As part of a mumming, a group of wives state: "And for oure partye þe worthy wyff of Bathe / Cane shewe statutes moo þan six or seven / howe wyves make hir housbandes wynne heven" (168–70), E. Hammond, "Lydgate's Mumming at Hertford," *Anglia* 22 (1899), 364–74.

6. John Lydgate, *Minor Poems*, ed. Henry Noble MacCracken, Early English Text Society, Original Series 192, Oxford, 1934.

7. John Skelton, *Poems*, ed. Robert S. Kinsman, Oxford, 1969.

8. Marshall H. Leicester Jr., "The Wife of Bath as Chaucerian Subject," *SAC: Proceedings* 1 (1984), 208.

9. Lee Patterson, " 'For the Wyves Love of Bathe': Feminine Rhetoric and Poetic Resolution in the *Roman de la Rose* and the *Canterbury Tales*," *Speculum* 58 (1983), 668. This article is reprinted in revised form in *Chaucer and the Subject of History*, Madison, Wis., 1991, where this comment is excised. On this comment, see Hansen, *Chaucer and the Fictions of Gender*, 45.

10. Lynne Dickson, "Deflection in the Mirror: Feminine Discourse in *The Wife of Bath's Prologue and Tale*," *SAC* 15 (1993), 61–90; Barrie Ruth Strauss, "The Subversive Discourse of the Wife of Bath: Phallocentric Discourse and the Imprisonment of Criticism," *English Literary History* 55 (1988), 527–54; W. F. Bolton, "The Wife of Bath: Narrator as Victim," *Women and Literature* 1 (1980), 54–65; Robert W. Hanning, "From Eva and Ave to Eglentyne and Alisoun: Chaucer's Insight into the Roles Women Play," *Signs* 2 (1977), 580–99.

11. On the historical basis of experience, see Joan Scott, "Experience," in *Feminists Theorize the Political*, ed. Judith Butler and Joan W. Scott, New York, 1992, 22–40.

12. Satya Mohanty, "The Epistemic Status of Cultural Identity: On *Beloved* and the Postcolonial Condition," in *Reclaiming Identity: Realist Theory and the Predicament of Postmodernism*, ed. Paula M. L. Moya and Michael R. Hames-García, Berkeley, Calif., 2000, 29–66; Sonia Kruks, *Retrieving Experience: Subjectivity and Recognition in Feminist Politics*, Ithaca, N.Y., 2001, 149–52.

13. On the status of the Wife's clothing in the *General Prologue*, see Gerald Morgan, "The Universality of the Portraits in the *General Prologue* to the *Canterbury Tales*," *English Studies* 58 (1977), 481–93. Laura Hodges, *Chaucer and Costume: the Secular Pilgrims in the General Prologue*, Cambridge, 2000, 161–86; Peter G. Beidler, "Chaucer's Wife of Bath's 'Foot-mantel' and Her 'Hipes Large,' " *CR* 34 (2000), 388–97. On the portrait of the Wife in the *General Prologue*, see Warren Ginsberg, "Chaucer's Disposition," in *The Endless Knot: Essays on Old and Middle English in Honor of Marie Borroff*, ed. Teresa Tavormina and R. F. Yeager, Cambridge, 1995, 129–40. On clothing and sexuality in medieval sexualities, see E. Jane Burns, "Refashioning Courtly Love: Lancelot as Ladies' Man or Lady/Man?" in *Constructing Medieval Sexuality*, ed. Karma Lochrie, Peggy McCracken, and James A. Schultz, Minneapolis,

1997, 111–34; Rhonda Knight, "All Dressed Up with Someplace to Go: Regional Identity in *Sir Gawain and the Green Knight*," *SAC* 25(2003), 259–84.

14. On the "animal-human" circuit, see Jeffrey J. Cohen, *Medieval Identity Machines*, Minneapolis, 2003, 41–71. Elspeth Probyn comments on erotics of women as riders, who "move gracefully outside of heterosexual clumsiness"; "Queer Belongings, the Politics of Departure," in *Sexy Bodies: the Strange Carnalities of Feminism*, ed. Elizabeth Grosz and Elspeth Probyn, London, 1995, 11.

15. *Livre de Leesce* 3800–831. Text from *Les Lamentations de Matheolus et le Livre de leesce de Jehan Le Fèvre, de Ressons*, vol. 2, A.-G. Hamel, Bibliothèque de l'école des hautes études 96, Paris, 1905. For a discussion of Jean le Fèvre, see Karen Pratt, "Analogy or Logic; Authority or Experience? Rhetorical Strategies for and against Women," in *Literary Aspects of Courtly Literature*, ed. Donald Maddox and Sara Strum-Maddox, Cambridge, 1994, 57–66; Renate Blumenfeld-Kosinski, "Jean Le Fèvre's *Livre de Leesce*: Praise or Blame of Women?" *Speculum* 69 (1994), 705–25.

16. Zacharias Thundy, "Matheolus, Chaucer, and the Wife of Bath," in *Chaucerian Problems and Perspectives: Essays Presented to Paul E. Beichner*, ed. Edward Vasta and Zacharias Thundy, Terre Haute, Ind., 1979, 24–58. See also Helen Phillips, "Chaucer and Jean le Fèvre," *Archiv für das Studium der neueren Sprachen und Literaturen* 232 (1995), 23–36.

17. A.-G. van Hamel, *Les Lamentations de Matheolus*. Ann Astell notes the connection between Matheolus' version of the "mounted Aristotle" and Chaucer's description of the Wife of Bath, see *Chaucer and the Universe of Learning*, Ithaca, 1996, 159.

18. For a discussion of the portraits in the Ellesmere manuscript see Richard K. Emmerson, "Text and Image in the Ellesmere Portraits of the Tale-Tellers," in *The Ellesmere Chaucer: Essays in Interpretation*, ed. Martin Stevens and Daniel Woodward, San Marino, Calif., 1995, 143–70. While Emmerson stresses that the portraits are placed at the start of each tale, he nonetheless reads them against the text of the *General Prologue,* and he does not find textual support for the whip and the youthfulness of the Wife in the Ellesmere portrait—though both are textually explained by the *Wife of Bath's Prologue* which immediately precedes the portrait. See also Martin Stevens, "The Ellesmere Miniatures as Illustrations of Chaucer's *Canterbury Tales*," *Studies in Iconography* 8 (1982), 113–34; Maidie Hilmo, "Framing the Canterbury Pilgrims for the Aristocratic Readers of the Ellesmere Manuscript," in *The Medieval Professional Reader at Work: Evidence from Manuscripts of Chaucer, Langland, Kempe, and Gower*, ed. Kathryn Kerby-Fulton and Maido Hilmo, Victoria, B.C., 2001, 14–71; Mary C. Olson, *Fair and Varied Forms: Visual Textuality in Medieval Illuminated Manuscripts*, London, 2003, 153–80. For the Cambridge manuscript, see M. B. Parkes and Richard Beadle, *The Poetical Works of Geoffrey Chaucer: A Facsimile of Cambridge Univ. Lib. MS. Gg. 4. 27*, Norman, Okla., 1979.

19. On the connection between premodern trade patterns and early modern colonialisms, see Eric R. Wolf, *Europe and the People without History*, Berkeley, Calif., 1982. See also Anne McClintock, *Imperial Leather: Race, Gender and Sexuality in the Colonial Contest*, New York, 1995.

20. See Mary Carruthers, "The Wife of Bath and the Painting of Lions," *PMLA* 94 (1979), 209–22; Paul Strohm, *Hochon's Arrow: The Social Imagination of Fourteenth-Century Texts*, Princeton, 1992, 139–44.

21. On vernacular versions of the *Remedia amoris*, see Reginald Hyatte, "Ovidius, Doctor Amoris: The Changing Attitudes towards Ovid's Eroticism in the Middle Ages as Seen in the Three Old French Adaptations of the *Remedia amoris*," *Florilegium* 4 (1982), 123–36.

22. For a reading of the Wife of Bath as a figure that encodes "female masculinity," see Glenn Burger, *Chaucer's Queer Nation*, Minneapolis, 2003, 79–100. Burger's powerful and insightful reading—in contrast to mine which places the *Prologue* in an Ovidian and continental tradition—is one that emerges when the Wife is read in the context of the *Canterbury Tales*. Burger's reading is shaped by a Deleuzian approach to issues of embodiment; by contrast, my theoretical approach to the question of embodiment is indebted to Elizabeth Grosz' reading of Deleuze; see *Volatile Bodies: Toward a Corporeal Feminism*, Bloomington, 1994, 160–183.

23. On the confessional discourse of the *Prologue*, see Karma Lochrie, *Covert Operations: The Medieval Uses of Secrecy*, Philadelphia, 1999, 56–61. Lochrie's analysis concludes by privileging gossip over confession in the case of the Wife of Bath. See also Jerry Root, " 'Space to Speke': The Wife of Bath and the Discourse of Confession," *CR* 28 (1994), 252–74.

24. Michel Foucault, *History of Sexuality*, vol. 1, New York, 1978, 62.

25. For the formulation of this idea I am indebted to Adale Sholock.

26. Judith Butler, *Undoing Gender*, New York, 2004, 172.

27. Dianne Chisholm, "The 'Cunning Lingua' of Desire: Bodies-Language and Perverse Performativity," in *Sexy Bodies*, 19–41.

28. See Carolyn Dinshaw, *Chaucer's Sexual Poetics*, Madison, Wis., 1989, 113–26.

29. For the term "lingual performativity," see Eve Kosofsky Sedgwick, *Tendencies*, Durham, N.C., 1993, 11; see also, Chisholm.

30. Joel Rosenthal argues that in late medieval England, old age would have begun at sixty, see *Old Age in Late Medieval England*, Philadelphia, 1996, 171–90. See also Alicia K. Nitecki, "Figures of Old Age in Fourteenth-Century English Literature," in *Aging and the Aged in Medieval Europe,* ed. Michael M. Sheehan, Toronto, 1990, 107–16. For a discussion of the figure of the old woman in medieval texts, see William Matthews, "The Wife of Bath and All Her Sect," *Viator* 5 (1974), 413–43; Margaret Wade Labarge, "Three Medieval Widows and a Second Career," in *Aging and the Aged*, 159–72. Chaucerian critics unquestionably consider the Wife of Bath to be old; see, for instance, Patterson, *Chaucer and the Subject of History*, 292–96. On the status of widows in medieval England, see Barbara A. Hanawalt, "Remarriage as an Option for Urban and Rural Widows in Late Medieval England," in *Wife and Widow in Medieval England*, ed. Sue Sheridan Walker, Ann Arbor, Mich., 1993, 141–64.

31. On the use of authority in the *Prologue*, see Susan Signe Morrison, "Don't Ask, Don't Tell: The Wife of Bath and Vernacular Translations," *Exemplaria* 8 (1996), 97–123; Ralph Hanna III, *Pursuing History: Middle English Manuscripts and Their Texts*, Stanford, 1996, 247–57; David Aers, *Chaucer, Langland and the Creative Imagination*, London, 1980, 143–51; Judith Ferster, *Chaucer on Interpretation*, Cambridge, 1985, 122–38; Susanne Sara Thomas, "What the Man of Law Can't Say: The Buried Legal Argument of the *Wife of Bath's Prologue*," *CR* 31 (1997), 256–71; Warren S. Smith, "The Wife of Bath Debates Jerome," ibid., 32 (1997), 129–45; Susan K. Hagen, "The Wife of Bath: Chaucer's Inchoate Experiment in Feminist Hermeneutics," in *Rebels and Rivals: The Contestive Spirit in the Canterbury Tales*, ed.

Susanna Greer Fein, David Raybin, and Peter C. Braeger, Kalamazoo, Mich., 1991, 105–24.

32. On the sermons on the marriage of Cana, see Andrew Galloway, "Marriage Sermons, Polemic Sermons, and the *Wife of Bath's Prologue*: A Generic Excursus," *SAC* 14 (1992), 3–30.

33. Chaucer's refashioning of the *Roman de la Rose* in the *Canterbury Tales* has long been recognized: scholars have catalogued and analyzed his adaptation of phrases, figures, and exempla from the *Rose*. See Dean Spruill Fansler, *Chaucer and the Roman de la Rose*, Gloucester, Mass., 1914; Charles Muscatine, *Chaucer and the French Tradition: A Study in Style and Meaning*, Berkeley, Calif., 1957, 204–13; F.N.M. Diekstra, "Chaucer and the *Romance of the Rose*," *English Studies* 69 (1988), 12–26; Derek Pearsall, *The Life of Geoffrey Chaucer: A Critical Biography*, Oxford, 1992, 80–82. On Chaucer manuscripts and manuscripts of the *Roman de la Rose*, see Joel Fredell, "The Lowly Paraf: Transmitting Manuscript Design in the *Canterbury Tales*," *SAC* 22 (2000), 213–80. The most synthetic discussion of the *Wife of Bath's Prologue* and the *Roman de la Rose* is Patterson, " 'For the Wyves Love of Bathe.' " On Chaucer and Ovid, see Michael Calabrese, *Chaucer's Ovidian Arts of Love*, Gainesville, Fla., 1994. Calabrese reads the wife as a "New Ovid," 81–107. See also John Fyler, *Chaucer and Ovid*, New Haven, Conn., 1979, 1–22; for a normative reading of Ovid and Chaucer, see Henry Ansgar Kelly, *Love and Marriage in the Age of Chaucer*, Ithaca, 1975, 71–100.

34. Text of the *Roman de la Rose* from Félix Lecoy, ed., *Le Roman de la Rose*, 3 vols., Paris, Champion, 1970. Translations from Frances Horgan, *The Romance of the Rose*, Oxford, 1994.

35. For a text of the *Art d'amours*, see Bruno Roy, *L'Art d'amours: Traduction et commentaire de la "Ars amatoria" d'Ovide. Edition critique*, Leiden, 1974; translations from Lawrence B. Blonquist, *L'art d'amours*, New York, 1987.

36. For a discussion of marriage and prostitution in medieval England, see Ruth Mazo Karras, *Common Women: Prostitution and Sexuality in Medieval England*, Oxford, 1996; Karras discusses the Wife of Bath, 91–92. For a feminist analysis of the ways in which prostitution queers heterosexuality, see Eva Pendelton, "Love for Sale: Queering Heterosexuality," in *Whores and Other Feminists*, ed. Jill Nagle, New York, 1997, 73–82; see also Sheila Delany, *Writing Women: Woman Writers and Women in Literature, Medieval to Modern*, New York, 1983, 76–92.

37. For a discussion of the legal structures that allow the Wife of Bath to acquire wealth through marriage, see Cecile Stoller Margulies, "The Marriages and the Wealth of the Wife of Bath," *MS* 24 (1962), 210–16. On marriage in Chaucer, see Kathryn Jacobs, *Marriage Contracts from Chaucer to the Renaissance Stage*, Gainesville, Fla., 2001, 15–92.

38. Glenn Burger has demonstrated Chaucer's engagement in the institutional discourses of marriage; see *Chaucer's Queer Nation*, 37–77.

39. As Elizabeth M. Makowski observes: "conjugal debt formed a cornerstone for canonical discussions of marital sex." "The Conjugal Debt and Medieval Canon Law," *Journal of Medieval History* 3 (1977), 99–114; see also Mary Flowers Braswell, *Chaucer's Legal Fiction: Reading the Records*, Madison, N.J., 2001, 21–48.

40. For transcriptions of the glosses from the Ellesmere manuscript, see Paul G. Ruggiers, ed., *The Canterbury Tales: A Facsimile and Transcription of the Hengwrt Manuscript with Variants from the Ellesmere Manuscript*, vol. 1 in Paul G. Ruggiers and Don-

ald C. Baker, gen. ed., A Variorum Edition of the Works of Geoffrey Chaucer, Norman 1979.

41. Clive Skidmore, *Practical Ethics for Roman Gentlemen: The Works of Valerius Maximus*, Exeter, 1996, 85.

42. For a discussion of Chaucer's use of exempla, see Larry Scanlon, *Narrative, Authority, and Power: The Medieval Exemplum and the Chaucerian Tradition*, New York, 1994.

43. The reading of "daungerous" in the Riverside editions is based on Skeat's reading; see Walter W. Skeat, ed., *The Complete Works of Geoffrey Chaucer*, Oxford, 1894, vol. 5, 295, 304.

44. George M. Braun, "Old French 'Dangier': A New Interpretation of Its Semantic Origin," *French Review* 7 (1934), 481.

45. See C. S. Lewis, *The Allegory of Love: A Study in Medieval Tradition*, Oxford, 1936, 364–66; as Lewis notes, "It must always be remembered . . . that the various senses we take out of an ancient word by analysis existed in it as a unity" (365). See also Elaine Tuttle Hansen, " 'Of his love daungerous to me': Liberation, Subversion, and Domestic Violence in the *Wife of Bath's Prologue and Tale*," in *Geoffrey Chaucer, The Wife of Bath*, ed. Peter G. Beidler, Boston, 1996, 273–89; Eve Salisbury, "Chaucer's 'Wife,' the Law, and the Middle English Breton Lays," in *Domestic Violence in Medieval Texts*, ed. Eve Salisbury, Georgiana Donavin, and Merrall Llewelyn Price, Gainesville, Fla., 2002, 78.

46. See Meradith T. McMunn, "The Iconography of Dangier in the Illustrated Manuscripts of the *Roman de la Rose*," *Romance Languages Annual* 5 (1993), 86–89.

47. For a discussion of the manuscript tradition of the *Wife of Bath's Prologue*, see Theresa Tinkle, "The Wife of Bath's Textual/Sexual Lives," in *The Iconic Page in Manuscript, Print, and Digital Culture*, ed. George Bornstein and Theresa Tinkle, Ann Arbor, Mich., 1998, 55–88; Beverly Kennedy, "Cambridge MS Dd.4.24: A Misogynous Scribal Revision of the *Wife of Bath's Prologue?*" *CR* 30 (1996), 343–58. On the glosses to the *Canterbury Tales*, see the magisterial article by Susan Schibanoff, "The New Reader and Female Textuality in Two Early Commentaries on Chaucer," *SAC* 10 (1988), 71–108; see also, Graham D. Caie, "The Significance of the Early Chaucer Manuscript Glosses (with Special Reference to the *Wife of Bath's Prologue),*" *CR* 10 (1976), 350–60; Daniel S. Silvia Jr., "Glosses to the *Canterbury Tales* from St. Jerome's *Epistola Adversus Jovinianum,*" *Studies in Philology* 62 (1965), 28–39; John M. Manly and Edith Rickert, *The Text of the Canterbury Tales Studied on the Basis of All Known Manuscripts*, vol. 3, Chicago, 1940, 526–27; Norman Blake, *The Textual Tradition of the Canterbury Tales*, London, 1985, 77–135. See also, Hanna, 247–45.

48. Helen Solterer, *The Master and Minerva: Disputing Women in French Medieval Culture*, Berkeley, Calif., 1995.

49. For a list of these glosses and their relation to other glossed manuscripts of the *Canterbury Tales*, see Manly and Rickert, 496–502.

50. Schibanoff, 79.

51. See Ralph Hanna III and Traugott Lawler, *Jankyn's Book of Wikked Wyves*, Athens, Ga., 1997; Robert A. Pratt, "The Development of the Wife of Bath," in *Studies in Medieval Literature in Honor of Professor Albert Croll Baugh*, ed. MacEdward Leach, Philadelphia, 1961, 45–77; Pratt, "Saint Jerome in Jankyn's Book of Wikked

Wyves," *Criticism* 5 (1963), 316–22; Pratt, "Jankyn's Book of Wikked Wyves: Medieval Antimatrimonial Propaganda in the Universities," *Annuale Mediaevale* 3 (1962), 5–27. Lawler and Hanna attempt to identify the parts of the Wife's discourse that are derived from the texts in Jankyn's book. See also, Ralph Hanna III, *Pursuing History*, 247–57.

52. Monica H. Green, " 'Traittié tout de mençonges':The *Secrés des dames*, "Trotula," and Attitudes toward Women's Medicine in Fourteenth- and Early Fifteenth-Century France," in *Christine de Pizan and the Categories of Difference*, ed. Marilynn Desmond, Minneapolis, 1998, 146–78. See also Morrison; Lorrayne Y. Baird-Lange, "Trotula's Fourteenth-Century Reputation, Jankyn's Book, and Chaucer's Trot," *SAC: Proceedings* 1 (1984), 245–56; Beryl Rowland, "Exhuming Trotula, *Sapiens Materna* of Salerno," *Florilegium* 1 (1979), 42–57; Edward F. Tuttle, "The *Trotula* and Old Dame Trot: A Note on the Lady of Salerno," *Bulletin of the History of Medicine* 50 (1976), 61–72.

53. John T. Noonan Jr., "Marital Affection in the Canonists," *Studia Gratiana* 12 (1967), 479–509.

54. Dinshaw recuperates the violence in this final scene: "the Wife thus describes a marriage relationship . . . that would acknowledge the desires of both sides and would yield satisfaction to both" (125).

55. Teresa de Lauretis, "The Violence of Rhetoric: Considerations on Representation and Gender," in *The Violence of Representation: Literature and the History of Violence*, ed. Nancy Armstrong and Leonard Tennenhouse, London, 1989, 239–58. See also Sharon Marcus, "Fighting Bodies, Fighting Words: A Theory and Politics of Rape Prevention," in *Feminists Theorize the Political*, 385–403.

56. Derek Brewer, *Chaucer: The Critical Heritage*, vol. 1, London, 1978, 39.

57. On the analogues to the *Tale*, see Sigmund Eisner, *A Tale of Wonder: A Source Study of the Wife of Bath's Tale*, Wexford, 1957. See also Colin A. Ireland, " 'A Coverchief or a Calle':The Ultimate End of the Wife of Bath's Search for Sovereignty," *Neophilologus* 75 (1991), 150–59; Christine Rose, "Reading Chaucer, Reading Rape," in *Representing Rape in Medieval and Early Modern Literature*, ed. Christine Rose and Elizabeth Robertson, New York, 2001, 36–37; Angela Jane Weisl, " 'Quiting' Eve:Violence Against Women in the *Canterbury Tales*," in *Violence Against Women in Medieval Texts*, ed. Anna Roberts, Gainesville, Fla., 1998, 115–36.

58. On this exemplum in relation to the figure of the Wife of Bath, see Alcuin Blamires, "Refiguring the 'Scandalous Excess' of Medieval Woman: The Wife of Bath and Liberality," in *Gender in Debate from the Early Middle Ages to the Renaissance*, ed. Thelma S. Fenster and Clare A. Lees, New York, 2002, 57–78. For a discussion of secrets in medieval literary cultures, see Lochrie.

Chapter 6. The *Querelle de la Rose*

1. On Christine's dealings with the English, see James C. Laidlaw, "Christine de Pizan, the Earl of Salisbury and Henry IV," *French Studies* 36 (1982), 129–43. On Christine's attitude towards the English see *Le Livre de l'Advision Cristine*, ed. Christine Reno and Liliane Dulac and Christine Reno, Paris, 2001, 3.2.

2. Text from *The Riverside Chaucer*, ed. Larry D. Benson, 3d ed., Boston, 1987.

3. *Livre de Leesce* l. 3800–31.Text from *Les Lamentations de Matheolus et le Livre de*

leesce de Jehan Le Fèvre, de Ressons, vol. 2, ed. A.-G. Hamel, Bibliothèque de l'école des hautes études 96, Paris, 1905. For a discussion of this passage, see Karen Pratt, "Analogy or Logic; Authority or Experience? Rhetorical Strategies for and against Women," in *Literary Aspects of Courtly Literature*, ed. Donald Maddox and Sara Strum-Maddox, Cambridge, 1994; Renate Blumenfeld-Kosinski, "Jean Le Févre's *Livre de Leesce*: Praise or Blame of Women," *Speculum* 69 (1994), 705–25.

4. On the *Legends* and Ovid's *Heroides* see James Simpson, "Ethics and Interpretation: Reading Wills in Chaucer's *Legend of Good Women*," *SAC* 20 (1998), 73–100; Lisa J. Kiser, *Telling Classical Tales: Chaucer and the Legend of Good Women*, Ithaca, 1983.

5. Text of the *Epistre au dieu d'amours* from Maurice Roy, ed., *Oeuvres poétiques de Christine de Pisan*, vol. 2, Paris, 1886; translation by Kevin Brownlee from *The Selected Writings of Christine de Pizan*, ed. Renate Blumenfeld-Kosinki, New York, 1997. See also Thelma S. Fenster and Mary Carpenter Erler, eds., *Poems of Cupid, God of Love*, Leiden, 1990.

6. See Lori Walters, "The Woman Writer and Literary History: Christine de Pizan's Redefinition of the Poetic *Translatio* in the *Epistre au Dieu d'amours*," French Literature Series 16 (1989), 1–16.

7. The *Epistre* was also adapted into English by Hoccleve in 1402. See Fenster and Erler. On Hoccleve's version of the *Epistre*, see Ethan Knapp, *The Bureaucratic Muse: Thomas Hoccleve and the Literature of Late Medieval England*, University Park, Penn., 2001, 45–75.

8. On the royal chancellery, see Octave Morel, *La Grande chancellerie royale et l'expedition des lettres royaux de l'avènement de Philippe de Valois à la fin du XIVe siècle (1328–1400)* Paris, 1900, 53–100.

9. For the origins of the *Querelle*, see Eric Hicks and Ezio Ornato, "Jean de Montreuil et le débat sur le *Roman de la Rose*," *Romania* 98 (1977), 186–219; Eric Hicks, "The 'Querelle de la Rose' in the *Roman de la Rose*," *Les Bonnes Feuilles* 3 (1974), 152–69; Hicks, "Situation du débat sur le *Roman de la Rose*," in *Une femme de letters au Moyen Age: Études autour de Christine de Pisan*, ed. Liliane Dulac and Bernard Ribémont, Orleans, 1995, 51–67. See also, Charity Cannon Willard, *Christine de Pizan: Her Life and Works*, New York, 1984, 73–90; Pierre-Yves Badel, *Le "Roman de la Rose" au XIVe siècle: Étude de la recéption de l'oeuvre*, Geneva, 1980, 411–91. For studies of Christine's role in the *Querelle*, see Kevin Brownlee, "Discourses of the Self: Christine de Pizan and the *Rose*," *Romanic Review* 79 (1988), 199–21; Karen Sullivan, "At the Limit of Feminist Theory: an Architectonics of the *Querelle de la Rose*," *Exemplaria* 3 (1991), 435–66; Helen Solterer, *The Master and Minerva: Disputing Women in French Medieval Culture*, Berkeley, Calif., 1995, 151–75; Helen Solterer, "Fiction vs. Defamation: The Quarrel over the *Romance of the Rose*," *Medieval History Journal* 2 (1999), 111–41.

10. Texts in the *Querelle* from Eric Hicks, ed., *Le Débat sur le Roman de la Rose*, Geneva, 1996. For a translation of the texts, see J. L. Baird and J. Kane, *La Querelle de la Rose: Letters and Documents*, Chapel Hill, 1978.

11. For descriptions of these manuscripts, see James C. Laidlaw, "Christine de Pizan—an Author's Progress," *Modern Language Review* 78 (1983), 532–50; and "Christine de Pizan—a Publisher's Progress." ibid., 82 (1987), 34–75.

12. The occasional poems, the *Epistre au dieu d'amours* and the *Dite de la Rose*, are

generally not considered to be part of the *Querelle*. For a schematic chronology of the documents and events in the *Querelle*, see Hicks, *Débat*, lii–liv.

13. See Giles Constable, *Letters and Letter-Collections*, Turnhout, 1976, 11: "in the Middle Ages, letters were for the most part self-conscious, quasi-public literary documents, often written with an eye to future collection and publication."

14. Brunetto Latini, *Li Livres dou Tresor*, ed. Francis J. Carmody, Berkeley, Calif., 1948, 322. For a discussion of this aspect of the *ars dictaminis*, see Ronald G. Witt, "Medieval 'Ars Dictaminis' and the Beginnings of Humanism: A New Construction of the Problem," *Renaissance Quarterly* 35 (1982), 17–19; Witt, "Brunetto Latini and the Italian Tradition of *Ars dictaminis*," *Stanford Italian Review* 3 (1983), 5–24.

15. In her letter to Pierre Col, she refers to Jean de Meun's prologue to his translation of Boethius, where he lists all the works he had translated; see Hicks, *Débat*, 121.

16. Martin Camargo, *Ars dictaminis, ars dictandi*, Turnhout, 1991.

17. Giles Constable, "The Structure of Medieval Society according to the *Dictatores* of the Twelfth Century," in *Law, Church and Society: Essays in Honor of Stephan Kuttner*, eds. Kenneth Pennington and Robert Somerville, Philadelphia, 1977, 253–67.

18. On the use of the term "corriger" see Karen Sullivan, "The Inquisitorial Origins of the Literary Debate," *Romanic Review* 88 (1997), 27–51.

19. On the *cour amoureuse* see Carla Bozzolo and Hélène Loyau, *La cour amoureuse: Dite de Charles VI*, 2 vols., Paris, 1982–91; Daniel Poirion, *Le Poète et le prince: L'Évolution du lyrisme courtois de Guillaume de Machaut à Charles d'Orléans*, Paris, 1965, 37–39; Arthur Piaget, "La Cour amoureuse: Dite de Charles VI," *Romania* 20 (1891), 417–54; Alma de L. Le Duc, *Gontier Col and the French Pre-Renaissance*, Lancaster, 1918. Montreuil and the Col brothers were also members of the *cour amoureuse*, though not at the time of the *Querelle*; see le Duc, 54–55.

20. On the *Querelle* and the tradition of the defense of women, see Alcuin Blamires, *The Case for Women in Medieval Culture*, Oxford, 1997.

21. See Pierre-Yves Badel, *Le Roman de la Rose au XIVe siècle*, 135–206; see also Sylvia Huot, *The Romance of the Rose and Its Medieval Readers: Interpretation, Reception, Manuscript Transmission*, Cambridge, 1993, 22–27.

22. A. J. Minnis, "Theorizing the *Rose*: Commentary Tradition in the *Querelle de la Rose*," in *Poetics: Theory and Practice in Medieval English Literature*, ed. Piero Boitani and Anna Torti, Cambridge, 1991, 13–36; Minnis, "Latin to Vernacular: Academic Prologues and the Medieval French Art of Love," in *Medieval and Renaissance Scholarship*, ed. Nicholas Mann and Birger Munk Olsen, New York, 1997, 154–86. For a further discussion of the implications of the academic prologues, see Rosalind Brown-Grant, *Christine de Pizan and the Moral Defence of Women: Reading Beyond Gender*, Cambridge, 1999, 7–51.

23. See Mary Carruthers, "Memory and the Ethics of Reading," in *The Book of Memory: A Study of Memory in Medieval Culture*, Cambridge, 1990, 156–88.

24. While Christine de Pizan was acquainted with the Valencia manuscript of the *Roman de la Rose*, that manuscript was produced in 1403–4, a few years after the composition of the letters in the *Querelle*. See Patrick M. de Winter, *La Bibliothèque de Philippe le Hardi, duc de Bourgogne (1364–1404): Étude sur les manuscrits à peintures*

d'une collection princière à l'époque du "Style gothique international," Paris, 1985, 298–99. For a discussion of the impact that the visual program of the Valencia *Rose* had on Christine's later work, see Marilynn Desmond and Pamela Sheingorn, *Myth, Montage, and Visuality in Late Medieval Manuscript Culture: Christine de Pizan's Othea,* Ann Arbor, Mich., 2003, 47–84.

25. For a discussion of the Col brothers and their approach to Ovid and the classics, see A. Coville, *Gontier et Pierre Col et l'humanisme en France au temps de Charles VI,* Paris, 1934, 99–114.

26. The *Art d'amours* would have certainly been available to Christine de Pizan, since the royal library and the dukes of Berry and Burgundy appear to have owned copies of this text; see Bruno Roy, *L'Art d'amours: Traduction et commentaire de la "Ars amatoria" d'Ovide. Edition critique,* Leiden, 1977, 7. On Christine's knowledge of Latin, see Thelma Fenster, " 'Perdre son Latin': Christine de Pizan and Vernacular Humanism," in *Christine de Pizan and the Categories of Difference,* ed. Marilynn Desmond, Minneapolis, 1998, 91–106.

27. "Se bien veulx et chastement vivre,/De la Rose ne lis le livre/ Ne Ovide de l'Art d'amer,/ Don't l'exemple fait a blasmer," *Oeuvres poétiques de Christine de Pisan,* vol. 3, ed. Maurice Roy, Paris, 1896, 39.

28. Helen Solterer, "Flaming Words: Verbal Violence and Gender in Premodern Paris," *Romanic Review* 86 (1995), 355–78.

29. See Coville, 65.

30. Claire Richter Sherman, *Imaging Aristotle: Verbal and Visual Representation in Fourteenth-Century France,* Berkeley, Calif., 1995, 25. See also Cary J. Nederman, "Aristotelian Ethics and John of Salisbury's Letters," *Viator* 18 (1987), 161–73; for a discussion of ethics and the *Livre de la cité des dames,* see Sarah Kay, "The Didactic Space: The City in Christine de Pizan, Augustine, and Irigaray," in *Text und Kultur: Mittelalterliche Literatur 1150–1450,* ed. Ursula Peters, Stuttgart, 2001, 438–66.

31. Text from Nicole Oresme, *Le Livre de éthiques d'Aristote,* ed. Albert Douglas Menut, New York, 1940.

32. Ibid., 446.

33. See Louis Mourin, *Jean Gerson: Prédicateur Français,* Bruges, 1952, 138–48.

34. Hicks, *Débat,* l.

35. Jean Gerson, *Oeuvres complètes,* ed. Palémon Glorieux, vol. 7, Paris, 1968, 862 no. 375.

36. Christine de Pizan, *Le Livre des trois Vertus,* ed. Eric Hicks and Charity Cannon Willard, Paris, 1989; Christine de Pisan, *The Treasure of the City of Ladies,* trans. Sarah Lawson, New York, 1985, 145.

37. "Marital violence . . . appears to have been remarkably common in the purlieus of Paris between 1384 and 1387," James A. Brundage, "Domestic Violence in Classical Canon Law," in *Violence in Medieval Society,* ed. Richard W. Kaeuper, Suffolk, UK, 2000, 191.

38. See D. W. Robertson Jr., *A Preface to Chaucer: Studies in Medieval Perspectives,* Princeton, N.J., 1962, 361–64; John V. Fleming, *The Roman de la Rose: A Study in Allegory and Iconography,* Princeton, N.J., 1969; David F. Hult, "Words and Deeds: Jean de Meun's *Romance of the Rose* and the Hermeneutics of Censorship," *New Literary History* 28 (1997), 345–66. For a discussion of Robertson and Fleming, see Joseph L. Baird and John R. Kane, "*La Querelle de la Rose*: In Defense of the Opponents,"

French Review 48 (1974), 298–307; J. L. Baird, "Pierre Col and the *Querelle de la Rose*," *Philological Quarterly* 60 (1981), 273–86.

39. Doris Sommer, "Attitude, Its Rhetoric," in *The Turn to Ethics*, ed. Marjorie Garber, Beatrice Hanssen, and Rebecca L. Walkowitz, London, 2000, 204.

40. See Helen Solterer, *The Master and Minerva*, 163–75; Brown-Grant; see also Desmond and Sheingorn, 46–97.

41. See Nadia Margolis, " 'The Cry of the Chameleon': Evolving Voices in the Epistles of Christine de Pizan," *Disputatio* 1 (1996), 37–70.

42. For a discussion of the category of experience in Christine's corpus, see Mary Ann C. Case, "Christine de Pizan and the Authority of Experience," in *Christine de Pizan and the Categories of Difference*, 71–87; Andrea Tarnowski, "The Lessons of Experience and the *Chemin de long estude*," in *Christine de Pizan: A Casebook*, ed. Barbara K. Altmann and Deborah L. McGrady, New York, 2003, 181–97.

Afterword

1. See Michel Foucault, "Sexual Choice/Sexual Act," in *Michel Foucault: Essential Works of Foucault: 1954–1984*, ed. Paul Rabinow, vol. 1: *Ethics*, New York, 1997, 151.

2. "Sex, Power and the Politics of Identity," ibid., 170.

✒ INDEX